THE RUSSIA
BALANCE
SHEET

ANDERS ÅSLUND AND
ANDREW KUCHINS

THE RUSSIA
BALANCE
SHEET

PETERSON INSTITUTE FOR INTERNATIONAL ECONOMICS
CENTER FOR STRATEGIC AND INTERNATIONAL STUDIES
WASHINGTON, DC
APRIL 2009

PETER G. PETERSON INSTITUTE FOR INTERNATIONAL ECONOMICS
1750 Massachusetts Avenue, NW
Washington, DC 20036-1903
(202) 328-9000   FAX: (202) 659-3225
www.petersoninstitute.org

C. Fred Bergsten, *Director*
Edward Tureen, *Director of Publications,
  Marketing, and Web Development*

**CENTER FOR STRATEGIC
AND INTERNATIONAL STUDIES**
1800 K Street, NW
Washington, DC 20006
(202) 887-0200   FAX: (202) 775-3199
www.csis.org

John J. Hamre, *President and CEO*
James Dunton, *Director of Publications*

Typesetting by BMWW
Printing by Edwards Brothers, Incorporated
Cover by Sese-Paul Design
Cover photo: © Lystseva Marina/
ITAR-TASS/Corbis

For reprints/permission to photocopy
please contact the APS customer service department at Copyright Clearance Center,
Inc., 222 Rosewood Drive, Danvers, MA
01923; or email requests to:
info@copyright.com

Printed in the United States of America
11 10 09   5 4 3 2 1

**Library of Congress Cataloging-in-
Publication Data**

Åslund, Anders, 1952–
   The Russia balance sheet / Anders
Aslund and Andrew Kuchins.
      p. cm.
   Includes bibliographical references and
index.
   1. Russia (Federation)—Economic
conditions—1991–   2. Russia
(Federation)—Economic policy—1991–
3. Post-communism—Russia (Federation)
4. Russia (Federation)—Politics and
government—1991–   I. Kuchins, Andrew.
II. Title.
   HC340.12.A85 2009
   330.947—dc22

                              2009007223

Contents

Preface   vii

Map   xi

Introduction: Why Russia Matters and How   1

1   Russia's Historical Roots   11

2   Political Development: From Disorder to Recentralization of Power   25

3   Russia's Economic Revival: Past Recovery, Future Challenges   39

4   Policy on Oil and Gas   57

5   International Economic Integration, Trade Policy, and Investment   69

6   Challenges of Demography and Health   83

7   Russian Attitudes toward the West   99

8   Russia as a Post-Imperial Power   115

9   Pressing the "Reset Button" on US-Russia Relations   139

Appendix: Key Facts on Russia, 2000–2008(p)   167

Bibliography   171

Timeline of Major Events   175

Abbreviations   185

About the Authors   187

About the Organizations   189

The Russia Balance Sheet Advisory Committee   193

Index   **195**

Tables

5.1 Merchandise and commercial services exports, world, Russia, and the United States   71

7.1 Response to "Is the United States a friendly country?" August 2003   101

7.2 Response to "Is Western society a good model for Russia?" 2004 and 2008   105

7.3 Response to "Which society is more just and fair—Russian or Western?" 2004Q3   106

Figures

2.1 Civil and political rights, 1991–2008   34

2.2 Corruption perceptions index, 2000–2008   36

3.1 GDP growth rate, 2000–2008   41

3.2 GDP growth in current US dollars, 1999–2008   41

3.3 Ease of doing business in Russia, 2008   49

4.1 Oil and gas production, 1985–2008   58

4.2 Energy intensity, 2005   66

4.3 Carbon dioxide emissions, 2004   66

5.1 Merchandise exports and imports, 1999–2008   70

5.2 Oil and gas exports compared with merchandise exports, 1999–2007   72

5.3 Russia's major export partners, 2007   73

5.4 Russia's major import partners, 2007   73

6.1 Natural increase/decrease in population, 1960–2006   84

6.2 Infant mortality, 1960–2006   85

6.3 Life expectancy, 1960–2006   87

6.4 Mortality among working-age people, 1960–2006   90

7.1 Response to "Is the United States a friendly country?" across age cohorts, August 2003   103

7.2 Response to "Is the United States a friendly country?" by income, August 2003   104

7.3 Response to "Is Western society a good model for Russia?" by income, 2004 and 2008   105

7.4 Support for market economy and democracy across 28 transition countries, 2006   107

7.5 Dynamics of life satisfaction and per capita GDP, 1994–2006   111

Preface

Russia has been on a wild roller-coaster ride for the past two decades with no end in sight. From global superpower in the 1980s to collapsed empire and nearly failed state in the 1990s to resurgent "energy superpower" during the past eight years, certainly no contemporary large emerging market and probably no great power in modern history has experienced such highs and lows in such a short period. Just in the past year as the global financial crisis deepened, the conventional perception of Russia, as this book went to press, has changed from a "safe haven" from the economic tsunami to one of the hardest hit larger markets in the world.

Russian international behavior has vexed policymakers and analysts alike in recent years. Early in his term Vladimir Putin endeared himself to the George W. Bush administration for his bold decision to strongly support US-led efforts to defeat the Taliban in Afghanistan after 9/11. Shortly thereafter US-Russia relations began to deteriorate steadily and reached their lowest point in more than two decades after the five-day Georgia-Russia war in August 2008. Many aspects of Russia's domestic development have seemed anomalous as growing prosperity over the last decade has occurred while the Kremlin has tightened its grip on power and eroded nascent democratic institutions. The middle class has grown tremendously, yet this newly prosperous generation is more anti-American than its parents' generation. Russia inspires strong and often contradictory reactions. Will Rogers noted decades ago that Russia is the only country about which you can say anything and it is true, which seems to remain the case today.

In spite of its changing, indeed quixotic, nature, understanding the sources of Russian behavior remains a priority for the successful pursuit of US foreign policy. Just the fact that Russia possesses the most hydrocarbon resources in the world and a nuclear weapons arsenal only comparable to that of the United States makes its significance clear. Add to this the vast geographic expanse of the Russian Federation and the fact that it borders on the most important regions of the world for US economic and security interests—from Europe to the Greater Middle East to Northeast Asia. Russia is also a significant player on some of the most crucial emerging challenges for the United States and its global partners including reducing global warming and reforming the international financial and economic architecture. In sum, Russia matters a lot but is not easy to understand.

As three years ago for the China Balance Sheet Project, the Center for Strategic and International Studies (CSIS) and the Peterson Institute for International Economics have teamed up again in an effort to provide a basis for sound and sensible judgments about Russia. Because we believe that US policies toward Russia must rest, first and foremost, on a firm and factual analytical footing, the Russia Balance Sheet Project's primary purpose is to provide comprehensive, balanced, and accurate information on all key aspects of Russia's developments and their implications for the United States and other nations. Seemingly everyday, we—policymakers and the public alike—are bombarded with bits and pieces of information and events involving Russia, making it more easy to lose sight of "the forest for the trees." With this book we hope to provide a comprehensive look at the complex dynamics of change in Russia and their implications for its international behavior.

As Stalin pithily put it, "Cadres decide all," and we are very fortunate to have this project codirected by two of the world's leading experts on Russian affairs, Anders Åslund, senior fellow at the Peterson Institute, and Andrew C. Kuchins, director and senior fellow of the Russia and Eurasia Program at CSIS, who together coauthored this book. The work of Åslund and Kuchins benefited enormously from draft contribution and materials from a "virtual" working group including Edward Chow, Thomas Graham, Sergei Guriev, Gary Clyde Hufbauer, Dmitri Trenin, Maxim Trudoliubov, Aleh Tsyvinski, Judyth Twigg, and Edward Verona.

The first chapter, written by Kuchins, examines the impact of Russia's past. Chapter 2, written by Åslund, records the evolution of the political system after communism. Chapter 3, with contributions from Åslund, discusses Russia's economic revival and the current financial crisis. Chapter 4, with contributions from Edward Chow, deals with Russia's policy on oil and gas. Chapter 5 on Russia's trade and investment policy was written by Gary Clyde Hufbauer, Edward Verona, and Jeffrey Barnett. Judyth Twigg first drafted chapter 6 on the demographic and health challenges. In chapter 7, Sergei Guriev, Aleh Tsyvinski, and Maxim Trudoliubov review what opinion polls reveal about the mood of the Russian population. Chapter 8 by Kuchins and Dmitri Trenin discusses Russia's foreign policy. In the concluding chapter, Åslund and Kuchins outline implications for US policy toward Russia.

Åslund and Kuchins have been fortunate to work with very strong teams at CSIS and the Peterson Institute in the research, editing, and publication process, which was noteworthy both for the compressed time deadline as well as the tumultuous impact of the global financial crisis on the subject matter. At CSIS thanks go to Amy Beavin, Anya Bryndza, Samuel Charap, Matthew Malarkey, Chad Miner, and Emma White. At the Peterson Institute for International Economics, gratitude is due to Olesya Favorska and especially to Madona Devasahayam for managing the editing. We also thank Cameron Fletcher for excellent copyediting and Susann Luetjen for production coordination.

We are very grateful for the support and contributions to the project from our eminent Advisory Committee (full list at back of the book), which met twice in the second half of 2008 to helped shape and inform the structure, style, and content of the book. In particular, Leon Aron, Thomas Graham, and Michael Mandelbaum read the entire manuscript in draft and provided tremendously insightful comments and suggestions. We are also enormously grateful to Zbigniew Brzezinski for his very keen critique and suggestions on the final chapter, which was also published as a policy brief in March 2009.

Finally, we are especially grateful to our corporate supporters of the Russia Balance Sheet Project, which includes AIG, British Petroleum, Caterpillar, Chevron, Coca-Cola, ExxonMobil, Microsoft, and Pepsi. The US-Russia Business Council, with its past president, Eugene Lawson, and current president, Edward Verona, has been a critical partner and supporter of the project.

John J. Hamre, President and CEO
Center for Strategic and
International Studies

C. Fred Bergsten, Director
Peterson Institute for
International Economics

March 2009

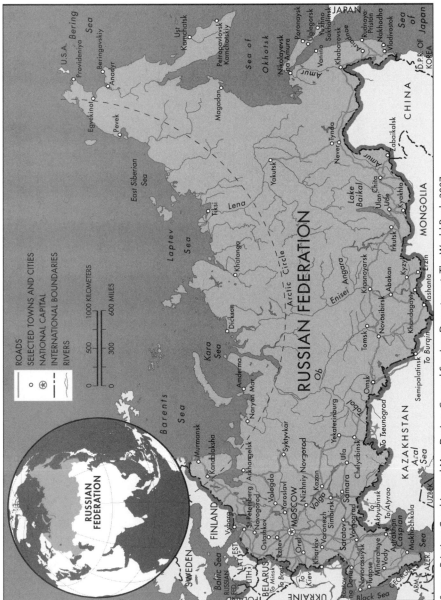

Source: Printing, Graphics and Map Design, General Services Department, The World Bank, 2007.

Introduction: Why Russia Matters and How

Whether one lives in Moscow, Mumbai, or Washington, 2008 will go down in modern history as one of the most tumultuous and difficult years. But newly elected Russian president Dmitri Medvedev must feel especially snake-bitten. Shortly after he was inaugurated in May, the Russian stock exchange reached an all-time high after 10 years of remarkable economic growth. In July the oil price peaked at $147 per barrel. Russia had gone through a remarkable economic recovery in the past decade, boosting its GDP nine times in current US dollars from $196 billion in 1999 to $1.75 trillion in 2008, becoming the eighth largest economy in the world. Its government had set ambitious development goals, including that of becoming the fifth largest economy by 2020. For the Russian government the biggest challenges were to control inflation and decide how best to allocate rapidly accruing reserves to promote modernization and sustained growth. The Kremlin emphasized rhetorically the political mantra of "continuity" and "stability" in the further implementation of the amorphous "Putin's Plan," and President Medvedev appointed his predecessor prime minister. Like medieval scholars speculating on the question of how many angels can dance on the head of a pin, Russia watchers guessed at the inner workings of Russia's new "tandemocracy."

But as so often happens in Russian history, shocking events in the form of a war followed by economic crisis intervened in the second half of 2008, bringing "tandemonium" to the Kremlin. On August 8, 2008, while people around the world were transfixed in front of their televisions by the stupendous Olympic Games opening ceremonies in Beijing, Russian and Georgian military forces engaged in large-scale combat in Georgia's separatist enclave South Ossetia. US President George W. Bush and Russian Prime Minister Vladimir Putin were together in Beijing observing the ceremonies and discussing the Georgia war. Despite the personal relationship they had cultivated through 27 meetings in the course of nearly eight years, they failed to stop what should have been a preventable war.

Russian forces routed their Georgian opponents, who had received training from American instructors to fight in Iraq but not American arms to use against Russian troops. The Russian military advanced well beyond South Ossetia and carried out bombing raids throughout Georgia. On August 12 French President Nicolas Sarkozy, in his capacity as president of the European Union, mediated a cease-fire agreement, and the war in Georgia became known as the five-day war. On August 26 the Russian Federation officially recognized the independence of South Ossetia and the other separatist region in Georgia, Abkhazia, but so far only one other country, Nicaragua, has recognized these two territories as independent.

Russian claims of "8/8 as their 9/11" were a crude exaggeration and soon forgotten, but the guns of August in Georgia shook the world for a moment. For the first time since the collapse of the Soviet Union, Russian military forces were used on a large scale outside the territory of the Russian Federation. Nearly 20 years after the fall of the Berlin Wall, this war tragically illustrated the failure to integrate Russia into a broader European security framework. US policy toward Russia and Eurasia was in tatters, and the credibility of US security assurances around the world had been devalued. The Kremlin complained that "US client" and virtual ally, Georgian President Mikheil Saakashvili, attacked Russia's "peacekeepers" in South Ossetia and that the United States failed to understand that the Russians were dead serious when they talked about "red lines" that could not be crossed. The Georgians were disappointed that the United States did not understand the danger of Russian military action or guarantee their security. The Bush administration was upset that Saakashvili ignored its advice not to let himself be provoked by the Russians or their proxies in South Ossetia.

International attention, however, did not linger on the Russia-Georgia war, as in mid-September 2008 the financial crisis in the United States took on global proportions at dizzying speed. Stock markets around the world plunged, and credit markets nearly froze up as world leaders from 20 leading economies (G-20) met in Washington in mid-November to discuss measures to control the crisis and begin thinking about reforming global financial institutions for future crisis prevention. In early 2008 Russian leaders talked about Russia as a safe haven as the subprime mortgage crisis began to overwhelm the US economy. But this notion was brutally debunked, as the Russian market tanked even more precipitously than other emerging markets in the wake of the global liquidity crisis in the second half of the year. Russian economic hubris was rocked as its risk was exposed. The ruble, which had been appreciating for nearly a decade, has fallen steadily by over one-third, and most economists predict further devaluation. Foreign exchange reserves, which had peaked at $598 billion in early August 2008, had fallen to $381 billion in early March 2009 as the Russian central bank was defending the ruble. The summer's heated discussions of the dangers of a resurgent Russia were replaced by chilled whispers about a possible third default in less than 20 years if oil prices fell to $30 per barrel and stayed there for more than a year.

The United States and its European allies have conflicting ideas about how to deal with Russia. Not only in Europe but around the world interests are more fluid and cross-cutting in this era of rapidly growing globalization. Perhaps most worrisome is that the understanding among American and Russian political elites about the US and Russian roles in the world was never as diametrically opposed in the last 20 years as it is today. Channels of communication between Washington and Moscow are thin and fraught with hostility and distrust.

The security challenges are obvious: Russia maintains the largest stockpiles of nuclear weapons and fissile materials; its military-industrial complex is second only to that of the United States; and its client list features countries such as China, Iran, Syria, and Venezuela, whose interests diverge in important ways from those of the United States. Russia is a regional power in many respects. It is the largest country in the world and borders Europe, East Asia, and the greater Middle East, theaters of greatest concern to US foreign policy, making its role as either a partner or a troublemaker most significant. Russia is important also in regional politics, energy, and the world economy. The inherent difficulties in anticipating what will happen in Russia make the stakes in getting it right all the higher for the United States.

An Elusive Subject

Historically, Russia has displayed a profound capacity to confound and confuse everybody, partly by design, partly due to an opaque political culture. Various blinders and biases among observers have also contributed. Moreover, Russia has tended to develop in a highly nonlinear and thus unpredictable manner. This quality is at the heart of the genius and the frustration of the country, a quality that Russians themselves simultaneously boast about and find vexing. Winston Churchill's famous 1939 comment about Russia as a "riddle wrapped in a mystery inside an enigma" or the 19th century Russian poet Fyodor Tyutchev's line that "Russia cannot be understood by the mind, only felt by the soul" sound like clichés, but clichés are usually grounded in some reality. Yet Churchill's less-quoted ensuing words indicate what to look for: ". . . but perhaps there is a key. That key is Russian national interest."

Today's Russia is also complex. Depending on one's perspective or source, one might conclude that the country is like a "Tale of Two Cities." Until the summer of 2008, observers who are more interested in economic and financial developments were impressed by the robust growth of the Vladimir Putin years and the macroeconomic revolution that transformed Russia from an economic basket case to an emerging-market powerhouse, with foreign debt amounting to 100 percent of GDP in 1999 repaid and the third largest foreign exchange reserves in the world. Those more interested in democracy, civil society, and human rights reached far less rosy conclusions. Policymakers, analysts, and scholars around the world concerned about international security continue to puzzle over how the Russians perceive and pursue their interests, from Iran to their European neighbors and China: Is Russia a partner or an unpredictable and unreliable troublemaker?

Looking back over the past 25 years, the unpredictability of Russia's development has been remarkable. Efforts to prognosticate the country's future have more often than not been woefully off the mark, as a broad expert consensus cautiously held that not much could change. Yet there have also been daring, and realistic, forecasts. Most prescient was probably the Soviet dissident Andrei Amalrik, who in 1969 recognized the preconditions of previous Russian revolutions in the contemporary Soviet Union:

> a caste-ridden and immobile society, a rigid governmental system which openly clashes with the need for economic development, general bureaucratization and the existence of a privileged bureaucratic class, and national animosities within a multi-national state in which certain nations enjoyed privileged status.[1]

In 1983 Zbigniew Brzezinski observed: "The Soviet Union is a world power of a new type in that it is one-dimensional. . . . [T]he Soviet Union is a global power only in the military dimension."[2] The following year, Richard Pipes rightly pointed out that Russia had entered a revolutionary situation.[3] In 1989 one of us wrote:

> The first [most likely] scenario is *radicalized reform with far-reaching democratization* [emphasis in original]. As Soviet reformist economics are waking up from their imposed lethargy, they are becoming ever more radical, because they realize that the state of the economy was worse than they had imagined and that half-measures do

---

1. Andrei Amalrik, *Will the Soviet Union Survive until 1984?* (London: Harper Collins, 1980).

2. Zbigniew Brzezinski, "The Tragic Dilemma of Soviet World Power: The Limits of a New-Type Empire," *Encounter* 6, no. 4 (1983): 12.

3. Richard Pipes, "Can the Soviet Union Reform?" *Foreign Affairs* 63, no. 1 (1984): 47–61.

not offer any results. Therefore, they want to go further towards a market economy and independent forms of ownership than they themselves had anticipated. The impressive resistance from the party and state bureaucracies is convincing them that little can be achieved without a considerable democratization. . . .[4]

Similarly, many sounded warnings of an authoritarian backlash with the ascension of a former KGB agent to the Russian presidency. In 1993 Daniel Yergin and Thane Gustafson published an excellent book outlining alternative Russian scenarios to the year 2010.[5] Ironically, they formulated one very positive economic scenario called *chudo* (miracle in Russian), which describes the remarkable economic growth that actually took place from 1999 until 2008. But they got the reasons for that growth wrong. In their *chudo* scenario, the Russian recovery would be driven by the diversification of the Russian economy, promoted especially by flourishing small and medium-sized enterprises. Economic reform is certainly part of the story of the Russian recovery, but skyrocketing oil and other commodity prices have been far more important drivers. And they make it more fragile.

Since we know that Russia is prone to nonlinear development, the current turn for the worse is not all too surprising, although it is part of a global trend. First, Russia is a quasi-authoritarian state, and such states are unstable almost by definition. Second, the decade-long economic boom has been driven not only by reforms in the 1990s but also by the high international oil price, which is cyclical and has now fallen. Third, Russia is an attractive target for large-scale terrorist attacks because of its vulnerabilities in domestic security and its failed policies in the northern Caucasus; an act of catastrophic terrorism could upset the status quo.

Under Putin or the Putin-Medvedev "tandem," Russia may project a newfound aura of power and resurgence that has unnerved many, but the sources and sustainability of this "comeback" are quite questionable and deserve focused research and analysis. Understanding Russia and informing American public debate about Russia's present and future are the principal motivations behind this book and our broader collaborative project, the Russia Balance Sheet.

Why The Russia Balance Sheet?

Given Russia's importance, it is vital to understand its possible trajectories of development. In this book we seek to address the key questions about possible trajectories of Russia's development through a rigorous,

---

4. Anders Åslund, *Gorbachev's Struggle for Economic Reform* (Ithaca, NY: Cornell University Press, 1989).

5. Daniel Yergin and Thane Gustafson, *Russia 2010 and What It Means for the World* (New York: Random House, 1993).

multidisciplinary, and comprehensive approach. Most importantly, we endeavor to keep an open mind in considering hard-to-imagine but possible outcomes, to avoid the shortcomings of previous projections that failed to imagine or anticipate what could and did happen in Russia.

The timing is ripe for such an effort, with President Medvedev having assumed office in Russia in May 2008 and the Barack Obama administration in Washington in January 2009. The two countries are embarking on a third epoch in post-Soviet US-Russia relations, following the Yeltsin-Clinton and Putin-Bush periods. The relative positions of the two countries in the world have changed considerably in the last eight years, with Russia's unexpected resurgence and the United States weakened by the costly war in Iraq. The sustained economic fallout from the 2008 global financial crisis will also affect how Washington and Moscow perceive their mutual interests. The United States has strong reasons to reengage with the world, both with its old European allies and with the large emerging economies, of which Russia is one. Russia is facing an existential choice: Will it opt for authoritarianism, state capitalism, and protectionism, or will it opt once again for political and economic liberalization? Our bet is the latter, but no certain prediction is possible at this time.

In the near term Washington needs to gain a sense of how the new Russian regime is shaping up—the broad outlines of the Kremlin's policies and of its ability to drive policy. In the longer term the administration will need to consider other questions, such as:

- What kind of power is Russia likely to be in the world?
- How will it define its interests?
- What capacities will it have to pursue those interests?
- How compatible will those interests be with US interests?

This book is the first product of the three-year Russia Balance Sheet project, and in it we seek to draw a clear and comprehensive understanding of the key drivers of contemporary Russia. Our goal is to be factual and objective, looking at Russia beyond the stereotypes, clichés, and historical perceptions and expectations. We chose the title *The Russia Balance Sheet* for both this book and the larger project for several reasons. The most superficial reason is that we are building on the brand name established by the very successful collaboration between the Center for Strategic and International Studies and the Peterson Institute for International Economics for the China Balance Sheet, launched in 2005 and widely supported by the business and policy communities. Like the China Balance Sheet, we seek to provide a comprehensive, objective, and balanced assessment of the key features of Russia's political economy and its foreign policy. While both of us have considerable experience in punditry at leading Washington think tanks, taking a side or position is not the goal of this exercise. Our aim is to present the relevant facts to allow readers to draw their own conclusions. We find that the dramatic polarization of the US policymaking and business communities involved with Russia is unproductive in serving the formulation of US policy toward Russia.

The US business community tends to view Russia as a large emerging market that cannot be ignored. Russia presents many challenges for trade and investment, but so do other large emerging markets such as Brazil, China, and India (with Russia, the so-called BRICs, adding Korea and Mexico, or the trillion-dollar club). It may be an exaggeration to call Russia a "normal country,"[6] but the American and international business communities do not view Russia as so different: They recognize it as both an important supplier and market, where all major global companies have to be present.

In the policy community, on the other hand, most high-level officials and analysts grew up during the Cold War, when the Soviet Union was the big, bad enemy, and current Russian realities are still too often looked upon through Cold War blinders. These skewed prisms were reinforced during the Putin years, when Russia reestablished itself as a much more centralized and authoritarian polity as well as a resurgent power whose unsubtle muscle flexing sent shivers down the spines of its neighbors, who themselves have a troubled history with Soviet and/or imperial Russia. Many features of contemporary Russia are not reassuring and to those living in Tbilisi or Tallinn or Warsaw they might even be alarming. The satirical publication *The Onion* struck a chord when shortly after the Georgia war it advised the small countries on Russia's border to move.[7]

Another problem for the US perception of Russia stems from the nature of the current media. The problem may not be so much old stereotypes such as the Cold War but rather that bad news makes the news much more often than good news does. Since the Soviet collapse, Russia has had no shortage of bad news from military conflicts, virtual civil war, terrorist attacks, contract murders of prominent journalists and businessmen, economic collapse, endemic corruption, renewed economic collapse—and the list goes on. One of us wrote in 2001 that Russia in the 1990s reminded him of the classic line from legendary bluesman Albert King: "If it wasn't for bad luck, I wouldn't have no luck at all."[8] That the average Russian

---

6. Andrei Shleifer and Daniel Treisman, "A Normal Country," *Foreign Affairs* 83, no. 2 (2004): 20–38.

7. "U.S. Advises Allies Not to Border Russia," *The Onion*, August 25, 2008, www.theonion. com (accessed on February 17, 2009).

8. Andrew C. Kuchins, *Russia after the Fall* (Washington: Carnegie Endowment for International Peace, 2002, 3).

consumer has just lived through the most prosperous decade in Russia's thousand-year history makes no headlines.

An additional motivation for naming this book *The Russia Balance Sheet* stems from our view that economic drivers are crucial to Russia's future, and neither Russia's political system nor its foreign policy can be well understood without a firm grounding in Russia's current economic realities, its goals, and the global economic system within which Russia operates. Russians are not only living more prosperously than ever but also are more integrated into the globalized economy than ever before.

In an article in 2006, one of us dubbed Putin "Vladimir the Lucky" because his presidency occurred during Russia's most felicitous conditions for economic growth, taking into account the dramatic increase in the oil price and the "global money party" that occurred during his tenure.[9] Especially from 2003 on, the Russian government needed to do little but float on high oil prices to maintain robust growth, and the structural economic reform agenda went into hibernation. Since Medvedev took over as president and Putin moved to the position of prime minister, however, those beneficial external circumstances have dramatically changed. The commodity price cycle has peaked and credit markets have become very tight around the world. Medvedev and company will have to be more than lucky.

As impressive as Russia's economic recovery has been over the last decade, if the country wants to rejoin the ranks of the world's great powers, it has a long way to go. The Russian government's plan for strategic economic growth to the year 2020, which was approved in the fall of 2008, has set the ambitious goal of raising the per capita income from today's level of $12,000–$14,000 to $30,000. Even in this best case, which the Kremlin calls the "innovation scenario," Russia's share of global GDP will grow from about 2½ to only 4 percent. Such growth would hardly support a new imperial foreign policy. To achieve it in the next decade, Russia will have to depend on greater integration with the postindustrial West: first and foremost Europe, but also the United States and Japan. Economic integration with China will continue to deepen, but it will probably exacerbate Russia's overdependence on commodity exports and not serve its goals of diversifying the economy.

One of the Kremlin's big choices is how Russia will opt to balance its foreign policy interests and economic growth goals. Historically, Russian governments have often seriously compromised optimal growth in favor of political control at home and domination abroad. In this book we hope to illuminate some current and potential tradeoffs and to explain how various economic, demographic, energy, political, and other drivers may

---

9. Andrew C. Kuchins, "Vladimir the Lucky," Carnegie Endowment Web Commentary, July 25, 2006, www.carnegieendowment.org.

interact to shape Russia's future. In so doing, we hope to clarify options for US and foreign policymakers and businesspeople in the months and years ahead.

Anders Åslund
Peterson Institute for
International Economics

Andrew C. Kuchins
Center for Strategic and
International Studies

March 2009
Washington, DC

1

Russia's Historical Roots

Russia's thousand-year history is replete with colorful leaders, global and continental wars, and the dramatic juxtaposition of brilliant culture with extreme brutality and poverty. Some Westerners find these qualities attractive, others repelling—there is little middle ground in how foreigners respond to Russia.

This chapter outlines some of the enduring legacies of Russia's political and economic organization and conveys Russia's perspective on both its global and regional position and its identity. For the last 500 years, Russia has been one of the traditional European powers,[1] with an inheritance both rich and complicated: Many of the peculiarities of tsarist Russia— some pertaining to geography, others to tradition—persist today; similarly, the Soviet period of 1917–91 is over, but it too has left indelible marks.

Over the past two centuries, occasional tsarist and even Soviet leaders have struggled to free Russia from the "path dependencies" of its centralized and authoritarian economic and political systems and its deeply territorial sense of security, which has fueled expansion and the domination of its neighbors. In addition to these challenges, the Russian reformers who came to power in 1991 strived to join the West but succeeded only partially.

The Muscovite, Tsarist, and Soviet Legacies

Looking at a map of the world, one cannot help but be impressed by the sheer vastness of Russia. From the beginning of the 16th century through

1. This point has been made most strongly by Martin Malia, *Russia under Western Eyes* (Cambridge, MA: Harvard University Press, 1999).

the middle of the 17th, Russia on average annually added territory equivalent to the size of the Netherlands, and it continued expanding until World War I. No other state in world history has expanded so persistently.[2]

Russia grew as a multinational and multicultural empire along with the Western European empires, but there was an important difference between them: The colonies of the Western European empires—those of Great Britain, France, Holland, Portugal, and Spain—were overseas, physically separated from their capitals. Russia, however, was a continental empire without a clear differentiation between the ruling core and its colonies, more like the Ottoman Empire. Although the Western European states developed national identities separate from their colonial possessions, Russia did not. Many historians have argued that Russia never was a nation-state but developed as an empire from the beginning.

The Muscovite principality marked the geographic center of the territory settled by ethnic Russians in medieval times, and the Muscovite court formed an efficient capital with a monolithic militarized political organization. Neighboring political-military groupings were comparatively weak and vulnerable to invasion.

Russia's centralized and militarized state has distinguished the country for centuries, although whether its militarization was offensive or defensive has been a matter of considerable historical debate. The country's need for expansion was self-perpetuating: It continually conquered or acquired territory populated by non-Russian ethnic and nationalist groups that formed a belt of regions of dubious political loyalty, arousing permanent insecurity in the core state, which responded with repression and the expansion of boundaries to create buffer zones.[3] As Russia grew, the demands of the administration and security of the vast territory resulted in an increasingly onerous tax and financial burden on the people, since the government extracted these resources chiefly from the agrarian population, which struggled for subsistence in climatically and geologically adverse conditions. As Russian historian Vasily Kliuchevsky famously remarked, "The state expands, the people grow sickly."[4]

Thus as one traveled east from Western Europe, regions became progressively poorer and the rule more autocratic. In their competition with Western adversaries, Russian governments resorted to the authority of the central sovereign—the tsar and later the head of the Communist Party of the Soviet Union—who allocated relatively large resources to the mili-

---

2. Richard Pipes, "Détente: Moscow's Views," in *The Conduct of Soviet Foreign Policy*, ed. Erik P. Hoffman and Frederic Fleron Jr. (New York: Aldine Publishing Co., 1980).

3. See Alfred J. Rieber, "Struggle over the Borderlands," in *The Legacy of History in Russia and the New States of Eurasia*, ed. S. Frederick Starr (New York: M.E. Sharpe, 1994, 61–90).

4. Quoted in Nicolas Berdyaev, "Religion and the Russian State," in *Readings in Russian Foreign Policy*, ed. Robert A. Goldwin (New York: Oxford University Press, 1959, 25–33).

tary. Because the Russians' deeply ingrained sense of territorial security created the need for a large and expensive state bureaucracy and military, Russia's commerce, economic growth, and technological development consistently lagged behind those of its European neighbors.

Yet Russia's vast natural resources, large territory and population, and ability to mobilize a large army made the country a formidable player in European politics. After the defeat of Charles XII and Sweden at Poltava in 1709 and the relocation of the capital of the Russian empire to the newly built St. Petersburg, on the Baltic Sea, in 1713, Russia continued to expand in the Baltic region. Later in the century, under Catherine the Great, Russia expanded in the west through the partitioning of Poland in 1772, 1793, and 1795, and to the south at the expense of the Ottoman Empire. In the 19th century the expansion continued to the south into the Caucasus and to the southwest into Central Asia. By 1837, Pyotr Chaadaev wrote in his *The Vindication of a Madman*, "Russia, it is a geographical fact."

Historians have argued that the geography of Eurasia was conducive for the Russians, as it had been for the Golden Horde and Tamerlane, to create a huge continental empire. Harvard University history professor Edward Keenan has suggested that Moscow was a pragmatic opportunist not inherently bent on expansion but simply taking advantage of opportunities as they emerged—in other words, Russia expanded because it could. Historian George Vernadsky embraced the argument of geographical determinism—that the peculiar geography of Eurasia encouraged a dynamic national grouping (i.e., Russia) to extend its domination as far as possible for security reasons:

> The fundamental urge which directed the Russian people eastward lies deep in history and is not easily summarized in a paragraph. It was not "imperialism," nor was it the consequence of the petty political ambitions of Russian statesmen. It was in geography which lies at the basis of all history.[5]

The two historians' views mesh well, suggesting that Russia's expansionism was normal behavior in an unusual geography. Richard Pipes suggests, however, that the Russians, and later the Soviets, adopted an ideology—be it "Moscow as the third Rome" or Marxism-Leninism—that promoted an extraordinary imperial appetite and that encouraged the government to be inherently aggressive and expansionist.[6]

Such views may not be all that contradictory. The geography of Eurasia presents a truly Darwinian dilemma given its susceptibility to invasion, and the imperative of security drove a peculiarly militarized economic development of both tsarist Russia and the Soviet Union.

---

5. George Vernadsky, *A History of Russia*, 3d ed. (Philadelphia: The Blakiston Company, 1944 , 6).

6. Richard Pipes, *Russia under the Old Regime* (London: Weidenfeld & Nicholson, 1974).

Russia's Early Identity Questions

A powerful national myth is required to dominate such extensive territories, and the Russians developed one, under first the tsars and then, with some adaptations, the Soviet Union. The 15th century saw the emergence of a messianic vision for the Russian state and the people of Moscow as the Third Rome, or the historical protector and purveyor of Orthodox Christianity. The first Rome was long gone, and the second Rome, Constantinople, fell in 1453. In 1472 Russian Prince Ivan III married Sofia Paleologue, the niece of Byzantium's last emperor, Constantine, and this marriage gave legitimacy to Russia's claim as Byzantium's historical successor. In 1520 the monk Filofey supposedly wrote in an oft-cited letter to the tsar,

> And now, I say unto them: take care and take heed, pious tsar; all the empires of Christendom are united in thine, the two Romes have fallen and the third exists and there will not be a fourth.[7]

In 1547 the Muscovite prince Ivan IV officially adopted the title of tsar, which was derived from the Roman *caesar*, emphasizing that the succession of Christian capitals was matched by a succession of rulers. Iver Neumann has argued that the Third Rome doctrine anointed Russia as the divine successor, but its borders were never clearly identified, thus providing religious justification for expansion. Throughout Russian history, Holy Russia has been invoked as the suffering savior of the world, and its historical mission was the crux of the Russian Idea. Russian philosopher Nikolai Berdyaev attributed the Russians' messianism to their unique combination of Western and Eastern qualities:

> The Russian people is not purely European and it is not purely Asiatic. Russia is a complete section of the world—a colossal East-West. It unites two worlds, and within the Russian soul two principles are always engaged in strife—the Eastern and the Western.[8]

The eternal question of East or West was at the heart of the 19th century debate between Russian Slavophiles and Westernizers.[9] The Slavophiles were aristocratic romantic intellectuals who believed in the superior nature and historical mission of Orthodox Christianity and in Russia as uniquely endowed with a culture transcending East and West. They touted traditional institutions such as the peasant commune as models of harmonious social organization and claimed that rationalism, legalism, and con-

---

7. Quoted in Iver B. Neumann, *Russia and the Idea of Europe* (New York: Routledge, 1996, 7).

8. Nikolai Berdyaev, *The Russian Idea* (Hudson, NY: Lindisfarne Press, 1992, 20).

9. Much of the following discussion is derived from Nicholas V. Riasanovsky, *A History of Russia,* 2d ed. (New York: Oxford University Press, 1969, 400–404).

stitutionalism would destroy Russia's natural harmonious development. The Slavophile movement was a reaction against the Westernizing efforts of Peter and Catherine the Great.

The Westernizers took the German idealism of Hegel as a starting point but argued that, while Russia possessed many unique and superior features, its historical mission required it to follow the path of Western civilization. They criticized Russian autocracy and took a more positive view of the rule of law and constitutionalism. While the Slavophiles' ideology was anchored in Orthodoxy, the Westernizers placed little value on religion; some became agnostic or even atheist, while the moderate Westernizers retained some religious faith and their political and social programs supported moderate liberalism with popular enlightenment.

Historians have pointed to a pendulum swing of Russian orientation between Europe and Asia. During the Kievan period from the 10th through the 13th centuries, Rus was closer to Europe both physically and culturally. Indeed, the Kievan Rus civilization may have been more advanced politically and commercially than Western Europe, which was then emerging from its dark age. But the Mongol invasion and the Tartar yoke interrupted this development, and the Russian civilization that subsequently emerged from Muscovy was more eastern both physically and culturally. This remained true until 1713, when Tsar Peter I moved the capital of the Russian empire from Moscow to St. Petersburg, which was to be Russia's window to the West, as Peter sought to modernize and Westernize Russia.

During the next century, Russian rebuffs or defeats in Europe were repeatedly followed by greater attention and expansions to the East. For example, the defeat of Russia in the 1853–56 Crimean War at the hands of a coalition of France, Sardinia, the United Kingdom, and the Ottoman Empire was followed by extensive Russian conquests in the East. In the Caucasus, Russia had been fighting for decades, but pacification was nearly complete when in 1859 the legendary Chechen leader Shamil was captured. In a series of successful military expeditions from 1865 to 1876 in Central Asia, Russia conquered the khanates of Kokand, Bokhara, and Khiva. The far eastern boundary of Russia had remained unchanged from the Treaty of Nerchinsk with China in 1689, but in 1858 China gave up the left bank of the Amur River to Russia through the Treaty of Aigun, and in the 1860 Treaty of Beijing, China ceded the Ussuri River region.

The Soviet Experience and the Emergence of a New Russia

World War I revealed that the Russian Empire was still economically and technologically lagging behind other European powers, geographically overextended, and burdened with an incompetent government headed by the weak and ineffective Tsar Nicholas II. While the defeats in the Crimean War and the Russo-Japanese war in 1904–05 had inspired some reforms of tsarist rule, World War I brought the system and Russian society to its knees. Driven to abdication in February 1917, Nicholas was succeeded by the Provisional Government, which proved no more effective. Strikes and food shortages in Moscow and St. Petersburg led to chaos, and in October Lenin's Bolsheviks successfully engineered a coup d'état.

The ideology of Marxism-Leninism was consonant with many features of the Russian security identity. Tsarist Russia was a very religious society, and Russian Orthodoxy was employed to legitimize tsarist rule; despite its aggressive atheism, Marxism is as much a teleological philosophy as Christianity. Indeed, many observers argue that Marxism-Leninism was a religion for the Soviet Union: It had a messianic quality and, instead of promising an afterlife in heaven, the Soviets strived to create a workers' paradise on earth. And in keeping with the country's imperial history and security concerns, Soviet propaganda stressed the unique role of the Soviet Union to lead the world toward socialism and combat the evil designs of world capitalism, especially the United States. The Soviet Union did not aspire to be an ordinary nation-state, and the expansionist implications of a proselytizing Marxism-Leninism matched the old Russian imperial mentality. As Russian historians Vladislav Zubok and Constantine Pleshakov commented,

> The traditional imperial legacy was an insurmountable obstacle to Russia's becoming an "ordinary" nation-state. Despite their intentions to build a brave new world form scratch, Russian Communists simply could not break with the imperial mode of thinking.[10]

Although the USSR's new Marxist-Leninist identity was important, Soviet leaders' perceptions of security were dominated by the traditional Russian dilemmas of geography and power. After seven debilitating years of World War I and the Russian Civil War, the Soviet Union in the 1920s was economically devastated and physically smaller than its tsarist predecessor. Joseph Stalin was concerned about the impact of Soviet economic and technological backwardness on its military power as European relations grew increasingly strained, and in 1930 he warned that if the USSR did not rapidly industrialize it would be overrun once again:

> To slow down the tempo [of industrialization] means to lag behind. And those who lag behind are beaten. The history of Old Russia shows . . . that because of her backwardness she was constantly being defeated. By the Mongol Khans, by the Polish-Lithuanian gentry, by the Anglo-French Capitalists. . . . Beaten because of backwardness—military, cultural, political, industrial, and agricultural backwardness. . . . We are behind the leading countries by fifty or a hundred years. We must make up this distance in ten years. Either we do it or we go under.[11]

---

10. Vladislav Zubok and Constantine Pleshakov, *Inside the Kremlin's Cold War: From Stalin to Khrushchev* (Cambridge, MA: Harvard University Press, 1996, 3).

11. Adam B. Ulam, *Stalin: The Man and His Era* (Boston: Beacon Press, 1973, 305–45).

For Stalin the experience of the 1930s and World War II strengthened his obsessive territorial view of international security, which fueled his cruel synthesis of Soviet domestic and foreign policies. He justified an internal regime of unprecedented terror in the 1930s by citing the supposed prevalence of capitalist spies and saboteurs who conspired to destroy the Soviet regime just as the capitalist powers had tried to "choke the baby in its crib" with the allied intervention in 1918. Show trials condemned to death many leaders of the Bolshevik revolution who were falsely accused of espionage and sabotage. Vladimir Lenin had referred to tsarist Russia as "the prisonhouse of nations"[12] but Stalin's purges and the gulag system were far more brutal than any oppression under the tsars. Stalin's key theoretical contribution to Marxism-Leninism argued that as socialism became more developed, opposition from the capitalist camp would grow more fierce, which required heightened vigilance on the home front.

From Cold War to Collapse

With the defeat of the Nazis in May 1945 Stalin stood triumphant as no Russian leader had since Alexander I's victory over Napoleon in 1812. During World War II the domestic reign of terror subsided and the leadership made ideological concessions to appeal to Russian nationalism. At a Kremlin banquet celebration in honor of his military commanders Stalin toasted the Russian people. Adam B. Ulam wrote of Stalin's toast:

> He acknowledged (uniquely) that the government, i.e., he himself had made many mistakes before and during the first phase of the war. Any other nation, he said, would have made short shrift of this government. Not the Russians! But he did not mention what rewards the grateful Leader was to bestow on his people.[13]

The dean of US Soviet specialists, George Kennan, captured Russia's outlook when he wrote in May 1945 from the US embassy in Moscow:

> By the time the war in the Far East is over Russia will find herself, for the first time in her history, without a single great power rival on the Eurasian landmass.[14]

Kennan intentionally referred to Russia rather than the Soviet Union because he believed that traditional Russian nationalist goals and concerns best guided US understanding of Soviet foreign policy under Stalin.

But Russia's newly comfortable position in the world did not presage improved international relations. Once again, like the war against

---

12. Lenin's reference had more to do with the oppressive treatment of the non-Russian nationalities in the Russian Empire.

13. Ulam, *Stalin: The Man and His Era*, 614.

14. George F. Kennan, *Memoirs 1925–1950* (New York: Pantheon Books, 1967, 533).

Napoleonic France, Russia had made huge sacrifices to "save the West" from another continental hegemon, Adolf Hitler, and Stalin considered that the West should pay its debt by allowing the Soviet Union to expand its domination to East-Central Europe. Stalin felt that the Soviet victory over Germany cemented the legitimacy of the Soviet regime, which did its utmost to ensure that the Russian citizenry did not forget. Although the Soviet Union in 1945 was in a stronger international position than ever, Stalin perceived weakness. The Soviet and European economies were largely destroyed, while the US economy was relatively stronger than ever, and because the United States had the atomic bomb Stalin pushed the Soviet science community and economy very hard to develop nuclear weapons.[15]

Stalin's clarion call in 1946 for the Soviet Union to catch up was similar to his admonition in 1930, as was his prescription for addressing the problem of perceived relative weakness. In 1949, the Soviet Union tested its first nuclear bomb. Yet Stalin continued to value territorial control and the development of heavy industry and military power. Throughout the Cold War, Soviet economic development focused on the requirements of the growing military-industrial complex.

The Soviet economic order was dubbed the command-administrative system. Its core features were complete state ownership, extreme centralization, and administrative control, minimizing the role of markets. It was effective in controlling society and mobilizing resources for the military sector but grossly inadequate at satisfying Soviet consumers, promoting efficient use of human and material resources, and encouraging technological innovation. Shortages and shoddy quality were pervasive features of the Soviet economy.

The dilemma of power and the Soviet position in the international system were in the forefront of Stalin's thinking. His obsession with power, expressed in terms of the "correlation of forces" between capitalism and socialism, and later between primarily the United States and the Soviet Union, would bedevil his successors for decades. Despite Nikita Khrushchev's denunciation of Stalin in 1956 and Leonid Brezhnev's détente policy in the 1970s, the Stalinist political and economic system endured until Mikhail Gorbachev's reforms in the late 1980s, and the Cold War defined international relations until the collapse of the Soviet Union in 1991.

Because of Stalin's obsession and that of his successors, the Soviet identity was increasingly defined by the USSR's superpower confrontation with the United States. Moscow and Washington maintained alliance relationships in Europe and Asia and balanced each other through nuclear

---

15. David Holloway, *Stalin and the Bomb: The Soviet Union and Atomic Energy, 1939–1956* (New Haven, CT: Yale University Press, 1994).

terror. When Brezhnev assumed power in 1964, he shaped his foreign policy around improving relationships with the United States and Western Europe in a superpower détente. Détente, a "relaxation of tension," resulted in important arms control agreements: the Anti-Ballistic Missile (ABM) Treaty in 1972 and the Strategic Arms Limitation Treaties (SALT) I and II, concluded in 1972 and 1979, respectively. The Brezhnev administration's achievement of nuclear parity with the United States was a seminal development that at last consolidated the Soviet international identity as a superpower equal to the United States.

But even at the peak of its powers the Soviet Union was, as Robert Legvold described it in 1977, like a "deformed giant . . . mighty in its military resources and exhilarated by its strength, but backward in other respects." Paradoxically, the Soviet Union of the 1980s was simultaneously a global superpower and a third world country.[16] In 1989 Aleksandr Bovin, a liberal deputy of the Soviet Congress of Peoples' Deputies, described his country as "Upper Volta with nuclear missiles."

The imbalance of Soviet power—a military superpower but an economic dwarf in comparison with the West—is essential to understanding the country's various motivations for economic, social, and political reform during the perestroika years. The Soviet leadership embarked on reform because of grave concerns about its aggravated economic backwardness. The Soviet system required reform to ensure long-term economic growth and technological development—otherwise Moscow would not be able to compete militarily or ensure future military parity with the United States. Nonetheless, in the mid-1980s the US Sovietological community still viewed the USSR as a powerful adversary, although it faced some daunting social and economic challenges that would eventually require far-reaching change.

When Gorbachev assumed power in 1985, he inherited an economy that had reached a developmental dead end. Allocations to the defense sector of at least 20 percent (the exact figure is not known) of the national product placed an unmanageable burden on long-term economic growth.[17] Gorbachev perceived that the Soviet Union was in a precrisis situation, so his major priority, and ironically his greatest failure, was domestic economic restructuring, or *perestroika*. His motivations were reminiscent of those of Peter the Great, of which Richard Pipes has written,

> The impetus for Westernization came largely from the awareness that the West was richer and stronger, and that if Russia hoped to attain the rank of a first-rate European power it had to model itself on the West. The initial motive for

---

16. Seweryn Bialer, *The Soviet Paradox: External Expansion, Internal Decline* (London: I.B. Tauris, 1986).

17. Anders Åslund, *Gorbachev's Struggle for Economic Reform* (Ithaca, NY: Cornell University Press, 1989, 17).

Westernization was military—namely, the inability of Russian troops in the seventeenth century to stand up to better organized and equipped forces of Sweden and Turkey.[18]

Perestroika did not proceed smoothly. Economic reform was aborted by bureaucratic resistance. In order to discipline the bureaucracy, Gorbachev unleashed *glasnost*, or greater public openness. When that did not help, beginning in January 1987 he attempted democratization.

As the political system started transforming, Russians' views of foreign policy also changed. In attacks on the traditional Soviet approach to foreign policy, those who embraced the new way of thinking sought to reduce the military's influence on Soviet security and foreign policy as well as its lock on domestic economic resources. And the Gorbachev team used diplomatic success with the West to justify reductions in defense spending. By demilitarizing its foreign policy, the USSR largely abdicated its role as global superpower and gave up its military-political "successes" since World War II: its (1) hegemony in East-Central Europe, (2) military parity with the United States, and (3) military-diplomatic gains in the Third World.

The Soviet people were supposed to be compensated for the geostrategic losses with the bountiful fruits of economic reform and growing integration into the world economy. Unfortunately for Gorbachev, it proved far easier to retrench strategically than to jump-start the Soviet economy and become a leading international economic power. The failure of Gorbachev's economic reforms left him without the increases he had promised in domestic economic production and in Western trade and investment. In fact, the half-hearted economic reforms destroyed the previous inefficient but functioning system and reduced the Soviet economy to chaos and near bankruptcy.[19]

Without the benefits of economic reform, the new political thinking amounted to a strategic giveaway with no near-term quid pro quo besides an improved image and much gratitude from the West for the de facto acknowledgment of losing the Cold War. After the revolutions in East-Central Europe, the unification of Germany, and Russia's siding with the United States in the 1991 Gulf War, the new political thinkers came under increased attacks for selling out the Soviet national interest.

Gorbachev's leadership made a difference. He proved to be remarkably flexible as he developed a deeper appreciation of his country's domestic and foreign challenges. He inherited a country that had been economically mismanaged for decades, had taken on foreign commitments far

18. Richard Pipes, "The Communist System," in *The Soviet System in Crisis: A Reader on Western and Soviet Views*, ed. Alexander Dallin and Gail W. Lapidus (Boulder, CO: Westview Press, 1991, 18).

19. Åslund, *Gorbachev's Struggle for Economic Reform*; Yegor T. Gaidar, *The Collapse of the Empire: Lessons for Modern Russia* (Washington: Brookings Institution, 2007).

outstripping its means, and had demoralized its citizenry. But he was very adept at playing a weak hand,[20] as he used the economic decline to catalyze reform. Yet Gorbachev could have played the hand differently. Ultimately he failed because he was too cautious on both domestic political and economic reform, and Boris Yeltsin capitalized on the forces of change unleashed by Gorbachev's policies to liberate the Russian Federation from its Soviet shackles.[21]

The New Russia

This brief survey of Russian history should leave the reader with a sense of the core continuities of domestic and foreign policy principles from Muscovite and tsarist to Soviet Russia. These deep grooves include highly centralized and unaccountable political authority, weak and often virtually nonexistent institutions of private property and rule of law, and a "great power" mentality that is deeply militarized as well as colored by messianism and xenophobia. Russia's experience of either being in or preparing for war for most of its history, coupled with its unique geography, engendered a very territorial sense of security that drove an impulse to dominate neighbors in order to expand a buffer zone against presumed and potential enemies. These crucial, long-standing realities did not change until very recently.

Boris Yeltsin was elected president of Russia on June 12, 1991, and by December he realized that the Soviet Union was finished after Ukraine voted with 90 percent majority for full independence. At two meetings that month (in Belovezhskaya Pushcha in Belarus and Alma-Ata in Kazakhstan), the remaining Soviet republics agreed to dissolve the Soviet Union, and on December 25 they did so peacefully, lowering the Soviet flag and replacing it with the Russian tricolor. Soviet President Gorbachev handed over the nuclear briefcase to Russian President Yeltsin.

Russia now had to create a new identity as a nation-state. It had been an empire since the 16th century. Now it was the last to decolonize, as the other empires had done after World Wars I and II. Yeltsin led Russia through a revolution that marked the most concentrated effort in the thousand-year history of Rus to break free of its traditional patrimonial and imperial paradigm. In retrospect, this effort has been remarkably success-

---

20. See Stephen Sestanovich, "Gorbachev's Foreign Policy: A Diplomacy of Decline," *Problems of Communism* (January/February 1988). This article was quite prescient, as Sestanovich wrote it before Gorbachev made his most notable concessions.

21. For excellent accounts of how Yeltsin seized the revolutionary moment while Gorbachev dithered, see Leon Aron, *Yeltsin: A Revolutionary Life* (New York: St. Martin's Press, 2000); and Michael McFaul, *Russia's Unfinished Revolution: Political Change from Gorbachev to Putin* (Ithaca, NY: Cornell University Press, 2001).

ful given the disastrous starting conditions. The new Russia was bankrupt. With the demise of the Communist Party and the Soviet Union, state power and authority were gravely weakened. Probably most devastating, Russia's economic system and infrastructure had relied for 70 years on nonmarket principles that resulted in one of the greatest misallocations of resources in human history.[22] The economist Gregory Grossman captured the magnitude of this legacy when in the 1980s he described the Soviet economy as "negative value added" and suggested Russia would make better use of its resources by simply shutting down its entire misdeveloped industrial structure.

Two months before the dissolution of the Soviet Union, on October 28, 1991, Yeltsin had made a great speech to the Russian parliament and declared his intention to build a normal market economy. He had appointed a government of young reformers, led by Yegor Gaidar, and they had started drafting the necessary legislation. On January 2, 1992, Russia freed most prices and liberalized both domestic and foreign trade. But the reform efforts faded quickly as Russia received no Western financing for its reforms and the reformers' economic and foreign policy plans came under increasing political attacks. By April 1992 the Yeltsin-Gaidar radical market reform was in rapid retreat.

Yeltsin had been hopeful—too optimistic, as it turned out—about the future of Russian foreign policy and Russia's place in the world order. Immediately after his election, he went to the United States and formulated his vision of Russian-American relations based on shared interests—creating a "common political and economic system in the Northeastern hemisphere in which the United States and Russia would play a leading role."[23] Former (and future) Finance Minister Boris Fedorov underscored this cooperative framework in a speech in London in September 1991 when he suggested that in the future Russia might become a member of the North Atlantic Treaty Organization (NATO) or whatever broader international structure might replace it.[24] And in a landmark article in the prestigious US journal *Foreign Affairs* in 1992, Western-oriented

---

22. For accounts of the extraordinary degree of misallocation of the Soviet economy, see Clifford G. Gaddy, *The Price of the Past: Russia's Struggle with the Legacy of a Militarized Economy* (Washington: Brookings Institution Press, 1996); and Fiona Hill and Clifford G. Gaddy, *The Siberian Curse: How Communist Planners Left Russia Out in the Cold* (Washington: Brookings Institution Press, 2003).

23. Sergei Goncharov and Andrew Kuchins, "Domestic Sources of Russian Foreign Policy," in *Russia and Japan: An Unresolved Dilemma between Distant Neighbors*, ed. Tsuyoshi Hasegawa, Jonathan Haslam, and Andrew Kuchins (Berkeley: University of California, 1993). This chapter was one of the first accounts of how the principles of Russia's foreign policy emerged in 1991–92.

24. "Fedorov on the Russian Foreign Policy" and "Russia's Stand Toward NATO," RFE/RL, no. 186 (September 30, 1991): 2.

foreign minister Andrei Kozyrev pointed out that the new Russia faced its most favorable security environment in centuries as the notion of a threat from the West had disappeared.[25]

But the dreams of deep partnership evaporated all too quickly. The political fate of the market reforms was closely tied to Westernizers like Kozyrev who were criticized as too idealistic and naïve. Russia's ambassador to the United States at the time, Vladimir Lukin, expressed a very different vision of Russia's national interests in the fall 1992 edition of *Foreign Policy*. Where Kozyrev found a friendly external environment, Lukin saw a multiplicity of security threats for the gravely weakened Russia, "a new encirclement." Although Russia did not face a hostile alliance, Lukin saw serious problems with nearly every nation on the periphery. Castigating "idealized democratic internationalism"—his characterization of Kozyrev's views—as a passing fad, Lukin called for a redefinition of Russia's national interests in the form of an "enlightened patriotism."[26]

Finally, the overly cautious approach of the George H.W. Bush administration to the reformist Yeltsin administration during the biggest window of opportunity (fall 1991 to spring 1992) for Russia's new mandate left an indelible stamp on relations between the two countries. Deputy Prime Minister Gaidar was deeply disappointed at the first meeting, in November 1991, with US Treasury officials, who showed no interest or concern in Russian reforms; their only goal was that the new Russia honor the Soviet foreign debt. It is impossible to know whether a more generous and activist US policy during those early days would have made a significant difference for the reformers. But it is clear that the November meeting was the first of many disappointments for the Russians, a perception that bedevils the bilateral relationship to this day, while the political demise of the reformers and consequent changes in Russian policy proved similarly disappointing to successive US administrations.

---

25. Andrei Kozyrev, "Russia: A Chance for Survival," *Foreign Affairs*, no. 71 (Spring 1992): 2.

26. Vladimir Lukin, "Our Security Predicament," *Foreign Policy*, no. 88 (Fall 1992).

2

Political Development: From Disorder to Recentralization of Power

After a brief period of nascent institutionalized democracy in the 1990s, from 2000 the Russian political system underwent a considerable reversal toward a precommunist Russian model. Brilliant historian Richard Pipes has described this original Russian model as "patrimonial authoritarianism."[1] Political institutions other than those of the highly centralized personal power are ineffectual—the parliament, political parties, legal system, regional governments, and civil society all are weak. When its coffers are full, as they were in mid-2008, the Kremlin is able to buy or intimidate potential competitors and appear strong, just as Vladimir Putin's government did during the last few years of his second term. But the system remains brittle and top heavy. It is inherently unstable and vulnerable to internal and external shocks.

The most important factor determining the government's popularity is economic performance. During Boris Yeltsin's term as president (1991–99), the Russian economy experienced a prolonged decline and his popularity ratings were consistently low, often in the single digits. In contrast, during Putin's presidency, the Russian economy grew at 7 percent a year for nearly a decade and his ratings were persistently high, even exceeding 80 percent at times.[2] However, the global financial crisis has deepened into what looks to be the worst recession in generations, and Russia is especially

1. Richard Pipes, *Russia under the Old Regime* (London: Weidenfeld & Nicholson, 1974).

2. Daniel Treisman, "The Popularity of Russian Presidents" (paper presented at the Frontiers of Political Economics conference, New Economic School, Moscow, May 30–31, 2008).

vulnerable because of its high dependence on hydrocarbon revenues and thus international oil prices. The risk of political instability is growing dramatically.

It is easy in hindsight to summarize the evolution of Russia's political system from the democratic breakthrough that occurred after the abortive hard-line coup in August 1991. The ensuing two years were characterized by serious strife between Yeltsin and the parliament. That period ended with Yeltsin dissolving the parliament, which responded with an armed uprising that he quashed with considerable bloodshed. The outcome was the adoption, through a referendum in December 1993, of a new constitution with strong presidential powers. But the nationalist and communist opposition to Yeltsin won parliamentary elections both then and again in December 1995. Thus Yeltsin and the oppositional parliament cohabited warily until the end of his term, while the regional governors and big businessmen enjoyed considerable autonomy.

Everything changed after the appointment in August 1999 of the unknown Vladimir Putin as prime minister. In December of that year, the newly formed pro-Yeltsin Unity party won the parliamentary election, giving Yeltsin a parliamentary majority for the first time. Yet on December 31, Yeltsin resigned voluntarily before the end of his term to the benefit of Prime Minister Putin, who was elected president in early elections in March 2000. Immediately after his inauguration, Putin curtailed the powers of the regional governors while the Kremlin manipulated regional elections through fraud and the disqualification of candidates. The new president also imposed his control over major television networks by antagonizing the two main media tycoons. In addition, in October 2003 Russia's richest man, Mikhail Khodorkovsky, the owner of Yukos oil company, was arrested and eventually sentenced on dubious grounds to eight years in prison for tax fraud, and his company was confiscated because of tax penalties. The Yukos affair signaled to the tycoons that they had better stay clear of any political opposition.

The popular Orange Revolution in Ukraine in November–December 2004 had a major impact on Russia's political system, as the Kremlin decided to tighten its political control. Beginning in 2005, governors were no longer democratically elected but effectively appointed by the Kremlin. Media control was reinforced. New legislation introduced strict control over nongovernmental organizations, public meetings, and popular protests. The registration of parties and candidates in elections became prohibitively complex, effectively excluding the possibility of actual opposition. Illegal protests were broken up with police force and many young protesters were jailed. Thus since 2005, the authoritative Freedom House has assessed Russia as "not free."[3]

---

3. Freedom House, *Freedom in the World 2008: Selected Data from Freedom House's Annual Global Survey on Political Rights and Civil Liberties*, www.freedomhouse.org (accessed on October 10, 2008).

Political Chaos, 1991–93

At the time of the collapse of communism in 1991, Russia had three important federal political institutions. The first and politically most important was a popularly elected president, Boris Yeltsin, who had a fresh democratic mandate through his election on June 12, 1991, by a popular majority of 57 percent against the communist establishment. The second political institution was the Congress of People's Deputies, the Russian parliament elected on March 4, 1990 (though those elections were not altogether democratic). The third institution was the Soviet Russian Constitution of 1978, a remnant of the Soviet Union Constitution (the so-called Brezhnev Constitution) of 1977, which was never meant to govern the state and was therefore not thought through.

Immediately after the failed coup of August 1991, President Yeltsin decided to disband the Communist Party of the Soviet Union in the Russian Federation, stripping Russia of its de facto government. Power fell into the hands of state institutions that lacked experience in governing.

Three ensuing developments were of particular importance. First, power rapidly devolved to the Russian Federation's 89 regions. Some ethnically based republics posed particular problems as they enjoyed greater rights than other regions. Notably, Chechnya insisted on treatment as a union republic and declared itself independent from Russia. Yeltsin had actually encouraged this stance in 1990 by telling Tatarstan and Bashkortostan, two large Muslim republics on the Volga, to "take as much sovereignty as you can swallow." But in March 1992, to stanch the flow of power away from Moscow after the breakup of the Soviet Union, Yeltsin signed a federation treaty, according the ethnically based republics a privileged position.

Second, strife developed between Yeltsin and his reform government, on the one hand, and the Russian parliament under the leadership of its chairman, Ruslan Khasbulatov, on the other. The parliament, the large and unwieldy Congress of People's Deputies, whose members had been elected on individual mandates in March 1990 before the electorate even knew who they were, was disorganized and not accountable to anybody. Increasingly, the parliamentarians opposed Yeltsin's market economic reforms and any financial stabilization. Most of all, they protested against his presidential power. Rather than seeking compromise, both sides escalated the struggle, and by August 1993 the situation was untenable. The parliament insisted on a huge budget deficit, which would have brought hyperinflation. On September 21, 1993, Yeltsin dissolved the parliament. But his hesitant handling of the situation provoked an armed uprising by the parliament. Finally, he mobilized special forces to defeat the parliament's troops, and some 150 people were killed, leaving a black mark on Russia's budding democracy.

Third, law and order collapsed and crime skyrocketed. Initially, crime was disorganized and carried out by individuals, but as public law enforcement did not do its job, crime became increasingly organized. As Vadim Volkov put it: "Since the actions of the state bureaucracy and of law enforcement remain arbitrary and the services provided by the state tend to have higher costs, private enforcers (read: the mafia) outcompete the state and firmly establish themselves in its stead."[4] Government officials, including policemen, were afraid and alienated, and they worked as little as possible. The state thus played a very small role in the early 1990s.

The Yeltsin Constitution of December 1993 and the Rise of the Oligarchs

The shootout at the parliamentary White House was traumatic for the new Russia; Yeltsin's rationale for his actions was comprehensible, but the actions seemed excessive. This was the obvious moment for Yeltsin to choose between democracy and authoritarianism, and he chose democracy, holding parliamentary elections as he had promised. On December 12, 1993, Russia held a referendum on a new constitution and elections to the new State Duma (the lower house) and Federation Council (the upper house). Together, they form the Federal Assembly.

Yeltsin no longer saw any need to negotiate the electoral rules—he simply imposed them by decree. He insisted on a system that gave the president strong powers and was even called superpresidential. The president had the right to nominate the prime minister, but the parliament had to approve the nominee. If it refuted the president's candidate three times, the president had to dissolve the Duma. And if the Duma passed two votes of no confidence in the government within three months, the president must either dismiss the cabinet or dissolve the Duma. Yet the president's powers were constrained. The president could veto a law passed by the parliament, but the parliament could override a veto by a two-thirds vote in each chamber. The new constitution also limited the scope of impeachment to high crimes.[5]

The president named the so-called power ministers: the minister of defense, the minister of interior, and the chairman of the Federal Security Service (FSB, the old KGB). He also appointed the minister for foreign affairs. These ministers reported directly to the president. The prime minister appointed all other ministers. No ministerial appointments required Duma approval. In effect, the president was responsible for foreign and

---

4. Vadim Volkov, *Violent Entrepreneurs: The Use of Force in the Making of Russian Capitalism* (Ithaca, NY: Cornell University Press, 2002, 19).

5. Thomas F. Remington, *Politics in Russia* (New York: Pearson Longman, 2006, 58).

security policy, while the prime minister managed economic policy. This division of labor worked well with Yeltsin and Prime Minister Viktor Chernomyrdin (1992–98).[6]

The lower house of the new parliament, the State Duma, confirmed the prime minister, legislated, and adopted the budget, performing the functions of a normal parliament. The Duma had 450 members, a customary size; half the members won their seats in a proportional election every four years through party lists with a threshold for representation of 5 percent of the votes. The other half were elected in single-mandate constituencies through a first-past-the-post system. The reason for this mixed approach was a fear that Moscow would be too dominant in a purely proportional system.[7] The aim of the proportional elections was to promote the development of parties. Mikhail Gorbachev's unusual innovation of indirect election to an inner parliament was terminated.

The upper chamber, the Federation Council, was somewhat inspired by the US Senate but probably more by the German Federation Council; its aim was to reinforce the representation of the regions. But it was never taken seriously. The constitution did not specify whether its 178 members (two from each of the 89 regions) would be elected or appointed, and the system changed repeatedly. In 1993, hasty Council elections in parallel to those for the far more important Duma virtually guaranteed the election of the regional rulers in the Federation Council. Beginning in 1995, the regional governors and the chairs of the regional legislative assemblies were automatically members of the Federation Council, until President Putin in 2000 usurped the right to appoint them.[8]

Notwithstanding the adoption of the new constitution, Yeltsin's power proved limited. In the first Duma election in December 1993, which the progovernment party, Russia's Choice, lost to a nationalist-communist opposition. A new progovernment party, Our Home Is Russia, fared even worse in the December 1995 parliamentary elections, which were largely won by the communists. In June–July 1996, Russia held presidential elections in two rounds; Yeltsin won the runoff against communist leader Gennady Ziuganov, but it was a tight race, showing both how comparatively democratic Russia was at the time—and how strong the reaction was against the not very successful reforms.

While the Russian state remained weak, private forces grew strong. Around 1994, big, new businessmen emerged. These oligarchs considered the fees of the pervasive protection rackets excessive and set up their own

---

6. Yeltsin had abolished the post of vice president after his many problems with Aleksandr Rutskoi in that position (1991–93). Michael McFaul, *Russia's Unfinished Revolution: Political Change from Gorbachev to Putin* (Ithaca, NY: Cornell University Press, 2001, 211–13).

7. The purely proportional system was introduced in 2007, when the threshold for representation was raised to 7 percent.

8. Remington, *Politics in Russia*, 58.

security and guard services. The oligarchs were powerful enough to ignore the old gangsters and also took advantage of the weakness of the state to purchase whatever state services they needed. They rose to particular importance in 1995–96 when, first, they acquired a dozen large enterprises through cheap loans-for-shares privatizations and then they provided Yeltsin with massive financial support for his reelection in the summer of 1996. The years 1996–98 are often described as the years of oligarchy.[9]

During his last term, Yeltsin accomplished few domestic reforms. He was in poor health and heart surgery put him out of commission for the second half of 1996. The communist-dominated parliament opposed his every step. Increasingly powerful businessmen seemed to roam the government corridors as if they owned them. The final blow was the financial crash of August 1998. In its wake, Yeltsin changed prime minister four times in 1998–99.

In retrospect, the political development under Yeltsin was confusing and idiosyncratic. He favored strong presidential powers and opposed a parliamentary system, and he sanctioned the manipulation of the presidential elections of 1996, interference that gradually undermined democratic standards in Russia. He believed in federalism and in the substantial powers of the regional governors, but condoned the start in December 1994 of the very bloody war against separatism in Chechnya. Toward the end of his rule, he was preoccupied with the question of anointing a successor. At the same time, he was amazingly tolerant of public and media criticism, never prosecuting anybody for libel. In a general sense, he identified himself with democracy, although his concept of democracy was vague.[10]

The Putin Centralization

In August 1999 Yeltsin appointed FSB Chairman Vladimir Putin prime minister, who soon emerged as Yeltsin's successor. In December 1999 the Kremlin won a majority in the State Duma for the first time. The election campaign focused on the second Chechnya war, begun in September of that year, and on the country's new financial stability and strong economic growth. On New Year's Eve 1999, Yeltsin resigned, and Putin became president in a snap election in March 2000.

---

9. Chrystia Freeland, *Sale of the Century: Russia's Wild Ride from Communism to Capitalism* (New York: Crown Business, 2000); David E. Hoffman, *The Oligarchs: Wealth and Power in the New Russia* (New York: Public Affairs, 2002).

10. Boris Yeltsin, *The Struggle for Russia* (New York: Crown, 1994); Boris Yeltsin, *Midnight Diaries* (New York: Public Affairs, 2000); Leon Aron, *Yeltsin: A Revolutionary Life* (New York: St. Martin's Press, 2000); Timothy Colton, *Yeltsin: A Life* (New York: Basic Books, 2008).

Putin was very different from Yeltsin, partly because of his career in the KGB, where he never reached a higher rank than lieutenant colonel. Although his political career rapidly took off in the late 1990s thanks to Yeltsin, he held very different views, as is evident from his early interview book.[11] He was determined to reverse Russia's trajectory by recentralizing the state and its power. He laid out his thinking on the Russian state in a document, *Russia at the Turn of the Millennium*, issued on the web shortly before he took over as acting president. In particular, he noted, "A strong state is not an anomaly for a Russian, it is not something to fight against; rather, it is the source and guarantee of order, the initiator and main moving force of any changes."[12] Accordingly, in his first months as president Putin vitiated three alternative bodies of power that had emerged under Yeltsin—the regional governors, the media, and the oligarchs—and recentralized power to the Kremlin, relying on a close circle of old collaborators from the KGB and St. Petersburg.

First, he reined in the regional governors by appointing his personal representatives to oversee seven newly created federal districts. The main tasks of these hand-picked representatives were to coordinate the activities of all federal agencies in their districts, bring regional laws in conformity with federal legislation and the constitution, and monitor tax collection and the flow of federal money in their districts. In addition, Putin reformed the Federation Council, the upper house of parliament, and effectively appointed members himself to deprive regional leaders of a direct voice in national policy. Elections of governors continued but were increasingly manipulated, especially by the last-minute disqualification of prominent candidates on the basis of technical minutiae. He fought a brutal war during the first years of his presidency to regain control over Chechnya. And in 2004 Putin used a large-scale terrorist attack on a school in Beslan in North Ossetia as a pretext for eliminating the popular election of regional governors in favor of presidential appointments.

Second, Putin moved against the media and their owners. He turned against the two major media oligarchs, Vladimir Gusinsky and Boris Berezovsky, who controlled large media empires, including the television networks NTV and ORT. Primarily through extralegal force, Putin imposed state control over these two television channels, and businessmen close to the Kremlin took over one media outlet after the other as Putin narrowed the field for political debate in the media. Television, the primary source of news for Russians, now reliably presents a Kremlin-approved viewpoint, although critical voices still make themselves heard in minor newspapers and on the Internet.

---

11. Vladimir V. Putin, *First Person* (New York: Public Affairs, 2000).

12. Vladimir Vladimirovich Putin, "Rossiya na rubezhe tysyacheletiy" ["Russia at the Turn of the Millennium"], December 30, 1999, in Richard Sakwa, *Putin: Russia's Choice* (London and New York: Routledge Press, 2004, 251–62).

Third, Putin launched well-publicized attacks on the oligarchs and then reached an informal agreement under which they would retain the rights to their property in exchange for a promise to stay out of politics. His message was: "You stay out of politics and I will not revise the results of privatization."[13] The Russian state was back and the era of the oligarchs was over. Big businessmen acquiesced to the Kremlin and minimized their public activities.

Putin thus centralized power to the federal government, or more specifically to the presidential administration and the FSB. Whereas Yeltsin had split up the KGB to weaken it, Putin reassembled and strengthened it. The secret police received increasing resources and enjoyed a legal monopoly on the use of violence.

In other areas, Putin continued the economic reform agenda of the 1990s from 2000 to 2002. He also undertook comprehensive judicial reform, which improved the quality and financing of the courts but made them dependent on the presidential administration rather than on the regional governors. Thus the reform did not depoliticize the courts; it only changed their political master.

The Arrest of Khodorkovsky and the Confiscation of Yukos

The oligarchs were still a major political force, but initially Putin limited his conflict with them to exiling the two big media oligarchs and telling the rest to stay out of politics. One oligarch, however, refused to comply.[14] Mikhail Khodorkovsky was the main owner and CEO of Yukos oil company. By 2003 he was the richest man in Russia, with an assessed fortune of $15 billion and more than 100,000 employees. Yukos had the highest market capitalization of any Russian corporation at $45 billion. He and his co-owners aspired to transparency and good corporate governance, publicizing their ownership. Yukos cleansed its corporate structures and financial system, abandoning transfer pricing, and the company was richly rewarded on the international stock market. Although Khodorkovsky had a reputation as one of the most ruthless oligarchs in the 1990s, from 2000 he became the foremost example of the gentrification of Russian capitalism as he and Yukos developed extensive charitable activities, supporting health care and civil society.[15]

---

13. Peter Baker and Susan Glasser, *Kremlin Rising: Vladimir Putin's Russia and the End of Revolution* (New York: Scribner, 2005, 86–87).

14. An excellent account of the Yukos affair is in Stephen Fortescue, *Russia's Oil Barons and Metal Magnates: Oligarchs and the State in Transition* (London: Palgrave Macmillan, 2006).

15. Baker and Glasser, *Kremlin Rising*, 272–92.

Khodorkovsky pursued numerous campaigns. By increasing Yukos' production and efficiency, he led the revival of the country's old brownfields, drawing on international technology and expertise. He advocated the construction of a private oil pipeline to China and another to Murmansk at Barents Sea, which would break the monopoly of the state-owned oil pipeline company Transneft. He criticized state-dominated Gazprom for inefficiency and advocated a bigger role for Yukos, complaining that his company was forced to flare billions of cubic meters of gas because of Gazprom's refusal to grant Yukos access to its monopolized gas pipeline system. In 2003 he conducted advanced negotiations with ExxonMobil and Chevron about selling a major equity stake of Yukos.

The collision between Putin and Khodorkovsky involved all the major issues of Putin's second term: nature of the political system, state or private control over resource industry, rule of law or vertical Kremlin power, some strategic aspects of foreign policy, the role of civil society, and, of course, the role of oligarchs. And Khodorkovsky accused Putin's close collaborators of corruption. Putin resolved all these conflicts in a way that made clear that oligarchs could not play an independent political role.

Khodorkovsky was arrested on October 25, 2003, and Putin used his control over federal bureaucracies and the courts to jail him and eventually dismantle Yukos (Rosneft bought most of Yukos' assets at much less than their value). The actual accusations were nebulous for a long time, but eventually Khodorkovsky was sentenced to eight years in prison for tax fraud, although Yukos was the largest private taxpayer in Russia. Putin denied that he had arranged for Khodorkovsky's arrest, but he explained to Western visitors that it was necessary because the CEO was buying up Russian politics.[16]

The Yukos confiscation was Putin's most important political act, framing his second term and changing Russia's political system. Putin and his party United Russia ran an antioligarchic campaign in the Duma elections in December 2003 and won an overwhelming majority of the seats, as the other parties had neither the financial resources nor the media access to compete. The Kremlin used "administrative resources" or multiple forms of minor fraud to control the election outcome, although Putin enjoyed a sky-high popularity rating of 70 to 80 percent, according to the remaining independent pollster, the Levada Center. In March 2004 Putin was reelected in an election completely controlled by the Kremlin.

Freedom House, which maintains an international index of freedom, assessed Russia as partially free in the 1990s, but Russia's ranking deteriorated and in 2004 Freedom House established that Russia was no longer free (figure 2.1).

---

16. Baker and Glasser, *Kremlin Rising*, 352.

Figure 2.1   Civil and political rights, 1991–2008

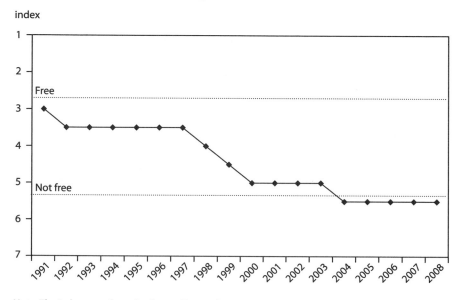

Note: The index runs from 1 = free to 7 = not free.

Source: Freedom House, *Freedom in the World Historical Rankings,* http://freedomhouse.org (accessed on September 16, 2008).

Further Political Centralization in Response to the Orange Revolution

Putin had successfully centralized political power during his first term, but he went further during his second term. His self-confidence was shaken by the Ukrainian Orange Revolution, a popular protest against a fraudulent presidential election in November–December 2004 that led to a regime change and democratization. In late 2005 Putin promulgated a restrictive law on nongovernmental organizations that allowed the government to deprive any organization of its right to exist. Foreign grants were severely restricted and many required explicit government permission. The tax authorities were mobilized to audit and raid nongovernmental organizations. Public protests and demonstrations were restricted and often prohibited. Criticism of public officials was proscribed by law as "extremism." Revised electoral legislation gave the government full control over the vote count and minimized independent electoral monitoring. Almost all opinion poll organizations came under Kremlin control, and businessmen close to the Kremlin purchased the last independent dailies.[17] Most

17. Anders Åslund, *Russia's Capitalist Revolution: Why Market Reform Succeeded and Democracy Failed* (Washington: Peterson Institute for International Economics, 2007, 248).

chilling were the many murders of Russian journalists and opposition politicians, most of which remain unsolved. Russia still ranks among the highest in the world in terms of the number of journalists murdered.[18]

Putin also changed the electoral rules to eliminate single-district constituencies in Duma elections in favor of proportional representation and then raised the threshold for parties to receive seats to 7 percent in an effort to reduce the chances of opposition politicians being elected. This too had the desired result, as Putin's party enjoyed a constitutional majority (two-thirds) after the Duma elections in December 2007. Once both the chambers of the official parliament had lost most of their significance, the State Council was given the role of a consultative upper chamber, and later a Public Chamber was created to mimic the lower chamber. In reality, however, both chambers were ceremonial rather than influential.

In 2006, hard-line KGB officers established a pro-Putin party called A Just Russia to capture dissatisfaction with corruption and inequality, providing a left-wing alternative to the purportedly center-right United Russia. The Kremlin formed a few youth "movements," notably *Nashi* (Ours). These Kremlin-directed "popular" initiatives were populist and nationalist, based on careful studies of opinion polls and focus groups.

According to the Transparency International corruption perceptions index, corruption declined slightly in Russia from 2000 to 2004 but has grown worse since 2005 (figure 2.2), as could be expected with decreasing transparency and a systematic weakening of all checks and balances. In 2008 Transparency International ranked Russia 147 out of 180 countries on its corruption index (the higher the number, the worse the corruption). According to a survey of large enterprises by the World Bank and the European Bank for Reconstruction and Development in 2002 and 2005, bribe frequency in Russia was the third highest among all postcommunist countries, and Russian businessmen reported that corruption increased significantly as a problem for business, while the dominant tendency among postcommunist countries was improvement.[19]

Political Succession or Instability?

Although Russia became somewhat nationalistic during Putin's two-term centralization of power, the regime did not have any clear ideology, and a persistent official complaint was the lack of a "Russian idea." The central message to the Russian electorate during the parliamentary and presiden-

---

18. See the annual reporting of the Committee to Protect Journalists, which tracks press freedom around the world.

19. James H. Anderson and Cheryl W. Gray, *Anticorruption in Transition 3: Who Is Succeeding. . . and Why?* (Washington: World Bank, 2006, 8, 11).

Figure 2.2 Corruption perceptions index, 2000–2008

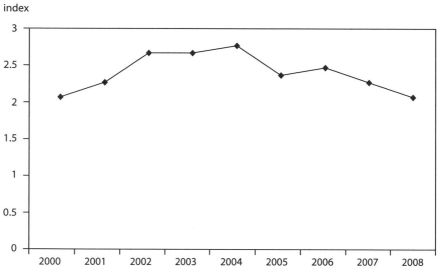

index

Note: The index runs from 10 = highly clean to 0 = highly corrupt.

Source: Transparency International, www.transparency.org (accessed on February 9, 2009).

tial campaigns of 2007–08 was stability and continuity of policy around the nebulous slogan of "Putin's Plan."[20]

Putin resigned after serving his eight years as president, in accordance with the 1993 constitution, which he had not amended. Like Yeltsin before him, he had picked his successor: Dmitri Medvedev, who had worked with Putin since 1991. The selection of Medvedev followed an internal power struggle between the different Putin clans with the arrests of several top aides. Immediately after Putin publicized his choice, Medvedev responded by promising to appoint Putin prime minister.

In March 2008 Medvedev was formally elected president, in elections controlled by the Kremlin, and in May he was inaugurated president while Putin became prime minister. Putin made clear that he planned to play a central role: In his last months as president, he issued a socioeconomic plan for Russian development to 2020, which he is now responsible for implementing as prime minister; he has also taken over the chairmanship of Russia's largest political party, United Russia.

Initially, the new configuration of power was confusing: In constitutional terms, Medvedev had assumed the top position, but Putin re-

20. Clifford G. Gaddy and Andrew C. Kuchins, "Putin's Plan," *Washington Quarterly* (Spring 2008): 117–29.

mained at center stage as prime minister and retained his widespread popular and elite support. There was at first speculation about this tandem, or diarchy, but after the August 2008 war in Georgia, Putin appeared all-powerful. Yet the question remains whether Medvedev will use any of his substantial formal powers. Will the diarchy be destabilizing?

In addition to the question of the stability of the leadership, numerous other serious challenges face Russia's current political system. We focus here on four: legitimacy, national identity, mediating capacity, and functionality.

Although there is much talk about Russia's return as a great power, nationalism remains quite moderate. Instead, the regime's legitimacy depends on stability and high economic growth (see chapter 7). But Russia is already experiencing a sharp decline in its growth rate, it is unlikely to see any economic growth in 2009, and forecasts contain a considerable downside risk. The current Russian regime may therefore face an existential question of survival or have to develop another source of legitimacy.

A shared identity is critical for the stability of any state, particularly to endure political and economic crises. Putin pursued the forging of a national Russian identity with vigor, stressing the continuity of Russian statehood by reaching back to both Soviet and imperial Russian traditions and giving the Russian Orthodox Church a central political role. That effort is evident in his decision in 2000 to restore the old Soviet anthem (with new words) as the national anthem, while maintaining the prerevolutionary tricolor and double-headed eagle as the national flag and herald. The Kremlin has supported the rewriting of school texts in Russian history to provide a more positive assessment, including of the Stalinist period. Over the past two years, the Kremlin has advanced patriotism by using anti-Western rhetoric as a rallying cry. Bolstered by robust economic recovery, these efforts were supposed to restore Russian pride. Yet the attempts to reinforce Russian nationalism have been accompanied by a tide of violent crimes by ethnic Russians against nonethnic Russian citizens. This strong ethnic component to the new Russian patriotism risks alienating the 20 percent of the population that is not ethnically Russian, particularly the millions of legal and illegal immigrants to Russia from Central Asia and the Caucasus, most of whom are Muslim. This risk will grow over the next decade as the share of Muslims in the population continues to grow.

If popular dissatisfaction grows, the ruling elites' natural reflex will be toward more repressive measures, particularly as there will be fewer resources to buy off activist, disaffected groups. However, without ideology or legitimacy, repression is not likely to succeed. The Russian government will need mediating structures to reach a compromise with dissatisfied groups, but at present such structures are missing. Only some mayors are genuinely elected, and the regional governors are effectively appointed, which has undermined Russia's constitutional federalism. President Medvedev himself was essentially appointed by Putin. The natural consequence will be that the Kremlin has to solve all problems, which is likely not possible.

Putin's Legacy and Medvedev's Prospects

In Russia, as throughout the postcommunist world, corruption is the most serious popular concern. Corrupt revenues are concentrated and controlled at the very top. One telling example is that, despite a sizable investment, Russia's paved road network has not been extended since 2000. The large amounts spent on investment are simply lost on corruption and incompetence. As oil revenues are now falling, the government's shortcomings will become all the more conspicuous.

President Medvedev has singled out corruption as one of the gravest domestic problems facing Russia, calling it a "systemic challenge, a threat to national security, a problem that engenders distrust among citizens in the ability of the state to produce order and protect citizens" from criminal activities. He called for strengthening the law enforcement agencies and judicial system to deal with the problem.[21] To underscore the seriousness of his intent, he put himself at the head of the Anti-Corruption Council. But substantial decisions have been slow in coming. A more efficient measure would be to protect independent investigative journalists.

In November 2008, in his first presidential address to the Federal Assembly, Medvedev called for an extension of the presidential term from four to six years. This was the first substantial amendment to the 1993 constitution. Within two months, it won approval from the Duma, the Federation Council, and all the regions. Medvedev signed it into law on the last day of the year.

Putin's central claim on political popularity rests on Russians' newfound sense of stability and prosperity. But as the impact of the global financial crisis becomes more evident to Russian workers and consumers, it is likely that the competence and effectiveness of the Kremlin's "power vertical" will be gravely tested. An optimistic scenario points toward the Russian government's return to an economic reform agenda and to domestic political, economic, and foreign policy decisions that promote national prosperity. A darker scenario depicts a Kremlin that cannot adjust rapidly enough to the social and economic impact with policy measures and so cracks down on dissent and social unrest and tightens the screws on its energy-rich neighbors.

---

21. See Medvedev's interview with Reuters, June 25, 2008, available at www.kremlin.ru.

3

Russia's Economic Revival: Past Recovery, Future Challenges

The Russian economy has gone through turmoil during the last two decades. In the 1980s the Soviet economy suffered from stagnation (although official statistics embellished the data), and in 1989–91, the Soviet economic system collapsed. Russia's GDP officially plummeted by 44 percent until 1998.[1] The real decline, however, was probably only half that, because an extensive unregistered economy developed after socialism.[2] From 1999 to 2007, the Russian economy grew rapidly by an average of 7 percent a year. But the global financial crisis has hit Russia hard. In 2008 growth slowed to 5.6 percent and even started falling in December. The question once again is, for how long and by how much will Russia's output fall?

Yet Russia today is vastly different from the country that was forced to devalue its currency and default on foreign obligations a decade ago. In 1998 the World Bank estimated that about 30 percent of Russia's population lived at or below the poverty line. By 2007 that number had fallen to less than 14 percent. Russians today are accustomed to traveling freely abroad and have a greater stake in an open, free market economy. Wealth has changed much, but many institutions remain unreformed.

1. United Nations Economic Commission for Europe, *Economic Survey of Europe*, no. 2 (2004): 80.

2. Anders Åslund, *Building Capitalism: The Transformation of the Former Soviet Bloc* (New York: Cambridge University Press, 2001, chapter 4); Simon Johnson, Daniel Kaufmann, and Andrei Shleifer, "The Unofficial Economy in Transition," *Brookings Papers on Economic Activity* 27, no. 2 (1997): 183.

This chapter assesses Russia's recent economic achievements and the government's goals for 2020. The old sources of economic growth have faded. What are the sources of Russia's renewed economic growth? What are the current challenges? Is Russia prepared to face them? Will it respond with the necessary reforms to face the challenges of less advantageous economic conditions? What are the potential outcomes?

Russia's Rising Economic Significance

In the past decade, Russia has emerged as one of the big, rising economies. Between 1999 and 2008, the Russian economy grew by an annual average rate of 7 percent, measured in constant rubles (figure 3.1). Because of the sharp real appreciation of the ruble, however, Russian GDP measured in current US dollars expanded by an amazing average of 27 percent a year over the same period, from $196 billion in 1999 to $1.75 trillion in 2008 (figure 3.2). According to the International Monetary Fund (IMF), Russia is now the eighth largest economy in the world, measured by GDP in current dollars, coming just before Spain and after Italy. If GDP is measured in purchasing power parity, Russia is already the sixth largest economy, after Germany but ahead of the United Kingdom and France.[3]

In a much-cited 2003 paper on the BRICs (Brazil, Russia, India, and China), Goldman Sachs projected that in less than 40 years these four economies together would likely be larger than the combined Group of Six (G-6) nations.[4] With a cautiously projected average annual growth of only 3.9 percent, Russia would overtake Italy in 2018, France in 2024, the United Kingdom in 2027, and Germany in 2028. By 2030, Russia would be the fifth largest economy in the world. Factors causing Russia's economic dynamism—in addition to abundant energy resources—are sound macroeconomic policies, an open economy, substantial investment, and high levels of education. Russia's weaknesses are institutions, governance, and the rule of law.

Among the BRICs, Russia has by far the highest GDP per capita in both current dollar and purchasing power parity terms: In 2008 these were $12,000 (four times that of China) and approximately $16,000, respectively—about one-third of those of the 15 old members of the European Union.[5] Goldman Sachs forecasts that Russia will be the only BRIC country to approach European per capita income levels by 2050.

3. International Monetary Fund (IMF), *World Economic Outlook* database, April (Washington, 2008).

4. Dominic Wilson and Roopa Purushothaman, *Dreaming with BRICs: The Path of 2050*, Goldman Sachs Global Economics Paper 99 (New York, 2003). The G-6 nations are France, Germany, Italy, Japan, the United Kingdom, and the United States.

5. IMF, *World Economic Outlook*.

Figure 3.1   GDP growth rate, 2000–2008

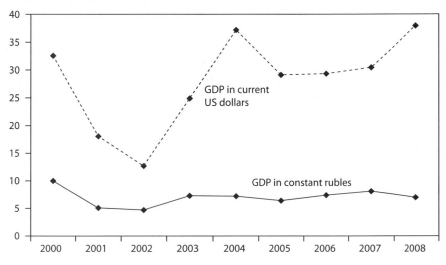

percent, year over year

Source: International Monetary Fund, *World Economic Outlook* database, October 2008 (accessed on November 22, 2008).

Figure 3.2   GDP growth in current US dollars, 1999–2008

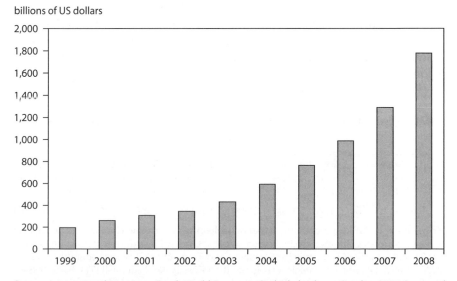

billions of US dollars

Source: International Monetary Fund, *World Economic Outlook* database, October 2008 (accessed on December 23, 2008).

Russia's higher income level is also evident in superior social indicators. In most regards, Russia is slightly more advanced than Brazil and Mexico but head and shoulders above China and India. Most impressive, increasing numbers of young Russians are opting for higher education. According to UNICEF statistics, the share of Russian college-age youth who pursue higher education nearly doubled from 25 percent in 1989 to 47 percent in 2005; and with a broader definition of higher education UNESCO arrived at 73 percent for 2007, more than the average for the European Union.[6] Another indication of Russia's strength is its swiftly growing middle class. According to the Russian research institute Center for Strategic Research, over 30 percent of Russians can now be considered middle class. Russians have 14 times more cars per capita than the Chinese and three times more computers.

The sophistication of Russian consumers makes the country all the more attractive to US exporters of merchandise and services. Yet it also means that Russia is likely to run out of high catch-up growth earlier than the other BRICs.

Russia's Goals for 2020

Russian politicians and economists are preoccupied with economic growth.[7] The nation is suffering from the trauma of its sudden demise as a superpower and is trying to come back through superior economic performance. The peer pressure from neighboring countries is also strong. This single-minded focus on economic growth permeates the Russian government, which has seized upon the Goldman Sachs vision of the BRICs as growth machines. In 2007–08, the Kremlin formulated a large number of goals for 2020; then-president Vladimir Putin laid out the program, Russia 2020, in a speech on February 8, 2008, and the Ministry of Economic Development and Trade presented a more detailed program in March with three alternative scenarios.[8]

The "innovation scenario" is the lead scenario of Russia 2020, with an average growth of 6.5 percent. It presupposes the development of a na-

---

6. TransMONEE database (Florence: UNICEF Innocenti Research Center), www.unicef-irc.org/databases/transmonee (accessed on December 8, 2008); UNESCO Institute for Statistics, *Public Report on Education*, http://stats.uis.unesco.org/ (accessed on July 30, 2008).

7. The best example is Yegor T. Gaidar, *Dolgoe vremya* [*The Long Term*] (Moscow: Delo, 2005).

8. Vladimir V. Putin, speech at the Expanded Meeting of the State Council on Russia's Development Strategy through 2020, February 8, 2008, www.kremlin.ru (accessed on October 15, 2008); Ministry of Economic Development and Trade of the Russian Federation, Rossiya 2020: Osnovnye zadachi strategicheskog razvitiya Rossiikskoi Federatsii [The Basic Tasks of the Strategic Development of the Russian Federation], photocopy (Ministry of Economic Development and Trade, Moscow, March 2008).

tional innovation system, competitive human capital, and regional development centers. It requires a comprehensive reform and investment program, but it has only been laid out in general reasoning in public speeches.

The Ministry of Economic Development and Trade also presented two less optimistic scenarios. The "energy and raw materials scenario" would result in 5.3 percent annual growth until 2020 based on faster development and modernization of the extractive sector. The "inertia scenario" assumes no significant improvement and forecasts an average growth of 3.9 percent a year.[9]

Russia 2020 conveys a vision of Russia as an innovation leader and a middle-class society. The key goal is to raise Russia's GDP per capita from $12,000 in 2008 to $30,000 in 2020—from one-quarter of the US level to half—and make Russia the fifth largest economy in the world after the United States, China, India, and Japan. Russia's GDP would increase on average 6.5 percent a year from 2008 to 2020, and its share of world GDP in current dollars from 2.5 to 4 percent. The share of the middle class would rise from 30 to 60–70 percent and the average life expectancy from 66.6 to 75 years. These are very ambitious goals but not impossible, with the exception of life expectancy. The question is whether Russia's government will pursue an appropriate economic policy.

In order to achieve the program's targets, labor productivity would have to increase by 2.5 times (slightly over 7 percent a year), the energy intensity of production decline by 55 to 60 percent, and spending on research and development increase from 1 percent of GDP in 2006 to 4 percent in 2020. At the same time, public expenditure on education and health care would rise significantly, and investment in infrastructure would skyrocket.

Energy is also a focus of Russia 2020. The energy windfall has facilitated Russia's economic rise, but the government favors diversification. The Russian Ministry of Economic Development and Trade estimated that energy in all its forms contributed 18 percent of GDP in 2007—a substantial fraction but far less than in pure "petrostates"—and accounted for 50 percent of federal revenues and 61 percent of export revenues. President Putin explained:

> So far we have only partially occupied ourselves with modernization of the economy. As a result, Russia has become increasingly dependent on imports of goods and technology, and our role as a raw material appendix to the world economy has been reinforced. In the longer term, this can lead to our lagging behind the leading economies of the world and our country being squeezed out from the world leaders.[10]

---

9. G.O. Kuranov, Kontseptsiya dolgosrochnogo sotsial'no-ekonomicheskogo razvitiya Rossiiskoi Federatsii [Concept of Long-Term Socioeconomic Development of the Russian Federation], photocopy (Ministry of Economic Development and Trade, Moscow, 2008).

10. Putin, speech at the Expanded Meeting of the State Council on Russia's Development Strategy through 2020.

The Russian government has focused on the most optimistic scenario, which is natural given that the country's growth has persistently been at the upper end of all forecasts during the last decade. But as long as current policies persist, this does not seem very credible.

Causes of Russia's Postcommunist Economic Recovery

To understand Russia's economic dilemma, it is necessary to comprehend the causes of its growth over the last two decades. They fall into three categories: capitalist transformation, the use of free capacity and structural change, and energy rents.

Capitalist Transformation

The primary reason for growth has been European or capitalist convergence, which Russia has enjoyed thanks to the hard-fought introduction of a market economy in the 1990s. The transition to a market economy consisted of deregulation, privatization, and financial stabilization. The most important step was to liberalize prices and trade to create a market economy, allowing economic decisions to be freely made by individuals and independent firms. Prices and trade are predominantly free and subsidies are small. No state planning committee tells enterprises what to produce or to whom to sell. Transactions are overwhelmingly monetized. According to the transition index of the European Bank for Reconstruction and Development (EBRD), Russia was a full-fledged market economy by 1996.[11]

Another feature of a free market economy is the dominance of private enterprise. Russia undertook the largest privatization in world history from 1992 to 1997. According to the EBRD, the private sector contributed 70 percent of GDP from 1997 until 2004, although, contrary to the trend in other transition countries, that share fell to 65 percent in 2005. Because essentially all economic growth has come from private enterprise, a decline in the share of the private sector bodes ill for future growth prospects. One-third of the labor force works in the public sector, which has expanded in recent years, aggravating Russia's structural drawbacks.

The government's contribution has been to keep the budget in surplus and taxation moderate. Until 1998, a persistent budget deficit of some 9 percent of GDP held back Russia's growth. In August of that year, it caused a financial crash so severe that Russia switched to prudent macroeconomic policies for a decade. As a result, since 2000 Russia has enjoyed large budget surpluses of several percent of GDP, amounting to 5.4 percent of GDP in 2007. In May 2008 Russia's stock-market capitalization ap-

---

11. Anders Åslund, *Russia's Capitalist Revolution: Why Market Reform Succeeded and Democracy Failed* (Washington: Peterson Institute for International Economics, 2007, 278–80).

proximately equaled its GDP, as is common in Western Europe. Russia's foreign currency reserves peaked at $598 billion in early August 2008, and its public foreign debt plunged from 100 percent of GDP in 1999 to 3 percent in 2008.[12]

From 1998 to 2002, Russia undertook a profound tax reform and adopted a liberal tax system, cutting the number of taxes sharply, reducing tax rates, and introducing a flat personal income tax of only 13 percent, while decriminalizing many tax violations. As a consequence, Russians started paying taxes, and public expenditures have hovered around a moderate 35 percent of GDP. The recovery was coupled with remonetization as Russia enjoyed a great credit boom.

Russia's structural reforms continued until 2002. Among the last important reforms were a comprehensive judicial reform—which means that businessmen sue both one another and the government on an increasing scale—and the adoption of a land code that legalized private ownership of agricultural land. New laws on licensing, certification, permits, and inspections eased restrictions on small enterprises, and a new customs code simplified the previously exceedingly difficult customs procedures.

Another important factor stimulating Russia's growth is the country's fast integration into the world economy: Total exports surged from $42 billion in 1992 to $472 billion in 2008 (roughly 30 percent of GDP) and the merchandise trade surplus to $180 billion.[13] Russia has enjoyed huge steady current account surpluses since 2000; even in 2008 it was $113 billion or 7.7 percent of GDP. Much of the increase has come from rising oil prices, but Russia's economy has been diversifying: The share of oil and gas in the country's exports has fallen to 60 percent from 90 percent in the late 1980s. With its exports now accounting for one-third of its GDP, Russia is quite an open economy.

Free Capacity and Structural Changes

The second set of reasons for high growth has been the huge free capacity in production, infrastructure, and human capital as well as significant structural changes since the collapse of communism. With the rise of the new capitalist service sector, a large-scale structural change spurred growth. The service sector expanded from 33 percent of GDP in 1989 to 57 percent in 2007. Even so, Russia's industrial sector is still large by international standards, contributing 38 percent of GDP in 2006, compared with 27 percent in the euro area.[14] The sizable industrial sector partly re-

---

12. Bank of Finland, Russia Statistics Online, www.bof.fi (accessed on various dates).

13. Statistics are from the Central Bank of the Russian Federation, www.cbr.ru (accessed on February 11, 2009).

14. World Bank, *World Development Indicators*, http://devdata.worldbank.org (accessed on various dates).

flects insufficient market adjustment (yet to come) and partly shows Russia's comparative advantage in raw material extraction.

Russia's structural changes are best illustrated with a quick review of its major industries. Economic growth took off with recovery in the privatized heavy export industries, oil and metals. In its wake, some related sectors recovered, notably mining, chemical industry, and partially heavy machine-building. With rising personal incomes, housing construction and retail trade expanded grandly, and their development is proliferating throughout the country.

A few industries that initially lagged are now evolving, and they will contribute to Russia's growth for years. Agriculture is reviving slowly but steadily. A very gradual redistribution of land is taking place from old state and collective farms, many of which have lain fallow, to huge agro-industries with a few hundred thousand hectares of land. But these companies are having serious trouble finding skilled management and labor. The agricultural revival started in grain production and other large-scale crop cultivation and is proceeding in poultry and pig farming, but Russia's cattle and dairy industry remains miserable. The country's burgeoning poultry industry has one of the strongest protectionist lobbies, whereas grain producers favor free exports. In the 1980s the Soviet Union imported an average of 38 million tons of grain each year, but in 2005–06 Russia exported 11 million to 12 million tons of grain a year.[15]

Another sector set to develop is the automotive industry. In 2010 Russia is forecasted to surpass Germany as the biggest car purchaser in Europe, with some 3.5 million cars. At present, Russia imports more cars than it produces because the old Soviet car producers have impeded the development of new domestic automotive companies. Yet most large car producers in the world either have or are about to establish production in Russia, and the country's automotive output will likely expand spectacularly. Similarly, Russia's forestry industry has been a laggard because of late reforms, but with huge resources and domestic demand it is set to develop fast.

One of the least noticed structural changes is the 7 percent a year rise in the number of registered enterprises. It is true that Russia remains dominated by big enterprises, but not to the extent commonly perceived. With 5 million registered enterprises and 3.4 million registered individual entrepreneurs, Russia has a total of 8.4 million firms[16]—one enterprise per 17 people, approximately as many as in Western European countries. Small and medium-sized enterprises contribute 45 percent of GDP, compared with about two-thirds in Western Europe.

---

15. Federal'naya Sluzhba Statistiki [Federal State Statistics Service] online database, www.gks.ru (accessed on September 11, 2008).

16. Federal'naya Sluzhba Statistiki [Federal State Statistics Service] online database, "Number of Individual Entrepreneurs," www.gks.ru (accessed on December 23, 2008).

A common feature of the postcommunist economies is a large pent-up need for investment and the remonetization of the economy. In 2006 Russia's M2 as a share of GDP was as little as 33.5 percent,[17] whereas 70 to 80 percent would be normal for a European market economy. As long as private property prevails, Russia has plenty of collateral for more than twice as large a credit volume without any apparent financial risks.

Together, Russia's systemic and structural changes represent the gigantic catch-up effect or capitalist convergence that all postcommunist reform countries have experienced. The average annual real growth in former Soviet states from 2000 to 2007 was 9 percent, but it reached only 7 percent in Russia, so Russia has actually been comparatively less dynamic than its cohort (the growth leaders are Azerbaijan, Armenia, Estonia, Kazakhstan, and Latvia).[18] Growth accounting shows that since 2000, about half of Russia's growth has been from capital and half from rising total factor productivity, while increased labor has contributed little.[19]

Energy Rents

The third factor behind Russia's growth is the oil price windfall since 2004. As international oil prices took off, a dominant theme in the Russian economic debate became the danger of an "energy curse" for the Russian economy. The curse actually encompasses several problems, such as overvaluation of the currency, the government ignoring reforms, and rent seeking.

After the Russian financial crash of 1998, the authorities were greatly concerned with any overvaluation of the exchange rate that would price out other exports, the so-called Dutch disease. As a consequence, talent has been focused on making money in the energy sector, and the development of other industries has been neglected, not least because Russian labor has been uncompetitive with its high salaries.

A second energy curse is that the abundance of energy revenues that has boosted the country's budget surplus, current account balance, and currency reserves makes it difficult to motivate policymakers and the population to pursue and accept economic reforms that often entail hardship in the short term. As a consequence, Russia has made no economic or social reforms worth mentioning for the past six years, as the government focused on the distribution of oil rents rather than on the improvement of policy.

---

17. EBRD, Economic Statistics and Indicators, 2008, www.ebrd.com (accessed on December 10, 2008).

18. Ibid.

19. Garbis Iradian, "Rapid Growth in Transition Economies: Growth Accounting Approach," IMF Working Paper no. 164 (Washington: International Monetary Fund, 2007).

A third energy curse is that the concentrated energy revenues facilitate the concentration of both political power and rent seeking. This is the cause of the extreme and rising corruption in Russia. As a consequence, Russia's business environment is poor, and it is getting worse. The state bureaucracy impedes efficient economic activity and adds to the cost of doing business in the form of time spent dealing with arbitrary regulations and the payment of bribes. The World Bank's Doing Business index ranked Russia 96 among 175 countries in 2006, but in 2008 it fell to 120 out of 181. Russia receives its best rankings for enforcing contracts (18), registering property (49), and starting a business (65), all of which make it comparatively easy to establish a firm. But the regulatory environment is bad (figure 3.3); in 2008, filing for and receiving the necessary permits and licenses for the construction of a warehousing facility took 704 days in Russia compared with 161 in the countries of Organization for Economic Cooperation and Development. But although there have been some official complaints about the public sector, Russia 2020 does not reflect any awareness that Russia's main problem is its huge, inefficient, and corrupt public sector.

The Kremlin's current economic problem is that most of the old sources of growth will soon be exhausted. Undoubtedly, some capitalist convergence will continue, being the engine of inertia growth, but it is bound to slow down. The qualitative improvement of human capital will also continue as will remonetization and structural changes. Yet the free capacity in production and infrastructure is probably coming to a sudden end. The most problematic sectors are those dominated by the state—natural gas, roads, railways, pipelines, aircraft, armaments production, medical services, education, and law enforcement.

The Global Financial Crisis: A Perfect Storm Revealing Old Sins

In July 2008 top Russian officials presumed that Russia would escape the international financial crisis and even be a safe haven. Instead, this hazard has served as rude a shock to Russia as to most other countries. This first became evident when the Russian stock market plummeted by 80 percent from its peak in May 2008 to its nadir (so far) in January 2009. The international oil price plunged from an all-time high of $147 per barrel in July to a low of $34 in December.

The particular Russian causes of concern are mainly structural and long term. It is easy to criticize Russia 2020. Its author, the Ministry of Economic Development and Trade, used to be Gosplan, the State Planning Committee, and its style is reminiscent of the Soviet 15-year perspective plans, which had no operative implication. As in the days of Nikita Khrushchev and Leonid Brezhnev, the new plan specifies how fast Russia is to catch up with the United States. After nine successful years the authorities just presumed

Figure 3.3 Ease of doing business in Russia, 2008

rank out of 181 countries

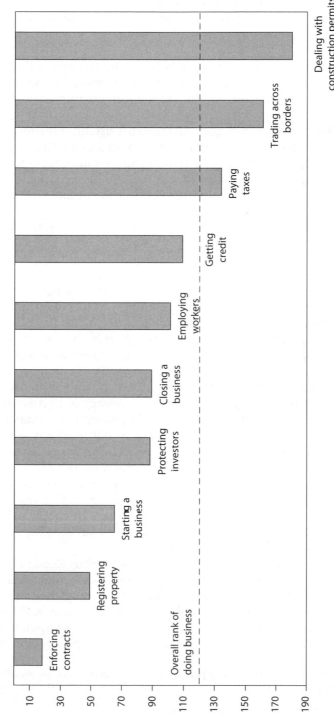

Source: World Bank, *Doing Business 2009*, www.coingbusiness.org (accessed on December 23, 2008).

that the same trend would continue for the next decade, but if the sources of growth are not maintained but undermined, it would be unrealistic to expect further improvement. Some of the goals—for example, to raise life expectancy from 67 to 75 years within 12 years—appear downright utopian.

The main problem with Russia's economic strategy is that it requires substantial and comprehensive economic reforms, but no such reforms have been planned. Russia 2020 ignores deregulation and improvement of the enterprise environment, instead vaguely emphasizing innovation and high technology; but catch-up growth is usually a matter of imitation, pragmatism, and opportunism rather than originality. The program seems to rely on the strength of growth momentum. But because it is predominantly a commodity exporter, Russia is liable to be particularly sensitive to the vagaries of the global business cycle, and currently the whole world is facing a vicious financial crisis.[20]

Problems abound. As its energy production stagnates, Russia's external account is bound to dwindle quickly with crumbling prices. Industrial production fell by 10 percent in December 2008, and GDP growth forecasts for 2009 have been revised from 7 percent growth to moderate decline. Russia's official international currency reserves sank from $598 billion in early August 2008 by more than one-third to $381 billion in early March 2009. Although the whole world was severely hit by the global financial crisis, Russia seemed to suffer more than other countries in spite of its vast reserves. For too long, the government denied the crisis and pursued other ambitions.

The greatest social shock is that the real disposable incomes of the population, which had been increasing by an average of 13 percent a year for several years, suddenly plummeted by 12 percent in December 2008. Surprisingly, the budget surplus of 4 percent of GDP in 2008 is expected to become a deficit of at least 8 percent of GDP in 2009. The current account surplus actually peaked at $99 billion, or 5.9 percent of GDP, because of the record commodity prices and contracting imports at the end of 2008. But the current account will possibly be balanced in 2009, though the size is highly dependent on the unpredictable oil price. A couple of these problems—the falling commodity prices and the global liquidity squeeze—are of external origin, but most are domestic.

The labor force is shrinking. Like most of Europe, Russia is facing a demographic problem as its native population is declining (as discussed in chapter 6); at best its population will increase only insignificantly until 2020. The labor force is set to decline from 90 million in 2007 to 78 million in 2020, according to the Ministry of Economic Development and Trade (or, at a minimum, 1 percent a year).[21] It may be possible to compensate

---

20. Two of the postcommunist star performers, Estonia and Latvia, have swiftly gone from 10 percent growth to decline.

21. Kuranov, "Kontseptsiya dolgosrochnogo."

for this decline with a more liberal housing market and a reduction in reliance on the public sector, but those will require substantial reforms.

Russia's investment ratio never reached more than 23 percent of GDP in 2007, and it is falling sharply in the current business environment, while the most successful transition countries have investment ratios exceeding 30 percent of GDP, as in East Asia. If Russia is to achieve high future growth, it needs to boost investment.

Infrastructure, especially roads, has become an extraordinary bottleneck, as any visitor to Moscow may notice in its horrendous traffic jams. The 2020 plans are full of grand infrastructure projects, but Russia seems to be unable to carry out major infrastructure projects. In 2000 the country had 754,000 kilometers of paved roads, according to official statistics; incredibly, by 2006 this figure had increased by only 0.1 percent, to 755,000 kilometers. The trunk (*magistral'nye*) oil pipelines were 47,000 kilometers in 2006, exactly the same as in 1995. The trunk gas pipelines increased from 213,000 kilometers in 2000 by 5 percent in 2006.[22] In all major infrastructure projects, the little that is built costs at least three times as much per kilometer as in the West. Russia's public administration has proven itself too incompetent and corrupt to undertake major projects. Unless that changes, none of the many large planned infrastructure projects will progress.

Russia's economic growth has also been driven by international economic integration. The World Bank and Russia's Economic Development Ministry estimated that World Trade Organization (WTO) membership would increase the country's economic growth by 0.5 to 1 percentage point a year for the next five years, primarily from finance, foreign direct investment, and services. If Russia's leaders abandon their attempts to join the WTO and aggravate protectionism, especially in agriculture and finance, a corresponding economic deterioration is likely.

Russia merits praise for its conservative fiscal policy, its accumulation of large currency reserves, and its limited domestic leverage, but it suffers from minimal domestic financial intermediation because inept state banks dominate the domestic financial market. Almost half of Russia's banking system is owned by five state banks: Sberbank, VTB, Gazprombank, Vneshekonombank (VEB), and Bank Moskvy. Because these banks are politicized, the banking system is inefficient and unreliable, and the national costs of a poor banking system rise over time. In effect, the Russian banking system works like this: The state takes money out of the country, while big Russian corporations are forced to borrow abroad, maximizing their currency risk.

Most of Russia's many private banks are quite small, while the Russian economy is dominated by large companies, leading to a mismatch be-

---

22. Federal'naya Sluzhba Statistiki [Federal State Statistics Service], *Russian Statistical Yearbook 2007*, www.gks.ru (accessed on October 16, 2008).

tween small banks and large creditors, which have to turn to international banks. Many small banks have failed or been merged with larger banks, but bank restructuring has only started. Moreover, large nonperforming loans need to be written off. If Russia had privatized its banking system like most other post-Soviet countries, its companies would suffer less from currency risks. Furthermore, if foreign banks owned a large share of the Russian banking system, Russia's access to international finance would be much better.

Russia's economic recovery has been generated by private enterprise, but since 2005 renationalization has prevailed, reducing economic efficiency and thus future growth. The renationalization of major companies such as Yukos, Sibneft, Vankor, United Heavy Machineries, VSMPO-Avisma, Sakhalin Energy, and Rusia (Kovykta) has aggravated corporate governance and political risk. The state now accounts for 83 percent of gas production and 45 percent of oil production, and the Kremlin is utilizing the financial crisis to promote renationalization that is economically unfounded and harmful. Strangely, in the midst of the financial crisis, the Russian government is preoccupied with further nationalization. A couple of companies, the mining and steel company Mechel and the potash producer Uralkali, seem to have been singled out for expropriation through major penalties, while the state corporations are buying up one distressed company after another with money from the state budget.

Yet Russia has not espoused a socialist ideology, and its big state corporations are moving toward 51 percent state ownership—Rosneft and VTB made limited initial public offerings in 2006 and 2007, respectively—exposing themselves to assessment by the stock market. Investors have reacted negatively, slashing Gazprom's market capitalization from $350 billion in May 2008 to $70 billion in October.

A major policy flaw has been the managed exchange rate, which caused annual inflation to peak at 15 percent in the summer of 2008. Global inflation rose with increasing food and energy prices, but Russia's inflation rate was about twice that of other emerging markets because its macroeconomic policy relied too much on fiscal policy and too little on monetary and exchange rate policy. The inflation was caused by the large current account surplus, which was monetized in rubles because the central bank purchased hard currency to defend the fixed ruble exchange rate (Russia's exchange rate was loosely pegged to a basket of $0.55 and €0.45). For years Russia had a negative real interest rate that boosted monetary expansion and inflation, as the central bank stated, but did not act on, its intention to move to inflation targeting within three years.

The Russian government has repeated its mistake from 1998, maintaining an untenable pegged exchange rate in the face of falling commodity prices. Until the summer of 2008, the pegged policy provoked speculative capital inflows that boosted the money supply and inflation. Since then the rate has left the ruble overvalued, promoting speculative capital outflows and rapidly reducing the currency reserves. At the end of 2008, Russia started to devalue, but rather than letting the exchange rate float, Russia devalued the ruble in many small steps. Repeated mini devaluations only convinced the market that a major devaluation was inevitable. All who could exchange their rubles for dollars or euro did so. Even so, Russia has not succeeded in letting the exchange rate float, though it has raised interest rates so that they correspond to inflation. The combination of loose fiscal policy, negative real interest rates, current and capital account deficits, and an overvalued ruble is unsustainable, clearly provoking capital flight: Russia's international currency reserves declined by over $210 billion from $598 billion in early August 2008 to $381 billion in early March 2009—more than one-third in half a year, though large amounts of the hard currency are held by Russian banks in Russia.

Russia should let the ruble float freely, move to inflation targeting, and boost interest rates to achieve positive real interest rates. A commodity-exporting country needs to let its exchange rate float up and down with international raw material prices to balance its foreign payments. As in 1998, speculators now sensibly bet on a ruble devaluation, which quickly depletes Russia's currency reserves and becomes a necessity. When the ruble is allowed to float, nobody knows whether it will rise or fall, which will reduce speculation and losses of currency reserves.

Russian big businessmen and their corporations have turned out to be much more leveraged than anybody had thought—total Russian corporate foreign debt was $488 billion in October 2008. Many of these big businesses have pledged their strategic holdings of Russian stocks against foreign bank loans, forcing the Russian state to bail them out (the government has made clear that it will refinance their foreign loans to secure "strategic" ownership). Initially, $50 billion was allocated to VEB for this purpose, but the government reduced this amount to $13 billion, directing the support to the banks instead.

For long the government persistently denied that anything was wrong with Russia's economic policy. Domestic and foreign businessmen realized that this did not tally with reality, and this incongruity undermined their confidence in the Russian market. Without free public debate, rational policy decisions are unlikely.

Short-term statistics from the winter of 2008–09 indicate how severe the situation is. In the spring of 2008, capital investment rose by some 20 percent over the corresponding month the preceding year. By December 2008, it fell by 2 percent. Similarly, in December 2008, industrial production plummeted by 10 percent, and gas production by about as much. These dramatic falls in output tally with the statistics of many other countries in the midst of the financial crisis, but the shocker is that in Russia, real disposable income dropped by no less than 12 percent, while the population had enjoyed a rise of an average of 13 percent a year during the six preceding years.[23]

Until 2009, the Russian government denied the crisis and treated it as a foreign phenomenon. Rather than trying to minimize the cost of adjustment, the government tried to minimize the adjustment itself. Its primary ambition seemed to be to promote renationalization, which deterred both domestic and foreign businessmen. It is too early to predict the overall decline in Russia's GDP, but it is likely to be a few percent, as large as or somewhat larger than in the Western world.

Russia has also alienated itself from the outside world just when it most needs worldwide support. At the Group of Eight (G-8) summit in Japan in July 2008, Russia promised not to block UN sanctions against Zimbabwe, after which it immediately vetoed them in the UN Security Council. Through its recognition of Abkhazia and South Ossetia, Russia violated multiple treaties guaranteeing the sovereignty and territorial integrity of former Soviet republics. At the G-20 meeting in Washington on November 15, 2008 Russia committed itself not to undertake new protectionist measures but immediately raised import tariffs on cars. Such blatant violations of top-level promises have boosted Russia's risk premium.

It is difficult to assess the impact of all these actions, but they are all potent and negative. How will the Russian people and leaders react? The positive scenario is that the rulers face reality and return to the progressive market reforms they pursued until 2002. The alternative is that they dig in and refuse to undertake necessary reforms.

A Time of Economic Challenge

After a decade of solid economic growth, Russia is now facing numerous acute challenges. A temporary economic slowdown is inevitable because of the global recession and falling prices of commodity exports. Russia's very high real estate prices are already rapidly declining, which will hurt the weak banking system, and domestic demand will be constrained. The big question is how Russia will respond to the economic slowdown. Three scenarios appear plausible over the next 12 years: an inertia scenario, a reform (or innovation) scenario, or a crisis scenario.

The inertia scenario presumes no major new reforms and average annual growth of 3.5 to 4 percent. The only growth drivers would be capitalist convergence, improved development and better allocation of human capital, continued economic restructuring, and some remonetization. Russia's resource wealth is so substantial that such a strategy can de-

---

23. Federal'naya Sluzhba Statistiki [Federal State Statistics Service] online database, www.gks.ru (accessed on January 29, 2009).

liver moderate growth for a long time to come, and the higher world energy prices will be, the more likely such a choice.

The reform scenario implies that the Russian government faces its main challenges and carries out the required reforms. This scenario requires the swift implementation of several critical measures. First, Russia should accede to the WTO to secure its successful international integration and an improvement of its legal standards. Second, to ease infrastructure bottlenecks, the Kremlin needs to introduce transparent procurement procedures for major investments. Third, property rights must be reinforced and renationalization stopped to ease the problems in banking and energy production. With this scenario, an average growth of 6.5 percent a year is feasible, but it is very far from Russia's current economic policy.

Finally, a crisis scenario not foreseen by the Russian government is possible. Russian officials do not discuss the possibility of outright systemic crisis, but the grounds for such a scenario are substantial. Russia is extremely sensitive to commodity prices, as commodities accounted for about 85 percent of Russia's exports in 2007; in the second half of 2008 international commodity prices fell sharply, and in 2009 they may very well be less than half of their average 2008 level. Such a drop would reduce Russia's exports by 40 percent, or some $180 billion. A political system whose legitimacy is based almost entirely on economic growth can easily collapse in such a situation and thus prompt a change of political regime.

So far, the Russian government has managed the financial crisis poorly. First, it denied the crisis. Second, it maximized capital outflows through an inadequate exchange rate policy. Third, its main endeavor has not been to deal with the crisis but to pursue other objectives, such as renationalization of major corporations. Clearly, this policy cannot continue because the results would be politically and socially untenable. When and how will Russia's government alter its economic policy?

Russia has gone through two impressive waves of structural reform, in 1991–93 and 1998–2002. In the interim, hardly any reforms were undertaken. The question today is whether Russia, facing a great need for a new wave of reform, can mobilize the political will to achieve it. This is, of course, a matter of political leadership, but the farther commodity prices fall—and with them economic growth—the more likely the leadership is to implement new reforms.

4

Policy on Oil and Gas

Russia's key dilemma lies in the conflict between its fast economic modernization and its centralized political system. This divergence is particularly evident in the country's dominant economic sector, energy. Russian leaders are calling their country an energy superpower with good reason: It is the biggest producer of primary energy in the world, with one-ninth of world crude output (roughly level with Saudi Arabia) and one-fifth of world natural gas output (in which Russia is the world leader). Russia holds about 27 and 6 percent of the world's known reserves of natural gas and oil, respectively.[1] Russia's reserves are likely to be far larger since exploration has been limited.

The importance of oil and natural gas to Russia's economy can be measured in three ways. First, according to official statistics, oil and gas account for only 9 percent of Russia's GDP, which is surprisingly little; the explanation is that energy overall and natural gas in particular have much lower prices on the domestic market because of export tariffs and price controls on gas and electricity. At world market prices, oil and gas account for 18 percent of Russia's GDP, which is the relevant statistic. The second measurement is the share of exports; in 2007 oil and gas accounted for 61 percent of Russia's exports. The third measure is the contribution of oil and gas to total federal revenues, which is about 50 percent.

Production of Oil and Natural Gas

Russia's oil production has been on a wild ride in the last two decades. From 1999 to 2004, it rose by no less than 50 percent (figure 4.1), but in

---

1. BP, *Statistical Review of World Energy 2008*, www.bp.com (accessed on December 12, 2008).

Figure 4.1   Oil and gas production, 1985–2008

million tons of oil equivalent

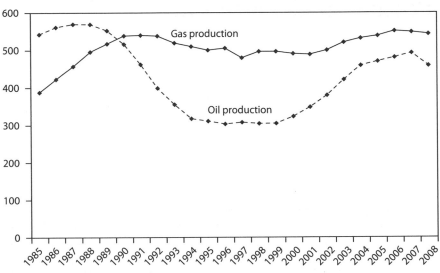

Source: BP, *Statistical Review of World Energy 2008*; Deutsche Bank; Russian Federal State Statistics Service; authors' calculations.

2005–07 the expansion slowed to 2.5 percent a year because of partial renationalization and high taxation, both of which limited exploration and development. Oil production peaked in 2007 at the very high level of 9.9 million barrels a day, almost as high as in the late 1980s, but declined by 0.9 percent in 2008 for the first time since 1998.

Russia's output of natural gas remained fairly constant in the 1990s, partly because the new giant gasfields in Western Siberia came on stream later than the oilfields. In 2000–06, the production of natural gas increased by about 2 percent a year, but only because of the contributions of independent producers. The state-dominated natural gas company Gazprom's aging giant fields were in decline, and Gazprom failed to develop both new and secondary fields. Therefore, Gazprom's output is now stagnating and fell by 0.8 percent in 2007 to 607 billion cubic meters.[2] A 1.4 percent recovery in 2008 was entirely due to independent producers, while Gazprom maintained a stable output of 83 percent of Russia's total output in 2008. At this point, large international investments in new oil and gas fields are needed just to keep up Russia's energy output. Expansion seems beyond reach for years to come.

---

2. Ibid.

Alternative Approaches to Risk Management

One of Russia's greatest challenges is the management of its oil and natural gas sector. Risk management has always been the key to success in oil and gas, a business inherently fraught with high geologic, technical, financial, and political risks. Balancing the risks and rewards is the true test of business acumen in the petroleum industry and is even more important for state policy. Companies that fail in the marketplace are replaced by smarter and better-performing competitors. The failures of governments have much more serious and enduring consequences.

Russia's former Prime Minister Yegor Gaidar has argued that one of the factors contributing to the collapse of the Soviet Union was an overreliance on the oil and gas sector after world oil price spikes in the 1970s, followed by the collapse of prices in the mid-1980s.[3] In 1988 the Soviet Union was the largest oil producer in the world, with peak production of 12.5 million barrels per day, 11 million of which came from Russia. The problem was that the world oil price dropped from almost $40 per barrel in the early 1980s (after the Iranian revolution and the start of the Iran-Iraq War) to well below $20 per barrel just before the Soviet Union collapsed in 1991. The nadir of $10 per barrel was in the midst of the financial crash of 1998.

This recent history is an object lesson for current Russian leaders about the long-term cyclical nature of the oil industry, which they have overlooked for the last five years. The reason is understandable. From the time Vladimir Putin emerged on the Russian national stage in 1999, the world oil price rose steadily during his first presidential term and then leaped during his second term to an all-time high (in inflation-adjusted terms). In light of this steady climb, Gazprom's CEO Alexei Miller boldly predicted in June 2008 that oil prices would rise to $250 per barrel in 2009. In fact, he almost perfectly called the top of the most recent oil price bubble: The world benchmark crude oil, West Texas Intermediate, reached a peak price of $147.27 per barrel on July 11 before promptly nose-diving. The next price level it tested was a floor of $35, which is where it stands as of this writing in February 2009.

Still the $35 price tag is historically high. If the real (inflation-adjusted) oil price returned to its level of the first half of this decade, it would drop to about $30 per barrel, which would not be an altogether shocking development given the current global financial meltdown, recession, and resulting decline in oil demand. Just as the price overshot on the upside, it is likely to overshoot on the downside as well before it finds a new equilibrium. Yet in September 2008 Minister of Finance Alexei Kudrin stated

---

3. Yegor T. Gaidar, *The Collapse of the Empire: Lessons for Modern Russia* (Washington: Brookings Institution, 2007).

that the Russian government needed an average price of Russian export blend crude oil of $70 per barrel for its budget to break even. Only in February 2009 did the government announce its intention to revise the 2009 budget to an oil price of $41 per barrel. Gas export prices to Europe follow European oil prices with a lag of 6 to 9 months, so what is true of oil prices is also valid for gas prices with a minor delay.

The Oil Sector: Reinforced State Control rather than Market Reforms

How have the fluctuations in prices informed Russian government policy toward the oil and gas sector? What are the consequences of this policy? And what are the implications for the future, including possible course corrections?

When Putin came to national prominence in 1999, the Russian oil industry had begun recovering as a result of ruble devaluation (which lowered production costs), privatizations that led to efficiency gains, reinvestment by oligarchs with newly acquired property rights, and the introduction of Western technology and management skills. Foreign investment was growing and demonstrating what could be achieved with international industry practices. Production improved rapidly with the use of modern oilfield techniques for brownfield projects in existing production areas. With lower domestic consumption from a slower economy and higher prices, oil exports grew steadily and became an important driver of the Russian economic recovery.

The reform process was incomplete, however. Trunk oil pipelines remain in the hands of the state-owned monopoly Transneft, with antiquated business practices and nontransparent access rules and regulations. For example, because of exchanges based on weight (tons) rather than volume (barrels or liters) and the lack of a crude quality adjustment mechanism, producers do not receive fair market value. This has the perverse effect of providing incentives to producers of low-quality heavy crude oil to increase their production, while producers of the higher-quality light crude oil are disadvantaged and seek less efficient methods of transporting their product. Extended production license periods would encourage larger investments that would take longer to pay back, but extensions are not granted. License renewal and award remain a capricious process subject to political interference and the whims and corrupt demands of bureaucrats.

In 2003 the entire reform process in the oil sector not only stalled but also went into reverse. The signal event was the arrest and imprisonment of Mikhail Khodorkovsky, the Yukos oil company CEO, who was at the forefront of modernizing the Russian petroleum sector under private ownership and the discipline of capital markets, outside of government's political control. Yukos was forced into bankruptcy and its prized assets acquired by the state-owned and -controlled oil company Rosneft. Other Russian oil oligarchs quickly fell into line to accommodate the Kremlin's new policy of state control and recentralization of decision making for the oil sector.

As world oil prices continued to rise, Russian oil export taxes rose to take as much as 90 percent of the incremental financial benefit for the government treasury, thereby reducing cash flow for Russian oil producers to reinvest in their businesses during a highly favorable market environment. Plans for privately funded major pipeline projects to Murmansk or China ceased. Instead Transneft proceeded to build economically suboptimal oil pipelines to the Baltic and Pacific coasts. Unlike Murmansk, the shallow Baltic ports in the Gulf of Finland cannot accept supertankers and they freeze in the winter.

Russian leaders rediscovered the political benefits of central control of the petroleum industry. The bonanza in oil income allowed them to parcel out wealth, pay social benefits, reward friends, punish enemies, buy electoral victories, and maintain power, all without seeking political legitimacy of the sort required by broad taxation of the public in a diversified economy.

The tradeoff is that centralization shifts the risks inherent in the petroleum business, especially commodity price risks, from a competitive private sector and capital markets to the state. It dries up investment flow, which is the lifeblood of a capital-intensive business like petroleum that requires long lead times. Responsibility for risk taking moves from market players to state bureaucrats, with accompanying loss of effectiveness and efficiency, after the easy improvements, such as enhanced oil recovery, have been made and frontier exploration and development are needed to replace declining oil reserves.

In 2005 the growth rate of oil production slowed considerably, and in 2008 Russian oil production actually declined. Russia joins the ranks of Venezuela and Iran as major oil-producing countries that have pursued policies that discouraged investment in future production capacity at a time of extremely favorable conditions of high prices and market premiums for access to resources. In contrast, Libya and Angola took advantage of the favorable climate by attracting foreign investment and increasing their productive capacity.

Producing-country governments often consider volume growth unnecessary at a time of high prices, but it can be critical when prices soften, particularly if the country is highly dependent on oil income. Again, balancing risks and rewards should be the key consideration. A farsighted host government attracts investment at a time of high prices when it can drive the best economic bargain as owner of the resource. A shortsighted host government appeals for investment after prices drop and bargaining leverage shifts in favor of oil investors. But political perception frequently lags market reality, and governments act late when it would be more prudent to respond in a countercyclical manner, getting maximum investments when prices are high so as to enjoy volume growth when prices soften, as they inevitably do.

The Gas Sector: A Serious Concern

In many ways the situation in Russia's gas sector, dominated by state-controlled Gazprom, is of more serious concern than oil. Unlike the oil sector, the gas sector never went through a period of reform and privatization. Gazprom is run much like the old Soviet gas ministry, with near monopoly control over the production, transport, distribution, and export of natural gas. Although Russia remains the largest gas producer and exporter in the world, with a quarter of all proven gas reserves, gas never enjoyed the boom in production growth that oil did.

Because of delays in instituting domestic gas pricing reform, fully two-thirds of Russia's massive production goes to domestic consumption, completely out of proportion to the size of the Russian economy and population, even after taking the cold climate into account. The waste is not limited to gas consumption. The Russian government estimates that 20 billion cubic meters of gas are flared every year because Gazprom restricts Russian oil producers on pipeline and market access for their associated gas; the producers, therefore, have little economic incentive to collect and process the gas associated with oil production. Estimates by international agencies such as the World Bank and the International Energy Agency put the actual figure for Russian gas flaring two to three times higher, which would make it equivalent to more than the annual gas consumption of France.

Meanwhile, production from three of Gazprom's four major fields—Medvezhye, Urengoy, and Yamburg—is past its peak and declining rapidly, and the fourth (Zapolyarnoe) is at its peak. In the short run, Gazprom is increasingly reliant on gas supply from Central Asia, particularly Turkmenistan, and is reducing its supply commitment to traditional customers in the former Soviet Union, such as Ukraine, in order to meet its domestic gas balance and contractual commitments to Western Europe. In the longer run, domestic pricing reform and massive investments in difficult greenfield projects are needed to maintain Gazprom's supply as well as its prominent roles both as exporter of gas to Europe and in Russian domestic politics.

In the gas industry, as in oil, Russia no doubt has a huge resource base. But many questions accompany the disposition of this resource. What are the right types of investments and what is the best way to ensure that they are timely and effective? Is continued centralization and government control the best way to achieve the desired results, for example, in the development of Eastern Siberia, the Yamal Peninsula, and the Arctic Region? Should the state assume sole risk in frontier projects or share the high risks—and rewards—with the domestic private sector and international capital? Should the government reconsider and resume market reform, perhaps in a more thoughtful and fair way than in the 1990s? Given the importance of the oil and gas sector to the Russian economy, foreign exchange earnings, and government revenue, the stakes are high.

The Changing Role of the Outside World

Even as the production growth rate slowed, the Russian government moved against foreign investors, notably Royal Dutch Shell in the Sakhalin II project, TNK-BP in the Kovykta gasfield, and ExxonMobil in Sakhalin I, in further reassertion of state domination.[4] On April 29, 2008, Russia adopted a new Law on the Procedure for Contributing Foreign Investments in Legal Entities Which Are of Strategic Importance for the Defense of the Country and Security of the State, commonly called the Law on Foreign Investments in Strategic Industries. It restricts foreign company access to large upstream opportunities. This measure is again contrary to the conventional industry wisdom that calls for spreading risks to foreign investors in expensive and challenging projects and for favoring domestic producers in smaller projects that they can easily handle and for which foreign investors are not needed.

Not only foreign companies but also private Russian corporations suffer from discrimination. Gazprom and Rosneft, the two national champions, now have the right of first refusal in new offshore exploration blocks. Gazprom has selected Norwegian StatoilHydro and French Total as partners for the development of the gigantic and difficult Shtokman offshore gasfield on the Barents Sea north of Murmansk. But with no license rights, it is unclear how StatoilHydro and Total will be able to book any gas reserve or what rights they can claim. The fate of that project is hard to discern at this point.

Russia's external energy relations present a more complicated picture. In an oil market dominated by the Organization of Petroleum-Exporting Countries (OPEC), Russia is a price taker, not a price setter, because it has neither the long reserve life nor the production flexibility of Saudi Arabia. However, it continues to exhibit tendencies of wanting to extend power beyond its borders by using oil and gas as foreign policy tools. The January 2006 gas cutoff to Ukraine after the Orange Revolution, disrupting gas supply to eight Western European countries in one of the coldest winters

---

4. Royal Dutch Shell and its Japanese partners were forced to give up a majority to Gazprom in the Sakhalin II oil and gas venture, and BP was compelled to give up the Kovykta gasfield in East Siberia to Gazprom.

in memory, was a vivid example. A year later, Belarus had the same experience. In 2008 Russia reduced its oil supply on the Southern Druzhba pipeline to the Czech Republic, right after Prague signed an agreement with Washington on radar installation for a missile defense system. In January 2009 Gazprom again cut gas supply to Europe through Ukraine, this time affecting no fewer than 20 countries; the disruption of gas flow was complete and lasted for two weeks. There are scores of other examples in the former Soviet space and in Central and Eastern Europe. Russia has become notorious as a very unreliable energy supplier.

Moscow's willingness to play outside the international system also means it uses oil and gas in unconventional deals, such as the Chinese bridge loan for Rosneft's takeover of Yuganskneftegaz and reportedly to meet its recent financial needs due to the global crisis. Russia has played one European country against another in securing supposedly favored business relationships in the energy sector for its national champion companies, such as E.ON, ENI, and Total. The recent experience of BP in its TNK-BP partnership may be an indicator that a 50-50 partnership with Russian companies is a dubious long-term strategy for Western companies. The Conoco-Lukoil relationship has yet to prove itself a commercial success. But as long as access to resources is restricted, companies, including those from China and India, will be tempted by special relationships.

Russia continues to talk about security of demand from Europe and about wanting to diversify markets for its oil and gas exports. As long as the basis for such diversification is economic, it poses no problems for the international marketplace; if not, then it raises concerns about whether arms sales and other geostrategic factors are part of the trade consideration. Similarly, Russia is promoting hugely expensive pipeline projects, such as Nord Stream and South Stream, that seem primarily intended to bypass transit countries like Poland and Ukraine and leave them more vulnerable to a supply cutoff. They would also increase the cost of gas to European consumers and reduce the netback price for Russian producers—seemingly another triumph of politics over economics.

In the past, when international energy prices plummeted, the market capitalization of Gazprom and Rosneft fell as well; the market value of Gazprom peaked at $350 billion in May 2008, but it has since fallen by no less than 80 percent to as low as $70 billion, and Rosneft has seen a similar drop, reflecting the market's distrust of these nontransparent state hegemons. Their considerable indebtedness also has raised concerns and is likely to limit future investments. The two tentative gas pipelines to China have always appeared unlikely. South Stream now seems out of the question as too expensive and without gas. The Shtokman project is in doubt, as is the much-promoted Nord Stream pipeline. Gazprom never had financing for its many pet projects, and now it is running short of cash for its current operations and prime capital expenditures.

The oil sector is also facing dilemmas. With lower world oil prices, Russia has revived discussions of cooperating with OPEC and has actively promoted the idea of forming a "gas OPEC" with Iran, Qatar, and Venezuela. This raises questions of whether Russia sees itself as part of the Group of Eight (G-8) industrialized democracies or as part of a cartel of oil and gas export countries seeking to extract the maximum economic rate by curtailing production from time to time in order to prop up prices.

The international actions of Russia as a major oil and gas exporter call for close monitoring and coordinated responses from the West, particularly when the vital interests of the United States and its allies are involved. However, as long as US imports of oil and gas from Russia are negligible, American and European approaches will necessarily be influenced by America's more geopolitical and Europe's more geoeconomic interests. Hot spots like Ukraine will be a test of the US ability to reconcile these interests into a coordinated position and course of action on Russia policy.

Energy Intensity and Climate Change

Climate change and the control of carbon emissions will be one of the greatest issues in the future. Russia has a rather peculiar starting position that influences its policies. The Soviet Union suffered from the greatest energy intensity of production of any country, because of its abundance of steelworks and other heavy industries and a wasteful economic system, while its GDP was relatively low. Since the end of communism, Russian industry has gone through impressive structural change. In the 1990s, unprofitable production that was also energy inefficient was closed down, which reduced Russia's energy intensity. As output growth resumed in 1999, heavy industry—and Russia as a whole—greatly improved energy efficiency as the most modern factories expanded and the obsolete ones stayed shut. Even so, in 2005, Russia was, together with China, among the least energy-efficient countries in the world (figure 4.2). Its energy intensity has declined but is still three times higher than Italy's.

As a consequence, Russia has very large emissions of carbon dioxide, although its carbon emissions declined from 13.3 tons per capita in 1992 to 10.5 tons in 2004, or by 21 percent over 12 years. Russia's GDP per capita is only one-quarter of the US level, but its carbon dioxide emissions are half that of the United States and still twice China's level (figure 4.3). In short, despite its improvements, Russia remains a major polluter.

Russia's economy has grown fast, but its potential for further cuts in energy consumption and carbon emissions remains huge. Because of price controls and export tariffs, the country's domestic energy prices have stayed far below world levels, but the recent decline in energy prices and

Figure 4.2 Energy intensity, 2005

GDP per unit of energy use (PPP dollars per kg of oil equivalent)

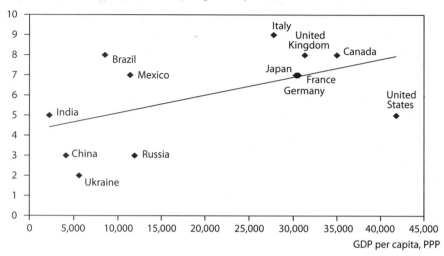

PPP = purchasing power parity

Source: World Bank, *World Development Indicators* database, www.worldbank.org (accessed on December 12, 2008).

Figure 4.3 Carbon dioxide emissions, 2004

metric tons per capita

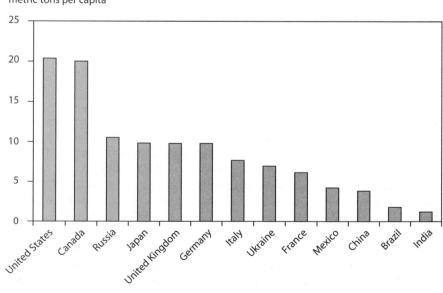

Source: Millennium Development Goals Indicators database, http://mdgs.un.org/unsd/mdg (accessed on December 12, 2008).

domestic price hikes have reduced that discrepancy. The Russian government has long professed the aim of raising energy prices closer to international prices (albeit not all the way), a move that would undoubtedly contribute to energy saving.

Russia's heavy industry, despite its trimming and restructuring, is still large as a share of GDP by any international comparison. However, most of the metallurgical and other commodity-producing industries are likely to be streamlined and rendered less polluting.

Given these preconditions, Russia is one of the big swing states in climate control negotiations. After long hesitation, Russia acceded to the Kyoto Protocol in 2004, in many ways as a goodwill gesture to the European Union as the European Union concluded its bilateral protocol with Russia on the latter's WTO accession. The decision was beneficial to Russia because, thanks to the decreased industrial production of the 1990s, it had already reduced its emissions so much that it could profit from selling certificates of reduced emissions. Russia also has a strong interest in pursuing cap and trade for the future, since it is likely to be the biggest seller of emissions certificates in the world given that the Soviet Union was an enormous polluter in the base year of 1990.

In contrast, Russia has no particular interest in any agreement on carbon or energy taxation. First, it would lose its comparative advantage of low energy prices, which the government strongly emphasizes. Second, it would not benefit from any sale of emissions certificates.

Naturally, Russia would prefer changes in absolute carbon emissions rather than per capita emissions. Russia should, therefore, be a strong ally of the United States against China, India, and the European Union. In addition, Russia strongly believes in nuclear power, which it sees as an important means to reducing carbon emissions. On this, too, it shares the US position.

Logically, Russia should engage strongly in discussions of climate change policy, pushing for cap and trade based on current levels of carbon emission and for expansion of nuclear energy. However, so far, the Russian government has been more ambiguous and less focused on climate change than an observer would expect on the basis of the facts.

Conclusion

The recent return to a degree of normalcy in world oil prices and its impact on Russian economic assumptions may give the Russian government reason to pause for strategic consideration. It is doubtful that such national policy decisions in Russia can be much influenced from the outside. It would be somewhat similar to America trying to influence Mexican oil policy 70 years after the nationalization of oil assets in that country. If and when Mexican policy shifts to include private investment, domestic and foreign, in oil, it will be due to the dynamics of Mexican politics and leaders creating a policy consensus that recognizes the benefits of such a policy change. It will not be because Westerners lecture the Mexicans. Similarly, the West will have to exhibit understanding, patience, realism, and astuteness about the extent of its influence on Russia's decision making in its oil and gas policy.

The United States can make clear to Russia that it does not have to be consigned to the natural resource–producing part of the world economy. Its oil and gas assets can ease the path toward reindustrialization and the modern global economy of technology and services, much as North Sea oil helped the United Kingdom in the 1970s and 1980s. If this is the path Russia chooses, then the West will welcome and embrace it. Certainly Western companies are prepared to share the risks and rewards of developing Russia's oil and gas resources, even after the unhappy experiences of recent years. The choice is Russia's.

5

International Economic Integration, Trade Policy, and Investment

Russia is integrated into the global economy to a greater degree today than at any time in its thousand-year history, and the contrast with its more recent Soviet autarkic past is stark. Russia is now a relatively open economy with an average import tariff of 12 percent. Its exports, heavily dominated by oil, gas, and metals, account for about 30 percent of its GDP; they skyrocketed with the high international commodity prices until 2008 but now are set to fall. As a consequence, the country's huge trade surplus is likely to turn into a deficit. Nonetheless, because of Russia's great comparative advantages in oil and other minerals, it is likely to remain predominantly an exporter of raw materials for the foreseeable future.

Russia has aspired to join the World Trade Organization (WTO) since 1993, longer than any other country, but its recent efforts stalled just before the completion of its accession. Although foreign direct investment (FDI), long a limited share of its GDP, has grown considerably, in the last few years Russia's investment climate has become more constrained, and FDI is not likely to expand in the midst of the global financial crisis. In addition, Russia's foreign economic policy has been growing more restrictive with regard to both trade and investment, and the question is whether this policy will continue and expand or whether renewed liberalization is possible.

In 2008 Russia's foreign economic policy took a serious protectionist turn. The decisive event was the war in Georgia. In its wake, the Kremlin announced that it was suspending its attempts to join the WTO and undertook special trade sanctions against the United States, Turkey, and

Figure 5.1   Merchandise exports and imports, 1999–2008

billions of US dollars

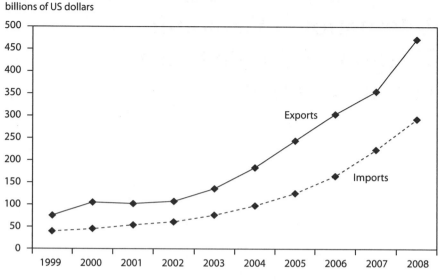

Source: Central Bank of the Russian Federation, February 2008.

Ukraine, because they had delivered arms to Georgia. In defense against the financial crisis, Moscow imposed prohibitive import tariffs on second-hand cars, and it is threatening to introduce equally hazardous export tariffs on lumber. In spite of having long benefited from open world trade, Russia has for the time being entered a more protectionist course. If Russia is to return to high economic growth, this is hardly a tenable policy.

Role in World Trade

Russian merchandise exports have driven the country's high economic growth. In only nine years, they multiplied six times from a low of $76 billion in 1999 to $472 billion in 2008 (figure 5.1). The share of exports in GDP contracted from 38 percent in 1999 to 27 percent in 2007, as the rest of the Russian economy caught up with the export sector. This means that the Russian economy is quite open—about twice as open as the US economy.

Still, Russia's share of world merchandise trade remains small, only 1.6 percent in 2000, rising to 2.5 percent in 2006, equal to its share of global GDP. Its share in world services trade is even less—1.1 percent in 2006 (table 5.1). Of Russia's total exports of goods and services in 2007, mineral

Table 5.1   Merchandise and commercial services exports, world, Russia, and the United States (billions of current US dollars)

Sector	1995	2000	2005	2006
Merchandise				
World	5,164	6,452	10,431	12,083[b]
Russia	81	106	244	305
United States	585	782	904	1,038
Share in world merchandise trade (percent)[a]				
Russia	1.6	1.6	2.3	2.5
United States	11.3	12.1	8.7	8.6
Commercial services				
World	1,185	1,491	2,414	2,755
Russia	11	10	24	30
United States	199	278	354	389
Share in world services trade (percent)[a]				
Russia	0.9	0.6	1.0	1.1
United States	16.7	18.7	14.7	14.1

a. Exports of each country divided by world exports.
b. Includes significant reexports or imports for reexport.

Source: World Trade Organization, www.wto.org.

fuels accounted for 61 percent. Soaring commodity prices, particularly for oil and gas, have, therefore, propelled the export boom, as is evident in figure 5.2, although merchandise export volumes also expanded rapidly. The second export group was base metals, primarily steel, accounting for 12 percent. Services and chemicals took third and fourth places, accounting for 10 and 4 percent, respectively. Exports of machinery and equipment also amount to 4 percent of total Russian exports.

The 1998 financial crisis and ensuing devaluation seriously curtailed imports, which hit a low of $40 billion in 1999. Since then, however, Russia's imports have dramatically increased to $292 billion in 2008. Imports were set to catch up with exports, growing 35 to 40 percent a year, but with the steep fall in commodity prices Russia's record trade surplus of $180 billion in 2008 (10.8 percent of GDP) is set to decline sharply in 2009. Depending on international commodity prices, Russia's exports are likely to decline by more than $200 billion in 2009, or more than 40 percent of their total in 2008. As a consequence, imports will have to be reduced.

Russia's imports are much more diversified than its exports. The biggest groups are machinery, services, chemicals, and agricultural goods. An important feature of Russian imports is the high proportion of con-

Figure 5.2   Oil and gas exports compared with merchandise exports, 1999–2007

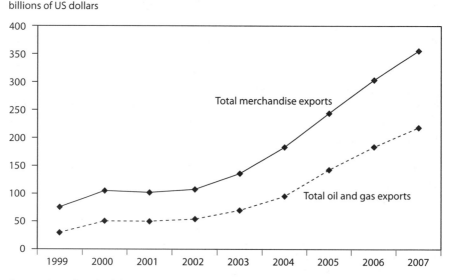

billions of US dollars

Source: Central Bank of the Russian Federation, June 2008; International Monetary Fund, *Russian Federation: Statistical Appendix,* December 2006; Russia Federal Customs online database (for 2006).

sumer goods, which is far higher than in the other BRICs: 28 percent for Russia, barely 9 percent for Brazil, and tiny shares for India and China.

Russia's foreign trade has such a regional orientation as the gravity model predicts: 80 percent of its trade is with East Asia, the European Union, and the Commonwealth of Independent States (CIS). The European Union alone accounted for as much as 53 percent of Russia's exports and 52 percent of its imports in 2007 (figures 5.3 and 5.4). The runner-up is East Asia, with 22 percent of Russia's imports but only 9 percent of Russia's exports, accounting for a large trade imbalance. The CIS, which used to dominate Russia's trade, has declined to an insignificant share of 12 percent of Russia's imports and 14 percent of exports. The US role in Russian trade is minor: only 5 percent of Russia's exports and 3 percent of its imports.

Are Russian Exports Competitive?

Raw materials dominate Russia's exports, and other goods are not very competitive in foreign markets. Julian Cooper has investigated Russia's competitiveness using an index of revealed comparative advantage—a country's share of world exports of a particular good divided by its share

Figure 5.3   Russia's major export partners, 2007 (percent)

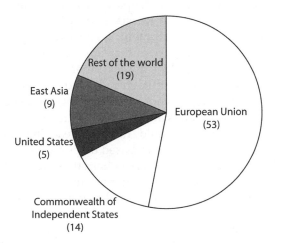

Figure 5.4   Russia's major import partners, 2007 (percent)

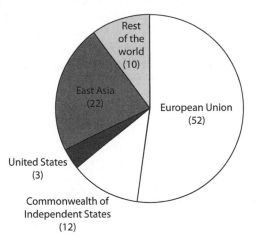

Source: International Monetary Fund, *Direction of Trade Statistics*, May 2008.

of total world exports.[1] The higher the ratio, the stronger the country's comparative advantage in that particular product. The results are almost a caricature of the conventional wisdom. Russia's revealed comparative advantage is overwhelmingly in hydrocarbons, other crude materials, met-

---

1. Julian Cooper, "Of BRICs and Brains: Comparing Russia with China, India and Other Populous Emerging Economies," *Eurasian Geography and Economics* 47, no. 3 (2006): 255–84; Julian Cooper, "Can Russia Compete in the Global Economy?" *Eurasian Geography and Economics* 47, no. 4 (2006): 407–25.

als, and chemicals, which benefit from Russia's low energy prices. By contrast, manufactured goods reveal comparative *dis*advantage.

Of 70 product groups in which Russia is competitive, only four pertain to machinery and transport equipment: nuclear reactors, condensers for steam boilers, rail freight wagons, and steam turbines, all traditional Soviet products with captive markets in the former Soviet Union. So far Russia is not breaking into new manufactured goods export markets of significance. Accordingly, Russia is not arousing protectionist concerns in the West, apart from ferrous metals and mineral fertilizers.

However, WTO accession would have far-reaching implications for the Russian economy, and inferences based on current trade patterns may not capture likely dynamic changes. An alternative calculation of Russia's competitiveness uses gravity model equations to suggest what would happen to its commerce if it followed general patterns of trade. The International Trade Commission, for example, uses disaggregated gravity model equations to identify destinations and sectors where Russian exports are below what might be predicted from world norms.[2] The authors conclude that, even excluding energy trade flows, current Russian exports to its neighbors (i.e., Eastern Europe, Kazakhstan, Turkey, and Ukraine), the European Union (15 members), Iran, and India are very strong and often above the export flows predicted by the model. By contrast, exports to China, Japan, Korea, and the United States are lower than predicted by the model, indicating untapped trade potential.

WTO Entry

Obstacles and Concerns

After its first application for WTO membership in 1993, Russia did not do much about the WTO for the rest of the decade. But in 2000 the Russian leadership woke up, primarily because China was about to join the organization. Over the next three years, Russia adopted most of the legislation necessary for WTO membership and in 2004 and 2006 concluded bilateral protocols with the European Union and the United States, respectively, about joining the WTO. Russia is now very close to accession.

It is important, however, to bear in mind that the WTO is a club, and club members can demand that applicants comply with the club rules (although the club cannot impose its rules equally firmly on existing members). Russia faces three significant obstacles to its WTO accession. Each new member has the right to ask for a bilateral protocol with applicants

---

2. US International Trade Commission, *Recent Trends in U.S. Services Trade*, 2006, Annual Report Investigation No. 332-345 (Washington, 2006). The model is based on Russian exports as of 2003.

on market access. The most recent WTO members—Cambodia, Saudi Arabia, the United Arab Emirates, and Vietnam—did so with Russia, which was compelled to offer each some benefits as long as it endeavored to become a member. On May 16, 2008, Ukraine became a member of the WTO. Thus the first and most complex impediment to Russia's WTO accession is a bilateral agreement with Ukraine, which will require months of negotiations. Trade between Russia and Ukraine is substantial, at some $30 billion a year, but Russia has imposed protectionist measures on its neighbor. Ukrainian trade negotiators can demand that Russia abandon all trade barriers that do not comply with WTO rules, and if Russia does not, other new members will enter the WTO and pose new difficult demands. To the Kremlin, this has become an important argument for forgoing the WTO.

The second impediment is Georgia, which is politically more difficult, especially since the Georgian-Russian war in August 2008. Although Russia has imposed multiple trade embargoes on the Georgians, the latter have focused on a single issue: border controls in Abkhazia and South Ossetia. The Georgians' area of concern may seem political and beyond the range of trade policy, but they have successfully defended their position. This issue can be resolved, and it should be in the Kremlin's interest to do so.

The last obstacle may seem prosaic by comparison. Finland and Sweden, and thus the European Union, do not accept that Russia has decided to impose prohibitive export tariffs on lumber in 2009. The European Union is likely to veto Russia's accession until Russia rescinds these tariffs.

For US companies, the overriding concerns are the Jackson-Vanik Amendment and the granting of permanent normal trade relations (PNTR) with Russia. Without repeal, or graduation, of the Jackson-Vanik Amendment and the granting of PNTR for Russia, US companies are at a disadvantage to their European and Asian competitors. They cannot take advantage of the preferential trade agreements that have been negotiated by the US government, but companies in other countries can. While the US Congress does not vote on Russia's WTO accession, it will have to vote to release Russia from Jackson-Vanik. A failure to do so would limit the access of US companies to a growing emerging market.

Naturally, other issues exist. Agricultural restrictions and poor defense of intellectual property rights may flame up again, as well as export tariffs and the role of state corporations in the economy. Yet Russia has hardly ever been so close to entering the WTO as it was before May 16, 2008, when Ukraine joined, showing that time does not necessarily work in Russia's favor in its quest for WTO accession.

By August 2008, as the war in Georgia flared up, the Kremlin feared possible political exclusion from the WTO. Instead, it declared that it was suspending its attempts to join the organization and that it would reconsider the commitments it had made preliminarily in its bilateral protocols for accession. Specifically, Russia reduced imports from Turkey through administrative impediments, because Turkey had delivered arms to Georgia. Then for sanitary reasons it disqualified 19 American poultry exporters, a significant step because Russia is the largest export market for US poultry. Russia has also threatened to abandon its 1993 free trade agreement with Ukraine because it too supplied Georgia with arms.

Impact on the Russian Economy

Several studies, mainly sponsored by the World Bank and the Russian Ministry of Economic Development and Trade for the benefit of Russian policymakers and citizens, have examined the effects of WTO entry on the Russian economy. The World Bank studies are probably the most authoritative, and they reach the following conclusions.[3] In the next five years, welfare gains to Russia from WTO accession will equal 7.2 percent of Russian consumption (and 3.3 percent of Russian GDP); in the long run, gains could be as high as 24 percent of Russian consumption (and 11 percent of GDP) after the investment climate has improved. These gains would come from:

- liberalization of barriers to FDI in service sectors;

- improved resource allocation as a result of Russian tariff reduction; and

- greater access for Russian products in foreign markets.

The most important Russian export products that are sensitive to protectionist measures, especially antidumping sanctions, are metals and chemicals, which account for one-fifth of the country's total exports. Dur-

---

3. The World Bank studies in question are Jesper Jensen, Thomas Rutherford, and David Tarr, "Economy-Wide and Sector Effects of Russia's Accession to the WTO" (Washington: World Bank, 2004); Jesper Jensen, Thomas Rutherford, and David Tarr, "The Impact of Liberalizing Barriers to Foreign Direct Investment in Services: The Case of Russian Accession to the World Trade Organization" (Washington: World Bank, 2004); Jesper Jensen, Thomas Rutherford, and David Tarr, "Telecommunications Reform within Russia's Accession to the World Trade Organization" (Washington: World Bank, 2004); Thomas Rutherford and David Tarr, "Regional Impacts of Russia's Accession to the WTO" (Washington: World Bank, 2006); Thomas Rutherford, David Tarr, and Oleksandr Shepotylo, "Poverty Effects of Russia's WTO Accession: Modeling 'Real' Households and Endogenous Productivity Effects" (Washington: World Bank, 2004); and Thomas Rutherford, David Tarr, and Oleksandr Shepotylo, "The Impact on Russia of WTO Accession and the Doha Agenda: The Importance of Liberalization of Barriers against Foreign Direct Investment in Services for Growth and Poverty Reduction," in *Poverty and the WTO: Impacts of the Doha Development Agenda*, ed. Thomas W. Hertel and L. Alan Winters (Washington: World Bank, 2005).

ing the boom, Russia's exporters of metals and chemicals did not suffer from limited access to export markets, but as global demand for metals has plummeted, market access is becoming important to the economy. At present, any country can prohibit imports from Russia without any legal repercussions, because the WTO is the only effective arbitration court for world trade and Russia has no rights under the agreement.

Membership in the WTO is also important for Russia's international status. About 96 percent of world trade takes place among organization members. Russia not only is the biggest economy outside the WTO but also accounts for most international trade outside the WTO. As a consequence, it is not a serious part of any discussion on world trade, rules of which are set by all the others. As long as Russia stays outside the WTO, it is difficult to fathom that Moscow could become a world financial center.

Foreign Direct Investment

Despite Russia's poor legal climate,[4] strong GDP growth and rising incomes have attracted increasing interest from foreign investors. Since 2002, FDI inflows have grown dramatically, reaching $45 billion in 2007, but both the total dollar stock of FDI and the share of GDP are still low by comparison with leading large economies.[5] As of end-2007, Russia had accumulated an inward FDI stock of $198 billion, some 15 percent of GDP according to the UN Conference on Trade and Development (UNCTAD), largely concentrated in energy, wholesale trade, and metallurgy. While Russia's FDI to GDP ratio is low compared with world leaders, it is the highest among the BRICs, and its FDI stock per capita is seven times higher than that of China.[6]

Property rights and legal protection remain central concerns for both Russian and foreign businesses. Russia has experienced quite a few property rights conflicts, and they are characteristically being fought out in international courts. The government takeover of Yukos oil company is a

---

4. The *FY2006 Russia Country Commercial Guide* emphasizes the lack of clarity in Russian tax law and administration, inconsistent government regulation, failures of the judicial system, and crime and corruption as factors that repel potential investors. In addition, the source notes that "recent economic reports have all concluded that corruption is getting worse in Russia" (*FY2006 Russia Country Commercial Guide*, US Commercial Service, International Trade Administraion, US Department of Commerce, chapter 6, 2).

5. For example, in 2005, the inward stock of FDI in the United Kingdom reached 37 percent of GDP, while the inflow of FDI contributed close to 45 percent of gross fixed capital formation.

6. UNCTAD *World Investment Report 2007*, available through the foreign direct investment database, http://stats.unctad.org (accessed on August 28, 2008).

familiar story (see chapter 2), and several examples of weak property rights protection in Russia have emerged since that company was effectively confiscated. US portfolio investors lost an estimated $12 billion in the Yukos confiscation and are not likely to receive any compensation.

There have been two major cases of foreign-owned companies losing out in property strife: Royal Dutch Shell and its Japanese partners, which were forced to give up a majority to Gazprom in the Sakhalin II oil and gas venture, and BP, which was compelled to give up the Kovykta gasfield in East Siberia to Gazprom. In both cases, administrative resources were deployed to pressure the foreign companies. A number of other, less significant cases have further undermined property rights and foreign investors' interest in Russia.

There are remedies to foreign expropriation, but the United States has not developed any of them with Russia. The most direct remedy is a bilateral investment treaty, which has been effective for many countries. The United States and Russia signed such a treaty in 1992 to guarantee "prompt, adequate and effective compensation in the event of expropriation" and provide "the right to third party international arbitration in the event of a dispute between a U.S. investor and the Russian government." The US Senate ratified this treaty in 1993, but the United States has failed to persuade Russia to ratify it, so it lacks legal force. The main reason for this failure to ratify was that a parliamentary majority opposed President Boris Yeltsin, but since December 1999 President Vladimir Putin could easily have had the treaty ratified in parliament, if the United States had only pushed for it. By contrast, Russia has concluded and ratified bilateral investment treaties with 38 countries, including Belgium, France, Germany, Ireland, Italy, Luxembourg, the Netherlands, Norway, Spain, Sweden, and the United Kingdom, allowing foreign claimants in those countries to sue the Russian government—recourse that is not available to American shareholders.

The United States has almost stopped concluding bilateral investment treaties since 1998. The government tried to make them more ambitious but as a result has concluded only two (Uruguay and Rwanda). The United States has instead tried to include investment guarantees in free trade agreements, but no such agreement is possible with Russia until it becomes a member of the WTO.

In 1994, 51 countries, including the former Soviet countries and most European countries, signed the Energy Charter and 46 of them have also ratified it. The treaty, which contains substantial clauses against confiscation, came into force in 1997. The United States is not a signatory because it abandoned the treaty negotiations in 1991. Russia signed but never ratified the treaty, although it has committed itself to abide by it. Major lawsuits are under way in Europe on the basis of the charter, an option that is, again, not available to US shareholders.

Citizens in European countries have a third legal option, namely to appeal to the European Court of Human Rights in Strasbourg. This court is attached to the Council of Europe, an organization of which Russia is a member but the United States is not. Thousands of cases concerning Russia have been raised there; the Russian government regularly loses but formally accepts the court's verdicts, which carry impact in commercial cases. One prominent case that the Russian government lost was against Vladimir Gusinsky. The European Court established that the Russian state had forced him to give his media empire to a state-dominated company. Again, US citizens have no recourse to this international court.

At present, several legal cases against nonresident Russian companies and individuals are pending in the United States. In the absence of any binding bilateral treaty, these cases focus on assertions that the defendants committed securities crimes in the United States, including insider trading and racketeering. It is too early to judge the eventual success of these legal suits.

The low US FDI figures probably signal an aversion among US firms to invest directly in Russia from a US-registered company. Many prefer to invest from a subsidiary based in a country with better investment protection in Russia. But the low numbers appear to reflect missed investment opportunities for US companies as well as commercial losses for Russia: When US multinationals establish a presence in foreign markets the recipient country benefits from imports of specialized inputs, production technology, and management expertise.[7] Thus more US FDI to Russia will expand US exports of goods and services. For these reasons, in the US-Russian Sochi Declaration of April 2008, both the US and Russian presidents committed themselves to negotiate a new bilateral investment treaty "to provide a stable and predictable framework for investment."

Russia has long maintained informal government intervention for major foreign investment, especially when related to national security. In May 2008, after years of deliberation, Russia adopted a Law on Foreign Investment in Strategic Industries, which identified 42 sectors of the economy as strategic. They include obviously military sectors as well as oil, gas, nuclear industry, fisheries, airspace, telecommunications, and media. The new law requires government approval for any foreign investor who seeks to buy a stake of over 50 percent in a company in these sectors. The control is stricter for state-controlled foreign companies, which have to seek permission to acquire more than 25 percent of the shares in a strategic enterprise. The law has been criticized in Russia as excessively restrictive, but foreign businessmen welcomed the enhanced legal clarity.

---

7. Edward M. Graham and Erika Wada, *Foreign Direct Investment in China: Effects on Growth and Economic Performance* (Oxford: Oxford University Press, 2001).

Russia's accession to the WTO will boost FDI by reinforcing Russia's commitments to international legal standards and mutual market opening. In 2002 Russian economist Ksenia Yudaeva estimated that WTO accession could result in an increase of FDI of up to $4 billion a year.[8] Today, this figure significantly understates the potential, since the Russian economy has grown sharply since 2002. Our own econometric analysis indicates that the total inward FDI stock in Russia could increase by 50 percent.

The potential for growth of US investment to Russia is probably far larger than these estimates imply. Simple arithmetic shows that the US FDI stock in Russia (currently at 5 percent) needs a fourfold increase to reflect the share of total US outward FDI stock in total world FDI stock (about 19 percent in 2005). Of course, in years to come Russian inward FDI will continue to grow strongly, as suggested by both the 2006–07 figures and our econometric estimates. If US firms approach their potential share, the annual dollar growth could be spectacular.[9]

Globalization of Russian Business

The great untold story of Russia's economic revival is the globalization of its businesses. Russia's foreign economic relations are no longer a matter of the transfer of Western money and technology into the country, as over the last four years Russian businesses have ventured outside the country to invest and set up elsewhere. These companies—predominantly in natural resources—have invested billions of dollars in acquisitions outside Russia. In fact, Russian investment abroad in 2007 surpassed the level of inward FDI, as Russian companies invested $47.8 billion globally. And in the first half of 2008, they invested $21.6 billion in global assets, including $4.2 billion in the United States.

Over the past five years, Russian companies have invested over $8 billion in the US economy. Severstal alone has invested $3.4 billion, including nearly $1 billion to build a steel plant in Mississippi, which created about 500 jobs in that state. Other companies, such as Evraz Holding, have invested in indebted US steel companies and used their expertise to revitalize run-down steel enterprises, thus breathing new life into these

---

8. Ksenia V. Yudaeva, Evguenia Bessonova, Konstantin Kozlov, Nadezhda Ivanova, Denis Sokolov, and Boris Belov, "Sektoral'ny i Regionalny Analiz Posledstviij Vstupleniya Rossii v VTO: Otsenka Izderzhek i Vygod ["Sectoral and Regional Analysis of Russia's Accession into the WTO: A Cost-Benefit Analysis"], Center of Economic and Financial Research at New Economic School (CEFIR), 2002.

9. Geographic distance might be read as an indicator of lower prospects for US investment in Russia. However, in a study of global FDI flows, Howard J. Shatz and Anthony Venables conclude that the influence of geographic distance plays a smaller role in sourcing decisions for FDI in larger markets, such as Russia (*The Geography of International Investment*, World Bank Policy Research Working Paper no. 2338, Washington: World Bank, 2000).

companies. Several Russian acquisitions, such as Evraz's purchase of Oregon Steel Mills and the Severstal's purchase of Esmark, have been supported by United Steelworkers on the grounds that the takeover would result in the preservation of the American jobs.

So far the focus has been on natural resource companies, but it is only a matter of time before Russian technology and consumer goods companies enter the global market. This is beginning to take place to a small degree as increasing numbers of Russian companies from all sectors undertake initial public offerings (IPOs) in London and New York as a means to finance growth, though they have taken a breather for a few years because of the international financial crisis.

An important benefit to the globalization of Russian business is the increased emphasis on transparency and good corporate governance. To raise the financing necessary for its foreign acquisitions—which have taken place primarily in Western capital markets—and undertake IPOs on Western exchanges, Russian companies have had to reform their business practices and internal governance to accord with global best practices and make themselves more attractive to Western shareholders and investors. Unfortunately, the global financial crisis has stalled this investment trend and will for some time.

Renewed Protectionism

The current Russian policy is to respond with protectionism, as evident in the government's many, substantial steps in 2008 toward greater protectionism in both foreign trade and FDI. The two biggest decisions were the adoption in May of the Law on Foreign Investment in Strategic Industries and the suspension in August of WTO accession efforts. In addition, as global food prices rose in the spring of 2008, Russia responded by introducing export tariffs and quotas on various agricultural products. And, as mentioned above, after the war in Georgia in August 2008, Russia imposed general trade sanctions on Turkey and on foods from the United States and Ukraine.

At the Group of Twenty (G-20) summit in Washington on November 15, 2008, the only substantial commitment by the heads of the 20 leading nations present was not to undertake any new protectionist measure in the next year:

> We underscore the critical importance of rejecting protectionism and not turning inward in times of financial uncertainty. In this regard, within the next 12 months, we will refrain from raising new barriers to investment or to trade in goods and services, imposing new export restrictions, or implementing World Trade Organization (WTO)–inconsistent measures to stimulate exports.[10]

---

10. Declaration of the Summit on Financial Markets and the World Economy, November 15, 2008, available at www.whitehouse.gov (accessed on December 24, 2008).

Yet Russia immediately announced that it would impose new import tariffs on cars, effective January 12, 2009. In some cases, these prohibitive tariffs could be as high as 200 percent, provoking popular protests in some 30 cities, particularly in the Far East.[11] Similarly, in steps to promote the domestic forestry industry, Russia increased its export tariffs on lumber, set for implementation in 2009.

Russia's critical economic vulnerability lies in its overdependence on revenues from exports of natural commodities, especially hydrocarbons. Despite a proliferation of official pronouncements, including the Russia 2020 plans, about the need to diversify its exports, such diversification is not easy and, as described in chapter 3, it is not clear that the government is taking effective measures to achieve it. In addition, the high oil price of recent years has reduced the incentives to diversify. But it is also not clear that much diversification of Russia's trade profile would make a great deal of economic sense. Russia's geography and rich endowments of natural resources have shaped its economic comparative advantages and disadvantages for decades, even centuries, and in all likelihood will continue to do so for the foreseeable future.

---

11. "United Russia Official Resigns after Protest," *Moscow Times*, December 23, 2008.

6

Challenges of Demography and Health

Russia's demographic challenges are so severe that they warrant a full chapter in this book. The country is facing acute natural depopulation. From the early 1990s until 2006 the population shrank at a predictable rate of 750,000 people per year—a loss of more than 0.5 percent annually, compared with steady population growth in the other BRIC countries (Brazil, India, and China) and in virtually all the advanced industrial democracies. Since the mid-1960s, births have not kept pace with deaths (figure 6.1). As a result, the overall population is aging, although mortality among working-age Russian men is the same now as it was a century ago. Life expectancy for men lingers at about 59 years, with overmortality concentrated among middle-aged men, while Russian women live 14 years longer than the men, the greatest gender gap in the world. The working-age population is dwindling even as unemployment rises. Widespread alcohol abuse contributes to half of all deaths, and the availability of low-cost cigarettes supports pervasive tobacco use.

However, there has been some improvement recently: The number of babies born in 2007 was the highest since 1991, about 120,000 more than in 2006—an increase of 8.3 percent in the fourth consecutive year of growth. Infant mortality, the single most reliable indicator of a nation's health, declined by half from 1993 to 2006 (figure 6.2), suggesting that the health care system is improving. The death rate has fallen and the rate of annual population loss is decelerating, with the death-to-birth ratio steadily declining.

The official interpretation is that several years of economic stability and prosperity have finally reversed almost two decades of demographic

Figure 6.1   Natural increase/decrease in population, 1960–2006

number of people

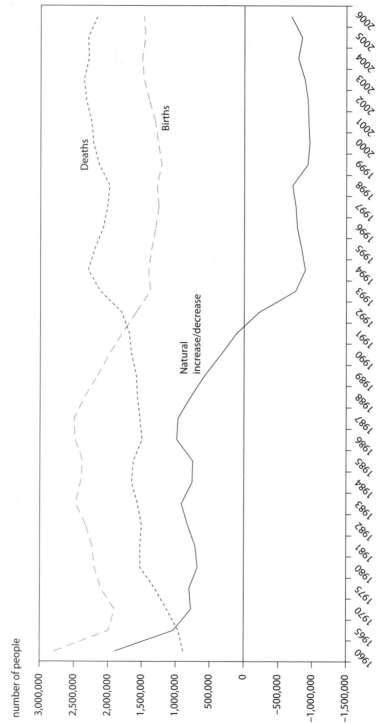

Source: Federal State Statistics Service of Russia, www.gks.ru.

Figure 6.2 Infant mortality, 1960–2006

deaths per 1,000 live births

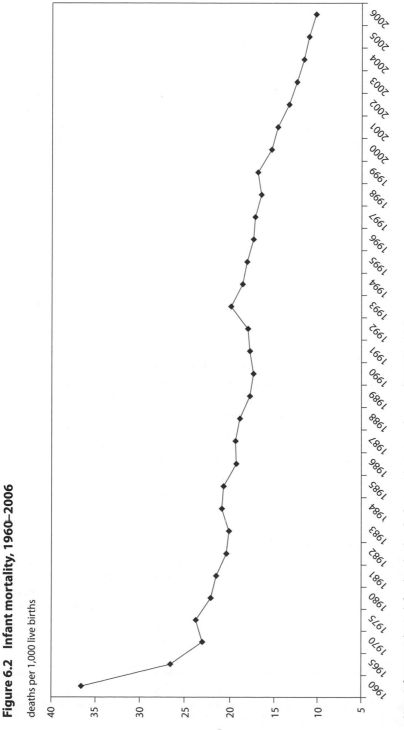

Note: Infant mortality is defined as deaths of infants under 1 year of age per 1,000 live births.

Source: Federal State Statistics Service of Russia, www.gks.ru.

disaster. A sizable, emerging middle class feels motivated to eat better, exercise, and drink in moderation; women feel sufficiently optimistic about their families' futures to have more children; and the government is pouring resources into a National Health Project. Extrapolating from these trends, Russia's long-term development concept now aims to increase life expectancy to 72 and the population to 144 million by 2020.

But progress is uncertain. Recent achievements in health and demography are offset by persistent low fertility and high morbidity. This chapter assesses the likely impact of recent policy initiatives on population dynamics and implications for labor markets, economic development, and national security.

Russia's Demographic Predicament

Russia's current population is about 142 million, down from a peak of nearly 149 million in 1993. The decrease is due in part to declining fertility, which is the norm in advanced industrial societies. But European birth rates have fallen because of positive overall developments, such as women entering the workforce and the transition from agrarian to industrial and service economies. In contrast, reproduction in Russia has fallen because, during the decline of living standards in the 1990s, socioeconomic conditions were not favorable for raising a child and the fear of poverty convinced women to delay or avoid having children.[1]

Russia differs dramatically from its European neighbors in its numbers, patterns, and causes of death. Male life expectancy declined from 64 in 1965 to 61.7 in 1984, briefly spiked to 64.9 in 1987 because of Mikhail Gorbachev's campaign against alcohol, plummeted to 57.6 in 1994, and now stands between 59 and 60, lower than in the early 1960s (figure 6.3).[2] That puts contemporary Russia in the company of Pakistan and Eritrea and considerably below the other BRICs: Male life expectancy is 68 in Brazil, 67 in India, and 71 in China.

Female life expectancy in Russia has followed roughly the same trajectory as for men, but women live 13 to 14 years longer than their husbands and brothers. By contrast, the gender gap in longevity in the United States is only five years. In fact, Russian women outlive men to a greater degree than anywhere else in the world. It appears that women's health has been less vulnerable than men's to the enduring impact of post-Soviet transition.

---

1. Valery Yelizarov, *Demographic Policy in Russia: From Reflection to Action* (Moscow: United Nations in Russia, 2008).

2. William C. Cockerham, "Health Lifestyles and the Absence of the Russian Middle Class," *Sociology of Health and Illness* 29, no. 3 (2007): 457–73.

Figure 6.3   Life expectancy, 1960–2006

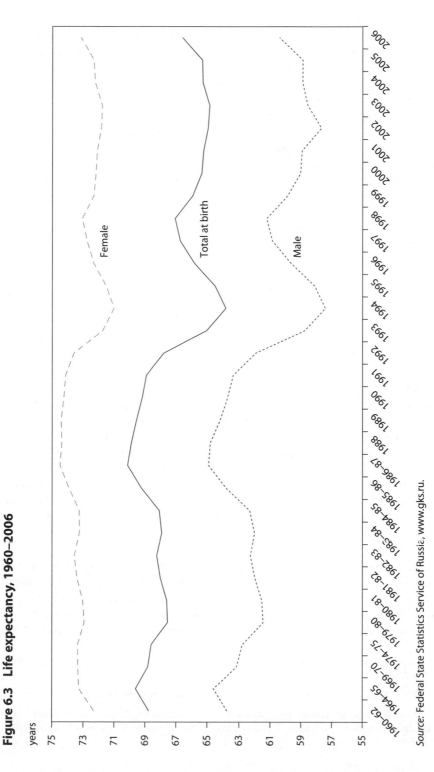

years

Female

Total at birth

Male

Source: Federal State Statistics Service of Russia, www.gks.ru.

The correlation between Russia's economic trajectory and life expectancy was as expected from the mid-1980s through 2000. After a rise due to Gorbachev's restriction on alcohol consumption, life expectancy plummeted sharply with the upheaval of the economy and society. Then as overall welfare improved slightly in the mid-1990s, so did life expectancy, until the two fell in tandem with the 1998 financial crisis. But life expectancy has not risen with the remarkable economic growth from 1999 to 2007. Instead, it has remained stagnant. Demographers remain puzzled, as this contradicts the health-wealth connection that prevails in the world.

Paradoxically, Russia's overall population is aging rapidly, in spite of low life expectancy, because of the anemic birth rates since the early 1990s. Over the next two decades, a shrinking workforce will be responsible for the pensions and long-term care of an ever-larger number of elderly retirees. In 2002 Russia had only 1.7 workers for every pensioner, and that ratio will steadily decline.[3] Yet pension reform has been insufficient to meet the coming increase in demand. The World Bank estimates that the greater need for pension and health services, along with more demand for education, will require an increase in social expenditures from 14.1 percent of GDP in 2008 to about 17.3 percent in 2016–20.[4]

In 2007 there were about 475,000 more deaths than births, down from more than 675,000 in 2006. Half of those deaths—about 1.1 million—were due to cardiovascular disease, and another half a million were due to trauma/accidents or cancer. Continuing widespread abuse of alcohol and tobacco lies behind all of these leading causes of death, primarily among working-age men. Although per capita alcohol consumption is as high in other countries as in Russia, nowhere are surrogate alcohols so widely used: Products such as aftershave lotions, lighter fluid, window cleaning solutions, and antifreeze contain substitute chemicals in the West but in Russia are based on highly concentrated alcohol, and they are not taxed.[5] In addition, binge drinking (i.e., not necessarily frequent but severe intoxication) is a greater problem in Russia than elsewhere and leads to deaths from higher blood pressure, heart attack, and stroke. The contribution of alcohol to overall mortality is estimated at roughly 50 percent.

About 60 percent of Russian men and 20 percent of Russian women smoke—more than twice as many as in the United States or the United Kingdom. And smoking is on the rise, as the share of women who smoke doubled from 1992 to 2003. Over 17 percent of Russian deaths each year are caused directly by tobacco consumption. The World Bank has called

---

3. Nick Eberstadt, "Growing Old the Hard Way: China, Russia, India," *Policy Review* (April/May 2006).

4. World Bank, *Russian Economic Report*, no. 16 (Washington, June 2008, 17–18).

5. Patricio Marquez, Marc Suhrcke, Martin McKee, and Lorenzo Rocco, "Adult Health in the Russian Federation: More Than Just a Health Problem," *Health Affairs* (July/August 2007): 1040–51.

smoking the single most preventable cause of death in Russia, linking it with cardiovascular disease, cancer, and chronic lung disease.[6] A pack of low-end cigarettes in Russia costs about 50 cents compared with $7 in Europe.

Noncommunicable disease and injury are thus the leading causes of premature mortality in Russia. Infectious disease causes a small minority of all deaths, but it remains a nascent threat. The Western press has highlighted HIV/AIDS; official statistics put the number of Russian HIV infections at 428,000, but the actual number is probably closer to a million. Both anecdotal evidence and scientific studies indicate that the spread of HIV remains largely confined to injection drug users and their sexual partners, and Russia is very unlikely to experience an HIV crisis as in sub-Saharan Africa. Since 2006, both government and international funding have put thousands of patients on life-saving antiretroviral medications. It is still imperative, though, to focus more effort and attention on prevention-oriented interventions. Russia also has Europe's highest tuberculosis mortality rate, 30,000 deaths per year, which is 20 times the Western average. Multi-drug-resistant tuberculosis is emerging as an increasing share of new tuberculosis cases. Hepatitis and tuberculosis coinfection with HIV are attracting attention as serious but previously neglected problems.

Economic Effects of Poor Health and Demography

From a humanitarian perspective, the level of sickness and death in Russia over the last two decades is tragic.[7] But these health and demographic trends also have an important impact on Russia's economic growth and national security. Absenteeism due to ill health is a drain on the economy, as employers annually lose an average of 10 days per employee due to illness, more than 25 percent more than in the EU-15 countries.[8] And the mortality rates of working-age men are almost four times those for women (figure 6.4). If Russia decreased mortality rates from noncommunicable disease and injury to EU-15 rates by 2025, its GDP would rise by 3.6 to 7.1 percent (depending on initial assumptions about future GDP growth).[9]

---

6. World Bank, *Dying Too Young: Addressing Premature Mortality and Ill Health Due to Non-Communicable Diseases and Injuries in the Russian Federation* (Washington: Human Development Department, Europe and Central Asia, World Bank, 2005).

7. This and some of the following sections draw from Judy Twigg, "Trends and Policy Priorities in Russia's Health Sector" (background paper for the National Bureau of Asian Research Discussion Workshop on Russia's Political Economy: Trends and Implications, Washington, April 24, 2008).

8. World Bank, *Dying Too Young*.

9. Ibid.

Figure 6.4 Mortality among working-age people, 1960–2006

deaths per 1,000

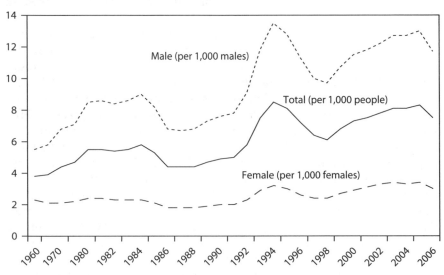

Source: Federal State Statistics Service of Russia, www.gks.ru.

According to Russian government statistics, by 2020 the working-age population will have fallen to 77.5 million people, resulting in a labor deficit as high as 14 million (another study cites a deficit of 19 million by 2025).[10] The Russian press is beginning to take note of these potential constraints on economic development.[11] Some trends are already visible. With increased economic growth, the demand for labor has risen, but the quality of the labor force is not rising accordingly, which has led to shortages in many categories of skilled labor and often extremely high salaries even by American standards.[12] Companies and regions will face a choice: to raise productivity dramatically, to attract migrants, or to abandon projects. Regions and industries are already competing with one another for labor.

National unemployment reached a low of 5.6 percent of the labor force in the spring of 2008 but rose to 7.7 percent at the end of 2008 and is likely to continue to rise sharply. In some areas (Kamchatka, Karelia, and Sakhalin), untapped labor reserves are sufficiently high that putting non-

10. Konstantin Gurdin, "Arguments of the Week," available at the website of the Higher School of Economics, Moscow, Russia, www.hse.ru (accessed on February 12, 2009).

11. Olga Kolesnikova, "2010–2020: Years When the Struggle for Human Resources Will Get Worse," *Rossiyskaya Gazeta*, June 5, 2008.

12. United Nations in Russia, *Demographic Policy in Russia: From Reflection to Action* (Moscow, 2008).

workers to work could plug at least part of the gap, but in most regions the unemployed have neither the skills nor the motivation to step in. People who traditionally have not worked, especially women with children, have already entered the labor force in droves in recent decades, but a successful strategy of encouraging higher birth rates and more children per family will likely keep many women out of the labor market.[13] Enactment of a long-standing proposal to raise the extremely low retirement age of 55 for women and 60 for men might help both to stave off collapse of the pension system and to expand the workforce. In any case about one-quarter to one-third of pensioners continue to work, not least because public pensions are extremely small.[14]

The projected impact of the shrinking working-age population varies with the direction of Russia's economic development. A resource-based economy does not require a large, diverse, skilled labor force; even a smaller and less healthy population can provide the number of qualified personnel necessary for the oil and gas sector. Challenges persist, however, even at this extreme: Oil and gas production takes place in remote regions with extreme climatic conditions; recent studies indicate that transplants to these regions suffer health problems that harm their productivity.[15]

If Russia is to continue diversification into modern manufacturing and services, it will be constrained by a lack of appropriately skilled personnel. Although investments remain concentrated in just a few sectors, non-tradable growth dominates: In 2007 wholesale and retail trade alone accounted for almost a third of economic growth, with construction and manufacturing responsible for another third, while growth in resource extraction practically stopped.[16] Yet in 2002–07, real wages increased by an average of 13 percent a year, outpacing real GDP growth of 7 percent a year as well as productivity growth.[17] As unemployment shrank to 6 percent of the labor force, the labor market was very tight in all dynamic regions. Rising labor costs, driven by labor shortages in some regions, are likely responsible for impeding growth in electrotechnical equipment, food, and chemicals. A June 2008 survey by the Institute for the Economy in Transition found 32 percent of enterprises in 2006, 35 percent in 2007,

---

13. Maxim Shishkin and Daria Nikolaeva, "Employment in Russia Is Reaching Its Limits," *Kommersant,* July 9, 2008.

14. Mikhail Sergeev, "Ministry of Finance Is Preparing to Raise the Pension Age," *Nezavisimaya Gazeta,* August 19, 2008.

15. M.P. Dyakovich, "Working Potential Evaluation in the Territory of an Oil-and-Gas Complex Development in Siberia," *Alaska Medicine* 49, no. 2 (2007): 228–30.

16. World Bank, *Russian Economic Report,* 4–5.

17. Russian State Committee for Statistics, Basic Social-Economic Indicators, www.gks.ru (accessed on January 16, 2009).

and 40 percent in 2008 reporting deficits of skilled labor as a factor preventing increased output.[18]

The demographic constraints also indicate that by 2016 the number of men of conscription age will be half what it was two decades earlier. Yet Russia has not undertaken any meaningful military reform and has failed to effect the long-promised professionalization of the military personnel. The army may find that even with all deferments eliminated, too few draftees will be available. An Armed Forces General Staff spokesman declared in September 2008, "It is quite possible that the state security bodies' demand for draftees will exceed the actual number of conscripts who can be enlisted by the armed forces by 2011."[19]

An increasing percentage of conscripted men are suffering nutritional, health, and substance abuse problems, all of which draw attention and resources away from the core mission of national defense. But such statistics are not reliable because they reflect the widespread use of medical excuses among young men to escape military service. Moreover, those who can afford it purchase exemption from military service with a bribe of a couple of thousand dollars, so only the poorest actually do their military service. Finally, there are significant negative synergies between the conscription and labor force challenges: The same limited cohort of healthy, capable young men needed by the military will also be in demand both by potential employers and for higher education.

Remedies

Reducing Smoking and Drinking

Russia must combat smoking and drinking. Meaningful policy intervention to address these issues has been missing for too long, although some recent policy developments are encouraging.

For example, Russia joined the World Health Organization Framework Convention on Tobacco Control (FCTC), the world's first public health treaty. It calls for comprehensive bans on tobacco advertising, promotion, and sponsorship. Since it came into effect in February 2005, 157 countries have ratified it, including most European countries, China, India, and, as of June 2008, Russia (the United States has signed but not ratified the convention). Russian government officials are drafting a national strategy against smoking that would comply with FCTC requirements and completely ban tobacco advertising within five years. In addition, the Duma

---

18. Daria Nikolaeva, "Ministry of Health and Social Development Is Preparing Amendments to the Labor Code," *Kommersant*, July 3, 2008.

19. Major General Andrei Kolesov, quoted in an Interfax-Agentstvo Voyennykh Novostey report, September 24, 2008.

in early 2008 legislated that each cigarette pack must carry a large-print warning saying "Smoking Kills" as well as 12 further warnings (on the back of the pack) that smoking causes premature death, lung cancer, heart attacks, and infertility, among other health problems. A forthcoming national strategy may ban the marketing and sale of cigarettes to children and teenagers.

This tobacco policy aligns well with Russia's recently passed three-year demographic policy plan,[20] the primary aim of which is to reduce mortality from controllable causes in 2008–10. The government's 2009 budget for the first time included significant funding for the promotion of healthy lifestyles, including anti-tobacco and anti-alcohol education. The Ministry of Health and Social Development formed a commission in 2008 to draft a strategy for health system development through 2020 (although formulation of the strategy did not include any significant input from reputable physicians, economists, and other experts). The plan calls for the 2009 launch of new initiatives to promote healthy lifestyles and reduce mortality from drinking and smoking, with a major cancer prevention program to follow in 2010. It also advocates the use of economic incentives: Smokers will, for the first time, pay higher public medical insurance premiums, and insurance will not cover injuries caused by drunkenness.

The most obvious area in need of intervention is alcohol policy. Decades of international research have consistently and convincingly revealed two kinds of policy actions that can effectively curtail alcohol consumption: price hikes and limits on availability. Yet increases of vodka excise duties have not exceeded the rate of inflation in Russia since 1998, even though real incomes have grown significantly. Although the mention of limitations on drinking in Russia is likely to produce a chuckle in most circles, recent public opinion studies indicate that well over half of Russians would support the reimplementation of Gorbachev's anti-alcohol campaign if it were proposed today.[21]

Education and Immigration

Much can be done to compensate for labor shortage through productivity gains, as Russian labor productivity lags behind the West by a factor of five to ten, although Russia's GDP per capita in purchasing power parities is already one-third of the US level.

One strength of the Soviet system was education. Russian youth do invest in their own human capital: More than two-thirds go on to tertiary ed-

20. "Demographic Policy of the Russian Federation up to 2025," Decree of the President of the Russian Federation, no. 1351, October 9, 2007.

21. Daria A. Khaltourina and Andrey V. Korotayev, "Potential for Alcohol Policy to Decrease the Mortality Crisis in Russia," *Evaluation and the Health Professions* 31 (2008): 272–81.

ucation—more than in the European Union—and most of them pay significant tuition fees. But most of the education is not of very good quality. Weaknesses persist in subjects barely taught in the Soviet Union—business administration, law, and the English language—and in the shortage of vocational training (enterprises typically have to provide it themselves). Traditional Soviet strengths were math, science, and engineering, and these remain, although diminished in quality since communism. Recent international tests of high school students put Russian students at the same not very high level as American students in math and science.[22]

The most easily available solution is immigration of labor. The European Union and the United States rely on tens of millions of immigrant workers to make up their labor shortfalls, and the same is true in Russia, although much of the immigration is illegal. Millions of illegal laborers populate Moscow, St. Petersburg, and other major cities, employed primarily in construction, transportation, and trade. One recent study cites a need for legal immigration of one million per year—three times the average official annual flow over the last 15 years—to compensate for the shrinking working-age population.[23]

In immigration, Russia benefits from a unique advantage: It has a huge pool to draw on—tens of millions of willing Russian-speaking residents of other former Soviet countries. Millions of immigrants from Ukraine, Moldova, the Caucasus, and Central Asia arrived after the collapse of the Soviet Union because all the former Soviet republics apart from the Baltic states and Kazakhstan have much lower wages. The most conspicuous recent migration consists of construction workers in Moscow from Tajikistan and Kyrgyzstan.

Most immigration is illegal, however, because of Russia's administrative barriers to migration, and the number of illegal immigrants is assessed at 6 million to 12 million. In late 2006 Russia adopted legislation to facilitate immigration from the former Soviet republics, but its effect has been the opposite. Overall, Russian immigration policy has been inappropriately complex and repressive, pushing migrants into the shadow economy. Trapped in low-skill jobs, these illegal migrants lag in productivity, although they remain attractive to employers offering very low wages and poor working conditions. In addition, illegal immigrants, especially from Central Asia, suffer from Russian xenophobia. Murders and hate crimes are shockingly frequent.

---

22. OECD Program for International Student Assessment (PISA), *PISA 2006: Science Competencies for Tomorrow's World*, volumes 1 and 2 (2007), www.pisa.oecd.org (accessed on November 15, 2008).

23. Yuri Andrienko and Sergei Guriev, "Understanding Migration in Russia," Policy Paper 23 (Moscow: Center for Economic and Financial Research, New Economic School, November 2005).

Internal migration also holds significant possibilities, as workers in many Russian regions still face low wages and high unemployment; the same study[24] estimates that over two million workers in these areas could easily find jobs in labor-scarce regions. Although it is easy to change jobs within one locality in Russia, it is exceedingly difficult to move from one region to another, primarily because of poorly functioning housing markets, and some regions, notably Moscow, remain closed to legal migration even for Russian citizens.

Limited Demographic Improvements

The increase in Russia's birth rate likely follows the recent improvements in the overall socioeconomic situation and general mood of society. The government heralds the recent rise in birth rate as a result of its pronatal policies of the last several years: lump-sum payments increasing for second and subsequent children and enhanced social benefits. But the size of these benefits is hardly sufficient to have prompted women to decide to have more babies.

Yet, whatever its causes, the rise in the birth rate cannot possibly produce a sustained overall population increase to counter the sharp declines in the birth rate in the early 1990s. Women of childbearing age will be dramatically fewer over the next 20 to 25 years. Even a significantly higher reproduction rate now would not be enough to boost Russia's population above its current low level. Consequently, international projections estimate that Russia's population in 2025 will shrink to 135 million or, in the worst-case variants, as low as 120 million.[25]

To the extent that the demographic situation has improved over the last few years, the Putin era's economic growth and stability can take much of the credit. The main cause of the sharply reduced infant mortality is presumably the improved general availability of pharmaceutical drugs and medical equipment in the post-Soviet period. Official Russian commentaries, however, emphasize the health reforms undertaken through the Priority National Health Project first proposed in the fall of 2006. During 2006–07, the government allocated just over 200 billion rubles (about $9 billion) to a set of explicit objectives: to improve the health of the population, to improve the accessibility and quality of medical care, to strengthen primary care as well as health promotion and disease prevention activities, and to increase access to tertiary care. The National Health Project has added resources and training for primary health care, including for

24. Andrienko and Guriev, "Understanding Migration in Russia."

25. US Census Bureau, International Data Base, www.census.gov (accessed on September 24, 2008); United Nations Population Division, *World Population Prospects*, http://esa.un.org/unpp.

pregnant women, funded HIV/AIDS prevention and treatment, and constructed new centers for high-tech tertiary care. Widely publicized new maternity incentives include expanded maternity leave and payments, educational vouchers for children, and "birth certificates" for pregnant women entitling them to free choice of facility for prenatal care and childbirth. During the first two years of the project, 13 million people received check-ups, 60 million were vaccinated, and 300,000 obtained high-tech medical care. Thousands of new ambulances were purchased and distributed to every region in the country.

Many of the National Health Project provisions are embodied in the Concept for the Development of Healthcare in the Russian Federation through 2020, finalized in December 2008 by the Ministry of Health and Social Development. But the project cannot guarantee the sustainability of the progress of the last few years. Russia is pursuing a classic, Soviet-style "storming" approach to its health and demographic challenge: throwing money at it. Money spent has been the primary official indicator of success. National Health Project spending has been chaotic and often thoughtless, with resources allocated according to political expediency. Equipment purchases have barreled forward seemingly without analysis of medical need, leaving millions of dollars' worth of machinery idle. Ambulances unable to withstand the rough Russian roads spend more time in repair than on duty, and emergency services prefer older, more reliable jeeps. Salaries for primary care providers are still insufficient to attract talented students. New high-tech centers are being built but often have no qualified personnel. Monitoring and evaluation are absent. A recent study by the International Monetary Fund shows that countries that spend 30 to 40 percent less on health achieve health outcomes similar to Russia's.[26]

The National Health Project has done little to address the structural imbalances that have plagued the Russian health care system since the Soviet period. Most care is still inefficiently provided by hospitals rather than by primary care providers. The compulsory national health insurance established in 1993 has neither functioned well nor delivered the intended market pressures for higher-quality, more cost-effective care. Doctors' basic salaries remain rigidly set by education and years in service, rather than by quality and success of treatment. As a result of this inefficient allocation of resources, people often pay for care that is constitutionally guaranteed to be free of charge: 30 to 60 percent of health care costs are paid out of pocket, and 50 to 70 percent of Russians report for-

---

26. David Hauner, "Benchmarking the Efficiency of Public Expenditure in the Russian Federation," IMF Working Paper 07/246 (Washington: International Monetary Fund, October 1, 2007).

going medical care because they cannot afford it. As in other sectors, corruption is rampant—as much as one-third of health care spending occurs outside official channels.

These problems are not new. Analysts identified the need for structural reform in the late 1980s and recognized that money was a necessary but not sufficient condition to create modern health care in Russia. Even if the resources flowing into the health sector were spent highly efficiently, no health system can overcome the poor choices of too many Russians—smoking, excessive and binge drinking, bad diet, and lack of exercise—and the unhealthy environment (air and water pollution, poor food quality, and unsafe roads) in which many Russians live.

Conclusion

For several decades, Russia has focused on solving its health problems by tinkering with its health care system. The National Health Project, for all its flaws, is an important demonstration of political will, backed by significant resources, to seriously address health problems. But health care reform alone cannot address the pathology behind Russia's health and mortality crisis: Behaviors such as smoking and alcohol abuse are the primary contributors to premature mortality.

Some may argue that getting Russians to curtail their destructive behavior is a futile proposition, but similar pessimism surrounded the release of the 1964 US Surgeon General's report on smoking in the United States, a landmark publication followed by a health education effort that reduced tobacco consumption immediately, significantly, and for the long term. In Russia a seat belt promotion campaign in 2006 doubled seat belt use (from 26.8 to 55.8 percent) in Bashkortostan in just a single month.[27] Behavioral interventions can also work in Russia.

27. Leila Akhmadeeva, Valentina A. Andreeva, Steve Sussman, Zolya Khusnutdinova, and Bruce G. Simons-Morton, "Need and Possibilities for Seat Belt Use Promotion in Bashkortostan, Russia," *Evaluation and the Health Professions* 31 (2008): 282–89.

7

Russian Attitudes toward the West

In the late 1980s the vast majority of Russians supported pro-Western economic and political transformation. Although the transition to a market economy and democracy has eventually delivered economic benefits, most Russians are now skeptical about Western economic and political values. In this chapter, we use polls and microeconomic data to understand what determines Russians' attitudes toward the United States, the West, private property, free market economy, democracy, and other hallmarks of Western polity.

Russians' negative attitudes toward Western values are strikingly uniform across economic and social strata—and across time (they have increased over the last four years but not substantially). While the oldest and youngest Russians are more anti-Western than those in their 30s and 40s, all age cohorts are quite negative. On a positive note, however, despite most Russians' dislike of the West, many incorporate Western pragmatism in their everyday economic lives.

Since the disintegration of the Soviet Union in 1991, Russia has undergone an unprecedented political, economic, and social transformation. The original goal was a transition to a Western-style democracy and market economy. Given the enormous challenges inherent in such a transition, it is not surprising that the transformation has not proceeded according to the initial plan. Nonetheless, although Russia's democracy and market economy are imperfect, the country is certainly more democratic and more capitalist than the Soviet Union was. What is unexpected is not the slow pace of progress but the change of destination. Both Russian policymakers and the majority of the population no longer view the Western model as the goal, and this change in orientation and expectation is important as it moves Russia away from rather than toward the Western model.

Why and to what extent are Russians negative about the West as a partner and as a model for Russian society? We summarize the results from recent opinion polls and large-scale datasets on values, attitudes, and perceptions.[1] To the best of our knowledge, ours is the first microeconomic analysis of these data. Thanks to these large-scale surveys we are able to go beyond analysis based on regular opinion polls (surveying 1,000–2,000 Russians) and investigate the relationship between attitudes toward the West and age, income, family, and social status, among other factors.

We find, first, that Russians' attitude toward the West is almost uniformly negative across all economic and social strata. There are some differences between rich and poor, young, middle-aged, and old, but these differences are not important compared with the breadth and depth of the negative sentiment, which applies to the West generally and to the Western social model, democracy, and markets. These attitudes are substantially more negative in Russia than in any other surveyed transition country.

Second, there is no reason to believe that the negative sentiment will fade with time. The idea that Russians will grow closer to Western values as their country grows richer and experiences generational change does not seem to be consistent with the data. Young Russians dislike the West more than their middle-aged Russian compatriots. Although every year of economic growth has brought more prosperity to Russia, Russian and Western perceptions are only diverging further over time, as Russians' approval of markets is sinking, not rising.

Third, Russians dislike the Western socioeconomic model and the United States in particular, even as they rely on Western economic values in their everyday life. Surveys show that Russians are über-capitalists, placing significant value on wealth, power, and achievement—they are in fact more capitalist than most other European nations.

These three findings seem hard to reconcile. Why are young Russians' values more similar to those of their grandparents than to those of their parents? How can the negative attitude toward Western society coexist with the embrace of everyday Western pragmatism? We consider the ori-

---

1. One is the *Life in Transition Survey* conducted by the European Bank for Reconstruction and Development and the World Bank in fall 2006; it surveyed about 10,000 Russians and 1,000 respondents in each of the other 28 transition countries about issues related to various objective and subjective measures of life. Another dataset, Georating, comes from the leading Russian pollster Public Opinion Foundation (Russian abbreviation FOM); it includes quarterly surveys of 34,000 Russians in 68 regions on various aspects of their life and their political, economic, and social views from 2003 through 2008. We also rely on multicountry opinion polls such as the Pew Global Attitudes Survey and the European Social Survey (ESS); the ESS, somewhat similar to the World Values Survey (www.worldvaluessurvey.com), has been administered every other year in 30 countries since 2002 and in 2006 included Russia for the first time.

Table 7.1   Response to "Is the United States a friendly country?" August 2003

Response	Percent of respondents
Certainly unfriendly	18.3
Rather unfriendly	30.8
Rather friendly	27.8
Certainly friendly	3.6
Difficult to say	19.4

Source: Public Opinion Foundation, Georating poll, August 2003, http://english.fom.ru.

gins and impacts of these conflicting perceptions and speculate about possible explanations.

Attitudes toward the United States

During the Cold War, the United States was the primary enemy of the Soviet Union and the main object of state propaganda. But one might imagine that perceptions had changed since the Soviet era, as American imports—McDonald's, Hollywood movies, and Hummers—are now everywhere in Moscow and many other cities. Nonetheless the official rhetoric often portrays the North Atlantic Treaty Organization (NATO) and the United States as unfriendly and even uses the old Soviet propaganda about militarism and imperialism.

In table 7.1, we present the answers to the question "Is the United States a friendly country?" from the Georating 2003 poll. The results show that the attitudes of 50 percent of Russians are negative.[2] Unfortunately, that negative attitude was not unique to Russia. Georating posed the question in mid-2003, when responses may have reflected feelings about the war in Iraq. At the time, the United States was unpopular in many countries, including its long-term allies. Similarly, the Pew Global Attitudes Survey of about 5,000 residents of nine European countries in March 2003 showed that Russians' attitude toward the United States was comparable to that of Germans and French and actually more positive than that of the Spanish and Turkish populations. In a similar survey of 44 countries prior to the war in Iraq, in April 2002, the Pew survey showed that the world on average, and Russians in particular, had a much more positive opinion of

---

2. Ideally, we would also have liked to see answers to the question "Is the West friendly toward Russia?" Unfortunately, we do not have such data. The dataset has answers to the statement, "Name three countries that are most sympathetic to you" from a list of 11 Western countries. However, inconsistencies in the coding of the data prevent us from including the results.

the United States. While Pew's sample in Russia was only 1,002 respondents in 2002, more than 50 percent of them held a very or somewhat favorable view of the United States and of Americans. By contrast, the 2007 Pew survey of 47 countries found that the United States is quite unpopular but, again, that Russians are more positive about it than most Western and Eastern European countries.

We further explore whether there are differences in Russians' attitudes toward the United States based on different characteristics. One of the most important dimensions to consider is respondents' age. One might anticipate that older Russians would dislike the United States more than the middle-aged and certainly more than the "McDonald's and Nintendo" generation. The older generations grew up in the Soviet Union with its anti-West propaganda in school and in the press. The younger Russians have grown up with many American products and influences and, one might have conjectured, would be more positive about the United States. If this were the case, one would expect a change to a friendlier attitude over time as the younger generation takes over.

The results are not consistent with expectations. The older generation does believe that the United States is not friendly to Russia, but so do young Russians, whereas the attitudes of Russians in their 30s and 40s are slightly more favorable. This result holds when controlling for the most common socioeconomic characteristics: gender, income, location (city, town, or village), and education (figure 7.1). The horizontal axis of the graph is the age of the respondent; the vertical axis is the average numerical value of the response as follows: "certainly friendly" (1), "rather friendly" (0.67), "rather unfriendly" (0.33), and "certainly unfriendly" (0).

We find an inverted U-shaped profile with regard to age. The youngest respondents (20 years old) dislike the United States to the same degree as the 60-year-olds; those who feel somewhat more favorably about the United States are the middle-aged (35 to 45 years old). The attitude of the older respondents (60 and older) is understandable, but it is surprising that young Russians dislike the United States so much. A similar age pattern appears in other measures of anti-Western sentiment from Georating as well as in the *Life in Transition Survey*,[3] where young Russians seem more negative about transition than middle-aged Russians.

We can only speculate why young Russians are less positive about transition and the United States than their parents. A possible explanation is that they have not witnessed the shortcomings of the Soviet system but have been influenced by the recent years' official propaganda. They may also have learned about the Soviet system and the West from their grand-

---

3. I. Denisova, M. Eller, and E. Zhuravskaya, "What Russians Think about Transition: Evidence from RLMS Survey," CEFIR/NES Working Paper no. 114 (Moscow: Centre for Economic and Financial Research, 2007).

Figure 7.1   Response to "Is the United States a friendly country?" across age cohorts, August 2003

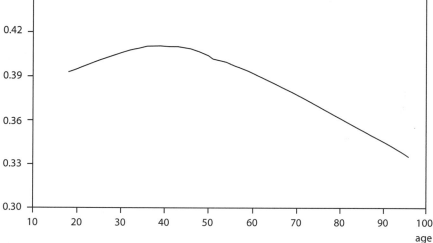

average numerical value of response

Note: The figure shows the average answer (technically speaking, a nonparametric smoother) to the question, "Is the United States friendly to Russia?" controlling for respondents' individual characteristics including income, education, gender, self-assessed social status, and location. The dependent variable is coded 1 "certainly friendly," 0.67 "rather friendly," 0.33 "rather unfriendly," and 0 "certainly unfriendly."

Source: Public Opinion Foundation, Georating poll, August 2003, http://english.fom.ru.

parents, who dislike the United States and the market economy more than the middle-aged Russians.

Other socioeconomic characteristics do not have a substantial effect. A graph based on respondents' income (figure 7.2) shows that the negative attitude toward the United States is virtually uniform across Russian society. If anything, the better-off and educated Russians perceive the United States to be less friendly toward their country. Only the upper class is slightly more positive about the United States, but the difference is very small.

The Negative Attitude toward the Western Model of Society

Given that the negative attitude toward the United States may be a reaction to US foreign policy—this would explain the low popularity of the United States among its Western allies—we analyze whether Russians

Figure 7.2   Response to "Is the United States a friendly country?" by income, August 2003

average numerical value of response

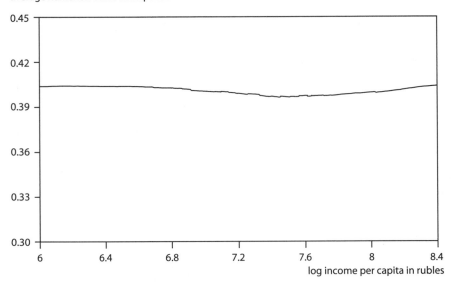

log income per capita in rubles

Note: This figure shows a nonparametric smoother controlling for respondents' individual characteristics including income, education, gender, self-assessed social status, and location type. The dependent variable is coded 1 "certainly friendly," 0.67 "rather friendly," 0.33 "rather unfriendly," and 0 "certainly unfriendly."

Source: Public Opinion Foundation, Georating poll, August 2003, http://english.fom.ru.

think that the West is a good socioeconomic model for Russia. The difference from the question in the previous section is that, while Russians may think that the West is "against them," they may nonetheless believe that Russian society should be built along the same principles.

We present the answers to the question "Is Western society a good model for Russia?" for polls conducted in the first quarters of 2004 and 2008 (table 7.2). These two polls also allow us to study the dynamics of the attitudes toward the West. They show a very negative attitude: In 2008 only 25 percent of the responses were positive or somewhat positive; among those who gave a definite answer in 2004, 30 percent were positive or somewhat positive. Thus the negative attitude toward the West increased from 2004 to 2008, although not significantly.

Again, income makes little difference. Figure 7.3 plots the average attitudes by income (2004 income is adjusted for inflation). The horizontal axis is the logarithm of income in 2008 rubles[4]; the vertical axis is the av-

---

4. We excluded the top and bottom 5 percent of the income distribution to facilitate comparison.

Table 7.2   Response to "Is Western society a good model for Russia?" 2004 and 2008

	Percent of respondents	
Response	2004Q1	2008Q1
Certainly not	27.1	30.2
Rather not	29.8	29.8
Rather yes	22.3	18.2
Certainly yes	7.3	7.2
Difficult to say	13.5	14.6

Source: Public Opinion Foundation, Georating poll, 2004 and 2008, http://english.fom.ru.

Figure 7.3   Response to "Is Western society a good model for Russia?" by income, 2004 and 2008

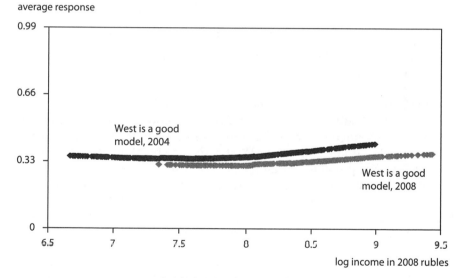

average response

West is a good model, 2004

West is a good model, 2008

log income in 2008 rubles

Note: The y-axis scale is 1 = "certainly yes," 0.67 = "rather yes," 0.33 = "rather no," and 0 = "certainly no." The x-axis is logarithm of income in 2008 rubles; top and bottom 5 percent of distribution excluded.

Sources: Public Opinion Foundation, Georating poll, 2004 and 2008; authors' calculations.

erage of the attitudes about Western society as a model for Russia. The top black line on the graph presents the results for 2004, the bottom grey one 2008 (all in 2008 rubles). (The 2008 curve shifts by about 0.5 to the right in logarithmic terms relative to the 2004 curve, representing the 13 percent annual growth in real incomes in 2004–08.) We summarize the results:

Table 7.3   Response to "Which society is more just and fair—Russian or Western?" 2004Q3

Response	Percent of respondents
Certainly Russian	6.8
Rather Russian	16.6
Rather Western	30.4
Certainly Western	17
Difficult to say	29.2

Source: Public Opinion Foundation, Georating poll, 2004, http://english.fom.ru.

1. *Russians do not like the Western model of society.* In both 2004 and 2008, the average response for all income categories was close to 0.66. In other words, Russians think that their country should not be like the West.

2. *Russians' attitude toward the Western model of society has worsened in the last four years.* The line of responses in 2008 shifted down, indicating that Russians like the West less across all levels of incomes.

3. *Rich Russians like the Western model more than the poor do, but the difference is small.*

While Russians do not think their country should imitate the West, they acknowledge that the Western model delivers good social outcomes and is fairer. Respondents were asked: "In your opinion, today, which society is more just and fair, Russian or Western?" The breakdown of responses (for 2004Q3) is presented in table 7.3. The responses are clearly positive about the fairness of Western society, at 47 percent compared with only 23 percent favoring Russian society—that is, twice as many Russians believe that the West is more fair and just than Russia. This pattern is true controlling for age, income, and other characteristics.

Are Russians Uniquely Nondemocratic?

Data from the Pew Global Attitudes Survey and the leading Russian pollster Levada Center as well as the European Bank for Reconstruction and Development (EBRD) and the World Bank illustrate Russians' view of democracy. The polls usually include only 500 to 2,000 respondents per country, but they allow international comparisons that help to benchmark Russians' attitudes in comparison with those of other nations.

Figure 7.4 displays survey data on attitudes toward market economy and democracy from the *Life in Transition Survey* conducted by the World Bank and the EBRD in 28 transition countries. These data show that Rus-

Figure 7.4 Support for market economy and democracy across 28 transition countries, 2006 (share of population)

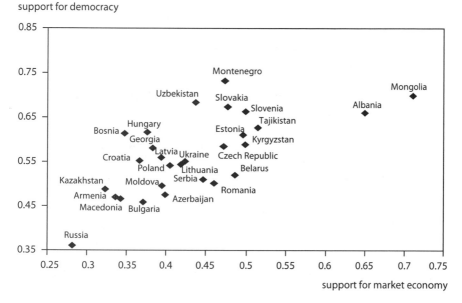

Source: World Bank and European Bank for Reconstruction and Development, *Life in Transition Survey,* fall 2006.

sia is an outlier, with the least support of any of the polled countries for both market economy and democracy—even less than the common straw man of Western criticism, Belarus. This pattern correlates with Russians' rejection of the West as a model for their society.

How have Russians' attitudes toward democracy changed over time? In 1991 many Russians were ready to discard autocracy. When asked whether Russia should rely on a democratic form of government to solve the country's problems or on a leader with a strong hand, 39 percent chose a strong hand and 51 percent a democratic government, a purely abstract concept at the time.[5]

The picture was very different in 2005, the latest year for which comparable data are available. Given the same choice, only 28 percent of Russians favored a democracy while 66 percent preferred a strong leader.[6] The growing incomes matter but are not crucial: Among Russians earning more than 8,000 rubles per month, 34 percent said democracy could solve

5. Times Mirror Center for the People and the Press, *The Pulse of Europe: A Survey of Political and Social Values* (Washington, 1991).

6. The Pew Research Center for the People and the Press, *Pew Global Attitudes Project: 15 Nation Survey* (Washington, 2006).

the country's problems compared with 27 percent of those making 4,000 to 8,000 rubles per month.

Perhaps the comparison itself played a role in the responses. When pressed to choose between a strong hand and a democracy, people may pick a strong hand because democracy sounds like a weak hand or one that does not provide well. It is likely that the respondents associate the opposites of weakness and strength with the opposites of (relative) poverty and (relative) prosperity. When asked whether a good democracy or a strong economy were more important, Russians overwhelmingly chose a strong economy by an 81 to 14 percent margin.[7]

The Levada Center has posed the same question in its regular polls but with different results. On the question, "Does Russia need a democracy?" 62 percent answered yes and only 20 percent said no in 2008.[8] But answers to further questions clarify how Russians understand democracy. Of those polled, 45 percent would choose a democracy that is "special, suited to Russia's uniqueness and national traditions"; only 20 percent prefer a democracy that is just like in "the developed countries of Europe and America." Only 13 percent chose "the democracy that was in the Soviet Union."

Can we reconcile these facts? In 1991 Russians were choosing between the known and unknown: They no longer wanted what they had but something else instead ("democracy"). Today, after being disappointed by "democracy" they again want something else, not a "Western-style democracy" but a "specially suited democracy." And this "special democracy" should accompany economic growth—unlike the "generic Western-style democracy" of the 1990s.

Russian Capitalist Pragmatism

The previous section could give the impression that Russians are very different from Westerners. But in their economic behavior Russians are much closer to the Western *homo oeconomicus*. When asked about common, everyday wisdom—rather than about general concepts like "the West," "market," and "democracy," which may be alien and abstract to them—Russians respond very much as they did in the 1991 survey conducted by Robert Shiller, Maxim Boycko, and Vladimir Korobov (see next section).

For example, the Georating survey asked respondents in 2003, "Please name the words that are the most important to the people living in your region." Respondents chose from 24 words of common human and eco-

---

7. Ibid.

8. Levada Analytical Center, *Russian Public Opinion 2007* (Moscow, 2008), www.levada.ru/eng (accessed on September 1, 2008).

nomic values. Most important to Russians were safety (37 percent), peace (33 percent), and material well-being (34 percent), followed by religion (27 percent), family (25 percent), and stability (25 percent). The terms "patriotism" and "national power" lagged far behind—as did "democracy" and "human rights."

In 2006 Russia participated in the large-scale European Social Survey (ESS), which allowed sociologists for the first time to compare Russian values with those of other Europeans.[9] Respondents considered descriptions of a variety of people and for each description indicated the degree of similarity to themselves on a scale from 1 to 6. The ESS describes a typical Russian as follows: "This person wants to have a lot of money and expensive goods. It is important to him/her to be respected. This person wants people to do what he/she wants. He/she wants to be successful." The survey results indicated, first, that Russia (together with Romania) is ahead of 17 other European countries on the power-wealth index that measures how important it is to be rich, respected, and have power over other people. Second, achievement is an important value for Russians (Russia is ahead of 14 European countries in this category). Russia lags behind the other countries on caring about others (i.e., caring about the well-being of others, fidelity to friends, and readiness to help) and universalist values (respecting the opinion of others and caring about the environment). Finally, the ESS data show that Russians score high on risk taking and openness to change. The data support our contention that Russians are no longer *homo sovieticus*. If anything, they are even more capitalist in their day-to-day life than Europeans.

Why Beliefs Matter

The first comprehensive study of Russian beliefs and whether they are similar or different from those in the West was the 1991 work of Robert Shiller, Maxim Boycko, and Vladimir Korobov.[10] In telephone interviews in Moscow and New York, they posed questions about attitudes to markets, inequality, and wealth. They followed this survey with another round extended to other Russian and Ukrainian cities.[11] They found that Russians and Americans were surprisingly similar in their attitudes about

9. Vladimir Magun and Maxim Rudnev, "Zhiznennye Tsennosti Rossiiskogo Naselenia" ["Values of the Russian Population"], *Vestnik Obschestvennogo Mnenia* 1 (2008): 34–59.

10. Robert J. Shiller, Maxim Boycko, and Vladimir Korobov, "Popular Attitudes Toward Free Markets: The Soviet Union and the United States Compared," *American Economic Review* 81, no. 3 (1991): 385–400.

11. Robert J. Shiller, Maxim Boycko, and Vladimir Korobov, "Hunting for Homo Sovieticus: Situational Versus Attitudinal Factors in Economic Behavior," *Brookings Papers on Economic Activity*, no. 1 (1992): 127–81.

most of these issues. The authors thus concluded that *homo sovieticus* did not exist or was at least not broadly different from the Westerner. A possible explanation for the lack of divergence is that the Russians were in the period of a honeymoon with the idea of the market economy—the interviews took place in the early 1990s when the average Russian was disillusioned with the state-run economy and had not yet seen the functioning (and fallibility) of the market economy.

Contrary to widespread beliefs, the reformers of the Russian economy in the 1990s understood the challenge of large-scale institutional transformation and knew that such a comprehensive reform could not be a top-down effort but required grassroots support. According to the initial Yegor Gaidar plan, reforms would be painful but as they brought results Russians would appreciate their value and support further reform.[12] But the painful reforms of the 1990s caused Russians severe disillusionment with the market economy. Partially in response to such negative popular sentiment, Russian policymakers have since undertaken a significant policy reversal. The early 2000s saw the first reversals of democratization policies, evident in the decline of Russia's rankings for democracy and media freedom.[13] Then came the reversal of liberal economic policy, starting with the nationalization of the Yukos oil company, as well as the development of state corporations and expansion of government spending.

The reversal of promarket and democratic policies coincided with a decade of spectacular economic growth (7 percent per annum on average). Moreover, contrary to the popular stereotype, this economic growth has not benefited just the lucky few but has trickled down to everybody. All measures of economic well-being have improved—unemployment and poverty fell by half and real wages tripled. Russians were buying cars, cell phones, and vacations abroad at a level that could not have been envisioned in the 1990s or, indeed, at any time in Russian history. The average Russian enjoyed this higher level of prosperity. Figure 7.5 presents a proxy for subjective well-being, an index of life satisfaction measured across a representative panel of Russians since 1994.[14] The graph shows that people are substantially happier than they were in the late 1990s.

---

12. Yegor T. Gaidar, "Inflationary Pressures and Economic Reform in the Soviet Union," in *Economic Transition in Eastern Europe*, ed. P. H. Admiraal (Oxford: Blackwell, 1993).

13. The Freedom House's Media Freedom Index for Russia changed by 12 points in just five years, 2000–05 (www.freedomhouse.org). This is a substantial change: The index is measured by a 100-point scale, and the standard deviation across countries is only 25 points. Larger declines in media freedom in the same period occurred only in Venezuela and Iran. In Polity IV's measures of democracy, Russia was ranked 61–69 (out of 150 countries) in 2000 and 69–78 (out of 152 countries) in 2005 (www.systemicpeace.org/polity/polity4.htm).

14. Sergei M. Guriev and Ekaterina V. Zhuravskaya, "(Un)Happiness in Transition," *Journal of Economic Perspectives* 22, no. 2 (2008): 53–72.

Figure 7.5   Dynamics of life satisfaction and per capita GDP, 1994–2006

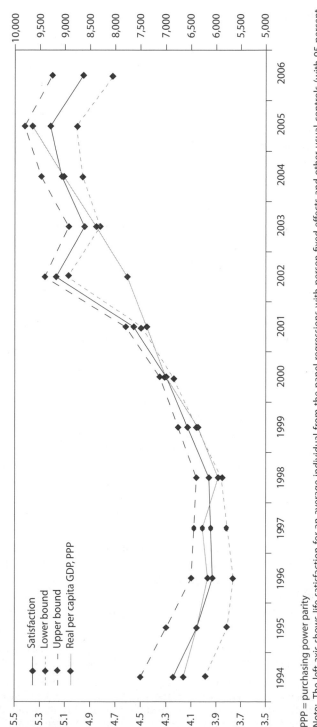

PPP = purchasing power parity

Note: The left axis shows life satisfaction for an average individual from the panel regressions with person fixed effects and other usual controls (with 95 percent confidence interval). There were no *Russia Longitudinal Monitoring Surveys* in 1997 and 1999, so we use linear interpolation. The right axis shows real PPP-adjusted per capita GDP in 2000 US dollars. According to the Penn World Tables, in 2004, the PPP-adjusted GDP per capita in Russia reached $11,794.

Source: University of North Carolina at Chapel Hill, Carolina Population Center, *Russia Longitudinal Monitoring Survey,* www.cpc.unc.edu/rims; World Bank, *World Development Indicators.*

There is little doubt that Russians are not only happier but also more prosperous than in the 1990s. What effect does this new prosperity have on their beliefs? The average Russian sees simultaneously the reversal of liberal policies and improved material outcomes. It is, therefore, not surprising that support for such a reversal is great, as Russians associate market reforms with the bad economic outcomes of the 1990s. Russia is not unique in this respect. French economists Augustin Landier and David Thesmar argue that the economic growth in France after World War II— probably due to the rebuilding of the economy and a natural bounce from a very low starting point—coincided with greater government involvement in the economy.[15] These two events changed the beliefs of the French that government is beneficial to economic growth and, hence, should play a larger role in the economy.

Why do Russians' attitudes toward the Western model matter now? One reason is that they lead to a tradeoff between economic growth and democracy. At the current level of GDP per capita, sustained economic growth is possible only by relying on capitalist or free-market values. But democracy requires policies that are inconsistent with the voters' preferences: The average citizen in Russia does not want markets or a capitalist economic model. Thus either a fully democratic Russia would vote for the reversal of many promarket reforms or a nondemocratic government could promote markets and private property.[16] In other words, Russians' beliefs and attitudes may become a constraint on the implementation of liberal economic reforms.

This constraint is even more important now as Russia has probably picked most of the low-hanging fruit of its economic growth. The catchup phase of economic growth since the slump following the collapse of the Soviet Union has ended. The main market infrastructure (e.g., a functioning financial market and a system of commercial banks) is in place. The benefits of the conservative macroeconomic policy, flat income tax reform, and administrative reform have come to fruition.

As Russia is growing richer, it is now facing a new economic challenge: how to embrace the innovation-based growth at the world's technology frontier. For such human capital–intensive economic growth, political and personal freedoms are important, but the values of Russians have to change. The present government seems to understand this conflict. Vladimir Putin's and Dmitri Medvedev's campaign speeches in February 2008 as well as the 2020 Strategic Economic Development Plan focus on build-

---

15. Augustin Landier and David Thesmar, *Le grand méchant marché: Décryptage d'un fantasme français* [*The Big Wicked Market: Deciphering a French Fantasy*] (Paris: Flammarion, 2008).

16. This distinction is evident in the divide between the two major pro-Western parties, the now disbanded Union of Right-Wing Forces (SPS) and Yabloko. While the former emphasized private property and economic reform even at the cost of political centralization, the latter focused on defending democratic values even at the cost of reversing privatization.

ing a prosperous and democratic society by 2020. While the speeches stress the value of freedom, they also acknowledge that political liberalization is a prerequisite for an "innovation economy" and that without innovation economic growth will inevitably slow down.

Conclusion

Multiple polls confirm that most Russians have negative attitudes toward the West, Western values, and the Western socioeconomic model. The data we have reviewed suggest that these attitudes are unlikely to change as Russia grows richer and the post-Soviet generation takes over: Wealthier Russians are only slightly more pro-Western than poorer ones, and the younger generation is even less happy about the West and the Western model than middle-aged Russians.

The fact that better-off and better-educated Russians have changed from liking the West (in the late 1980s) to disliking it is not new for Russia—waves of fascination and disillusionment with Western ways have followed each other for centuries. Russia's identity emerged when tsars started seeing themselves as standard-bearers of the Orthodox world after the fall of Constantinople in the 15th century, and the idea of Russia as a political and spiritual alternative to the West has been developing ever since. This messianic narrative is matched by an equally strong growing drive to catch up with the West economically (see chapter 1). The two motivations alternate, as an urgency to develop prevails for a certain period until the messianic calling proves time and again to be a deep-seated instinct.

Interestingly, both Slavophiles and Westernizers, the two major opposing schools of thought in 19th century Russia, agreed on the country's unique identity. "In the West the soul is in decline . . . conscience is replaced by law, inner motives by regulations. . . . The West has developed the rule of law because it felt a lack of truth in itself," wrote Konstantin Aksakov, a leading Slavophile. Leading Westernizer and dissident Alexander Herzen looked for truth in the West but became disillusioned with democracy, calling it a "collective mediocrity." This led him to believe that Russia should not repeat the West but should follow its own way instead: "Should Russia follow all the stages of European development? No, I reject the need for repetition." A messianic discourse of Russian national identity endured even as the Moscow Empire fell and a new state replaced it.[17]

The current wave of disillusionment with the West may be due to the coinciding policy reversals and the economic growth in the past 10 years,

---

17. Judith E. Kalb, *Russia's Rome: Imperial Visions, Messianic Dreams, 1890–1940* (Madison, WI: University of Wisconsin Press, 2008).

when Russia experienced both a decline in personal and political freedoms and stellar economic growth. This combination of developments may have convinced the Russian public that a Western-style democracy and market may function well in the West but are not suited for Russia. Russians do not seem to believe that Russia can build an effective democracy and a developed market economy. Whether the ongoing crisis will again bring a new tide of Westernization is yet to be seen.

8

Russia as a Post-Imperial Power

Russia's extraordinary economic recovery since 1999 has fueled its trans-formation from a reluctant follower in the 1990s to an obstructionist with aspirations to revise the world from a unipolar to multipolar order.[1] Russia's initiatives have been colored with such *schadenfreude* over the trials of the George W. Bush administration that Russian leaders often come across as self-appointed critics-in-chief of the United States rather than genuinely interested in reform of the institutions of global governance.

Russia's recovery is only part of Moscow's rather Darwinist perspective of the increasing tilt in the global economic balance of power toward large emerging-market economies and hydrocarbon producers—two categories in which Russia figures prominently. Thirty years ago when the Group of Seven (G-7) was formed to manage the global economy, its member countries constituted more than 60 percent of the world economy; today those countries are no longer so dominant and account for only 40 percent.

During the 1990s, both Presidents Bill Clinton and Boris Yeltsin considered that they shared the same Western values, which could be described as market democracy. Today, the Russian leadership no longer subscribes to those values. Its capitalism persists but is increasingly becoming state capitalism, and political freedom in the Western sense has been curtailed.

Given these changes in Moscow's perspectives, it was bound to re-evaluate its interests in the international system. President Vladimir Putin did so starkly in his famous February 10, 2007, speech at the Wehrkunde Security Conference in Munich, when he made essentially two points: (1) that the United States was behaving irresponsibly in managing global

1. Sections of the chapter derive from Andrew Kuchins and Richard Weitz, "Russia's Place in an Unsettled Global Order: Calculations in the Kremlin," in *Powers and Principles: International Leadership in a Shrinking World* (Stanley Foundation Project, 2009, forthcoming).

affairs and (2) that the international system of American hegemony was evaporating and being replaced by genuine multipolarity. Most commentary focused on the first point and missed the importance of the second, which Putin summarized:

> The combined GDP measured in purchasing power parity of countries such as India and China is already greater than that of the United States. And a similar calculation with the GDP of the BRIC countries (Brazil, Russia, India and China) surpasses the cumulative GDP of the EU. And according to experts this gap will only increase in the future. There is no reason to doubt that the economic potential of the new centers of global economic growth will inevitably be converted into political influence and will strengthen multipolarity.[2]

Putin and his colleagues elaborated on this theme in a series of important speeches in 2007, and the call for a "new international architecture" of global governance became a campaign theme of the Russian parliamentary/presidential electoral cycle of 2007–08.[3]

Russians are right to point out that institutions of global governance are anachronistic and often ineffective, but their own capacity to contribute to a solution is less obvious because of their emotionally charged view of the past 20 years. The Kremlin considers many changes since the late 1980s illegitimate, because Russia was too weak to assert its positions. In its narrative, the West, mainly the United States, took advantage of Russian weakness through North Atlantic Treaty Organization (NATO) enlargement in 1997, the bombing of Yugoslavia in 1999, abandonment of the Anti-Ballistic Missile (ABM) Treaty in 2001, endorsement of regime change (the "color revolutions") on Russia's borders in 2003 and 2004, promotion of missile defense, and recognition of Kosovo in 2008.[4] The Russian elite sees these Western moves as detrimental to Russia's national interests.

Russian political leaders see themselves as "realists" and describe their foreign policy as pragmatic and driven by national interests. When they discuss international relations, they rarely talk of public goods or norms, and they receive US and European references to them with cynicism or, more often, with defensive hostility about double standards. They view American efforts to promote US values as hypocritical justifications for the promotion of US interests—and, ultimately, influence and hegemony.

Rather than norms and public goods, Russian leaders and political analysts frame their country's international cooperation in terms of *realpoli-*

---

2. Vladimir V. Putin, speech and the following discussion at the Munich Conference on Security Policy, February 10, 2007, www.kremlin.ru (accessed on February 20, 2008).

3. For more on this point see the article by Clifford Gaddy and Andrew Kuchins, "Putin's Plan," *Washington Quarterly* (Spring 2008): 117–29.

4. This argument is set forth in Gaddy and Kuchins, *Washington Quarterly.*

tik bargains and tradeoffs of interests. For example, if the United States wants Russia to take a stronger position to isolate Iran, Washington is expected to compensate Moscow by halting NATO enlargement or the deployment of missile defense systems in Poland and the Czech Republic. One of Russia's most oft-repeated grievances is the US betrayal of the supposed gentleman's agreement between George H. W. Bush and Mikhail Gorbachev in 1990 to allow the unification of Germany as long as NATO would not deploy new bases on the territory of former Warsaw Pact countries. US officials contest the Russian interpretation, thus illustrating the problem with such unwritten exchanges. In reality, such "tradeoffs" on major issues seem fairly rare in international relations. And in the case of perhaps the most significant such example during the Cold War, the US withdrawal of nuclear forces in Turkey to resolve the Cuban missile crisis remained secret until decades after.[5]

The Russian government holds one norm dear, that of national sovereignty, but it applies it very selectively. Russian policy is itself rife with double standards when it comes to the sovereignty of countries like Georgia and Ukraine. President Dmitri Medvedev made this eminently clear in his September 2008 remarks on Russian television presenting the five principles that would guide his country's foreign policy:

> First, Russia will comply in full with all of the provisions of international law regarding relations between civilized countries.
>
> Second, Russia believes in the need for a multipolar world and considers that domination by one country is unacceptable, no matter which country this may be.
>
> Third, we are naturally interested in developing full and friendly relations with all countries—with Europe, Asia, the United States, Africa, with all countries in the world. These relations will be as close as our partners are ready for.
>
> Fourth, I see protecting the lives and dignity of Russian citizens, wherever they may be, as an indisputable priority for our country, and this is one of our foreign policy priorities.
>
> Fifth, I think that like any other country, Russia pays special attention to particular regions, regions in which it has privileged interests. We will build special relations with the countries in these regions, friendly relations for the long-term period.[6]

This formulation, which analysts dubbed the Medvedev Doctrine, is a striking contrast to the idealistic universalism that marked Mikhail Gorbachev's new political thinking of the late Soviet period. It bears a strong resemblance to traditional realist balance-of-power thinking. Many

---

5. Interestingly, President Medvedev spoke out against consideration of such "tradeoffs" as detrimental to Russia's interest in a major speech in Berlin in June 2008. See his speech to political, parliamentary, and social representatives, June 5, 2008, www.kremlin.ru.

6. Dmitri Medvedev, interview on Euronews television channel, Moscow, September 2, 2008, www.kremlin.ru (accessed on February 17, 2009).

Western analysts interpreted Medvedev's speech as aiming at a diminished role for NATO and the Organization for Security and Cooperation in Europe (OSCE). A European security framework that would allow for Russia's privileged relations with neighbors and special spheres of interest sounds straight out of the 19th century playbook of great powers, including the American Monroe Doctrine that justified the United States' repeated violations of the sovereignty of its neighbors. Such anachronistic notions are nonstarters in 21st century Europe, where the trend is toward common and cooperative security institutions.

Yet there have been indications of Russian willingness to be more cooperative and constructive. In the early months of the Medvedev administration, prior to the conflict with Georgia, the new Russian president used distinctly different language regarding the challenges of global governance—offering positive proposals rather than complaints about Kosovo, missile defense, NATO enlargement, and other contentious issues.

In his June 2008 speech in Berlin, President Medvedev proposed that Europe, Russia, and the United States draft a binding treaty on European security.[7] This proposal, which Medvedev repeated in a major speech in Evian, France, in October,[8] strikes at the heart of the contradictory nature of contemporary Russian foreign policy. Although it seemed to signal a move toward improved international relations, the Russian invasion of Georgia in August 2008 offered the starkest evidence that nearly 20 years after the fall of the Berlin Wall and the end of the Cold War, Americans, Europeans, and Russians together have not succeeded in making Europe "whole, free, and secure." Europe will not be secure until Russia feels fully vested in regional security institutions.

But there is an even more fundamental contradiction between Russia's domestic economic growth goals and its increasingly belligerent insistence on its "hypersovereignty." Russia is more integrated today in the global economy than it has ever been. But as its ambitious strategic economic goals for 2020 make clear, the best-case growth scenarios for Russia require much deeper integration with the West, first and foremost Europe but also the United States and Japan.[9] These partners are far more important for trade, investment, technology, and management transfer than the Commonwealth of Independent States (CIS), China, Iran, Venezuela, and the rest of the world. Despite its deepening economic integration and the imperative for more such integration, Russia's political ties

---

7. Speech at footnote 5.

8. Dmitri Medvedev, speech at World Policy Conference, Evian, France, October 8, 2008, www.kremlin.ru (accessed on December 15, 2008).

9. Andrew Kuchins, Amy Beavin, and Anna Bryndza, *Russia's 2020 Strategic Economic Goals and the Role of International Integration* (Washington: Center for Strategic and International Studies, 2008).

with the West have been worsening in recent years. This unsustainable contradiction is counter to Russia's national interest.

Russia: A Post-Imperial rather than Neoimperial Power

Until recently, Russian foreign policy was characterized by geopolitical decline, which began with the Soviet Union's failed invasion of Afghanistan in 1979 and a draining war that spotlighted Moscow's overextension during a decade of economic stagnation. The ensuing demise of the Warsaw Pact and the collapse of the Soviet Union, both in 1991, dramatically accelerated the process. With the Soviet collapse, Russia was transformed overnight from an international superpower to a recipient of international humanitarian aid. It experienced the nadir of its global power and influence during the 1990s, a traumatic period when Russia lost a civil war on its own territory in Chechnya and twice found itself virtually bankrupt. Most Russians regard this decade as a modern-day Time of Troubles (*Smutnoe Vremya*), the designation for the interregnum between the Rurik and Romanov dynasties from 1598 to 1613.

For much of the post-Soviet period, Western policymakers were principally concerned about the implications of Russia's weakness, its ability to secure nuclear weapons and materials, and more broadly its ability to effectively govern its territory. After the financial crisis in 1998, however, the Russian economy began to dramatically recover, and pundits and policymakers qualified Russia as resurgent. With the cutoff of gas to Ukraine in January 2006, the term "energy superpower" gained currency. In the wake of the August 2008 war in Georgia, many observers describe Russian foreign policy as expansionist, even neoimperial.

Russia continues to transition from its historical empire toward becoming a nation-state. As Dominic Lieven has pointed out, no empire has ended as peacefully as the Soviet Union (although the bloodshed was significant in Chechnya and Tajikistan).[10] But the country is less than two decades into this transformation; this largest land empire in world history was built over the course of several centuries, so it is reasonable to expect that its transformation will require at least another generation.

As Russia redefines itself, it seems clear, even with the Georgian war, that its territorial ambitions are largely a thing of the past. No serious political actor seeks to incorporate Georgia, Ukraine, Uzbekistan, or other neighboring former Soviet nations into a Russian state. Russia does not have sufficient financial, demographic, or military resources for such a grandiose project; Russia's rulers have their hands full with the sparsely populated and resource-rich lands in Siberia and the Far East and North.

---

10. Dominic Lieven, *Empire: The Russian Empire and Its Rivals* (New Haven, CT: Yale University Press, 2000).

Russian territory in the northern Caucasus presents other challenges, with its dense Muslim population that is not welcoming to ethnic Russians. Aside from a few overly quoted theorists of Eurasian geopolitics like Aleksandr Dugin, the Russian population has hardly any imperialist appetite. Russians have realized the costs of empire that helped catalyze the movement for their country's independence nearly two decades ago.

The current Russian political elite sees the megalomaniacal ambitions of the Soviet Union as an aberration in Russian history. They prefer the 19th century's concert of powers as a model for global governance. They believe Russia is a great power and should be treated as one, which is, of course, a major departure from the early 1990s' notion of a democratic Russia as a fundamentally new state and close ally of the world's old democracies in North America and Europe. In contrast, Putin and Medvedev present themselves as succeeding the Russian tsars—the style of their inaugurations (or coronations) is unmistakable.

By the standards of the current *realpolitik*, the Russian leaders measure states in terms of power and influence. One modification of the traditional realist approach is to distinguish not only hard but also soft power. Russia wants the ex-Soviet states to defer to Moscow on issues such as foreign policy orientation and military alliances with third parties. The concept of "near abroad" as a sphere of privileged Russia access is central to Moscow's demands on its neighbors, and the Kremlin sees this as its Monroe Doctrine.

The Kremlin opposes democracy at home but is even more concerned about new democracies serving as fig leaves for the expansion of US power in Russia's backyard. The vehemence of the Russian response to the Georgian attack in South Ossetia reflected Moscow's view of Georgia as a US "client" state. Putin and company view Mikheil Saakashvili's status as a democratic leader with utter cynicism and disdain; their reaction to Washington's support for Saakashvili brings to mind John McEnroe's attitude toward tennis umpires: "You cannot be serious!" Russia's armed response was designed to deter another "US client," Ukrainian President Viktor Yushchenko, from testing Moscow's resolve to protect its interests in that country.

President Medvedev is just the most recent Kremlin leader to have claimed privileged interests in the CIS. It is important, however, to distinguish a sphere of interest from a sphere of influence, a term both Putin and Medvedev have been careful not to use. A sphere of influence is a well-known concept of the imperialist 19th century when Russia's sphere included Northern Persia and Manchuria: When necessary, Russia could militarily occupy those territories and place them under its direct rule. In the 20th century, Moscow exercised even tighter control over its satellites through the Warsaw Pact. In contrast, in a sphere of interest third parties have limited rights, which, in the cases of Georgia and Ukraine, according to Russia means no NATO membership or foreign military bases.

The Commonwealth of Independent States: A Marginal Organization

The Commonwealth of Independent States has been far more like the British Commonwealth than a successor to the Soviet Union. It has been reasonably successful in helping the former Soviet republics to manage their independence: In 1991 few among them knew how to conduct foreign policy; all needed some mechanism to communicate with the other parts of the former empire; and all wanted guarantees that their borders would remain intact. The populations were mostly content with continued access to the former imperial space for ordinary people—no visas were needed for travel, and people could choose their country of residence and citizenship. To the leaders, the CIS provided a platform for regular summits, which they used for solving problems bilaterally. The early CIS summits resembled the meetings of the former Soviet Communist Politburo, but without the general secretary: only a *primus inter pares*. Compared with the former Yugoslavia, the dismantlement of the USSR was very gentle.[11]

Thus the CIS was a useful tool to support nation-building. All 12 new states have so far survived, which was hardly a given in 1991; relations among most of the former Soviet republics are bilateral; and all of the CIS countries are now securely integrated in the global community.

The CIS has completely failed, however, as an instrument of post-Soviet integration between Russia and its neighbors. The CIS and its suborganizations have signed many agreements, but few have been ratified and even fewer implemented. Furthermore, the CIS has no mechanisms for imposing its rules, rendering it ineffective. Moscow tried to push for more integration than the other states were interested in, while gradually reducing the resources it offered. Curiously, when Russia obtained sufficient money to change course in the 2000s, it chose the commercial expansion of Russian companies rather than regional integration.

For Russia, the CIS has proven unwieldy. It has created several smaller arrangements; the three most important are the Russia-Belarus Union State, the Collective Security Treaty Organization (CSTO), and the EurAsian Economic Community (EurAsEC). None of these organizations is particularly tight-knit. Nations join them to improve relations with Russia, but since these organizations are largely consultative, they do not generate any real benefit to Russia.

With respect to the Russia-Belarus Union State, the union-state is a fiction; Belarus is emerging as a separate nation-state, and its merger with Russia can be ruled out. Russia has a notoriously difficult relationship with Belarusian autocrat President Aleksandr Lukashenko. Yet improba-

---

11. Martha Brill Olcott, Anders Åslund, and Sherman Garnett, *Getting It Wrong: Regional Cooperation and the Commonwealth of Independent States* (Washington: Carnegie Endowment for International Peace, 1999).

ble as it may sound, Lukashenko, the most "Soviet" figure in the entire post-Soviet space, has turned out to be the true father of Belarusian independence, having accomplished what early nationalists failed to do: He gave the new nation a sense of identity.

The CSTO, originally established in 1992 as the CIS Collective Security Treaty, was founded in 2002 by the presidents of Armenia, Belarus, Kazakhstan, Kyrgyzstan, Russia, and Tajikistan; Uzbekistan joined in 2006. It should certainly not be compared with the Warsaw Pact as there is neither political control exercised by Moscow nor an integrated military structure. The CSTO is a consultative body where Moscow is not challenged, but national interests clearly prevail over collective ones. Tellingly, no member of the CSTO apart from Russia has recognized the independence of Abkhazia and South Ossetia.

EurAsEC was founded as the CIS Customs Union in 1995 and renamed in 2000. Until recently, it included Belarus, Kazakhstan, Kyrgyzstan, Russia, Tajikistan, and Uzbekistan—that is, the countries closest to Russia. (Uzbekistan, the last to join, suspended its membership in 2008.) Although its purpose was to be a customs union, it has never been and is not likely to become one, because Russia is unwilling to negotiate customs tariffs and as a large producer of many products prefers higher tariffs than the other member states do.

Despite the existence of these regional organizations, the real problem behind Russia's tenuous relationships with its "near abroad" is that Moscow does not offer anything to its close neighbors. It has cut virtually all subsidies and has not formed any effective trade community or security alliance. Meanwhile, it threatens its neighbors with cuts of gas or oil supplies and frequently imposes unannounced trade sanctions. As a consequence, the post-Soviet states focus on improving relations with other countries and not with Russia.

NATO Enlargement: A Thorn in Russia's Side

NATO's first collaborative program with Russia and other postcommunist nations was the strictly bilateral Partnership for Peace, launched in 1994. After the Czech Republic, Hungary, and Poland were accepted as members of NATO in 1997, the organization, in order to accommodate Russia, adapted the Partnership for Peace to sign the Founding Act on NATO Cooperation with Russia. The purpose was to give Russia a strong institutional position vis-à-vis NATO but keep it outside the organization, an approach described as a "voice but no veto." In the spring of 1999, however, Russia experienced its most severe crisis with NATO, when the organization bombed Slobodan Milosevic's Yugoslavia in response to his ethnic cleansing in the Serbian province of Kosovo. Russia-US and Russia-NATO relations reached a post-Soviet low. Yet in 2002 NATO and Russia formed the NATO-Russia Council, which was supposed to raise their relationship to a new level.

On September 11, 2001, President Putin was the first international leader to reach President Bush after the attack on the World Trade Center in New York—apparently he was able to do so thanks to the old hotline between the Kremlin and the White House. That telephone call and the NATO members' evocation of Article V of the organization's statutes on mutual defense aroused high expectations for NATO-Russia cooperation. Until the Georgia war, the NATO-Russia Council was a useful vehicle for cooperation between the alliance and Russia. Significantly, Moscow has signed and ratified agreements with NATO allowing it to transport military goods to Afghanistan, although NATO has largely preferred transporting through Pakistan.

Increasingly, however, Russia views NATO as a tool for the expansion of US power. Moscow has little or no trouble with the European Union or with the membership of European countries such as France, Germany, and the United Kingdom in the Atlantic alliance because the Russian leadership has some confidence in those countries' ability to say no to the United States. In contrast, Moscow regards the excommunist states, and particularly the former Soviet republics, as anti-Russian, weak, and not fully sovereign. When Poland and the three Baltic states became members of the European Union in 2004, Moscow foreign policy pundits started calling these four countries the "new aggressive minority" in the European Union. From the Kremlin's perspective they are not states so much as platforms for use by the Pentagon as Washington pleases. Because Russians have an exaggerated sense of the importance of their country as a US adversary, they wonder, Why does the United States want so many platforms so close to Russia's borders? What is the United States really up to? What is the hidden agenda? All too often their answers presume worst-case scenarios.

According to Moscow, NATO has no role in the CIS. The Partnership for Peace was all right, but NATO membership for any CIS country or US permanent military presence threatens Russia's security interests; thus in Georgia, for example, Russia demonstrated that it was ready to act to make others respect its security interests. Russia is more relaxed toward lower levels of NATO involvement: It tolerates symbolic participation of CIS countries (for example, Armenia and Kazakhstan) in US-NATO operations outside the CIS; and it did not protest the dispatch of troops from Azerbaijan, Georgia, Kazakhstan, and Ukraine as part of the coalition of the willing. The US military air base Manas in Kyrgyzstan was established in the wake of 9/11 with Russian consent. Similarly, Uzbekistan let the alliance use its Karshi-Khanabad air base, but in July 2005, soon after the Andijan massacre, the Uzbeks, supported by Moscow, asked the US Air Force to leave. At present, however, Moscow is focusing its anti-Western, anti-NATO protests on membership action plans for Georgia and Ukraine.

Mutual concerns about Afghanistan's security appeared to engender a modicum of Russia-NATO cooperation. After the April 2008 NATO summit in Bucharest, however, Foreign Minister Sergey Lavrov suggested that Russia might suspend Moscow's agreement with NATO for the transportation of nonlethal equipment through Russia and through consenting Central Asian countries for use in Afghanistan. He pointedly told reporters that "The fate of NATO is being decided in Afghanistan" and that "Russia needs cooperation with NATO no more than NATO needs Russia."[12]

Looking ahead, however, when Russia and the West begin looking for areas to restore their relationship, Afghanistan and Central Asia may offer opportunities. Russian policymakers express less unease about the Western military presence in Central Asia than about NATO military activities in Eastern Europe, Ukraine, or the southern Caucasus. Of course, it helps that no influential voices call for extending NATO membership to the Central Asian governments. In addition, Russia and NATO share an interest in preventing a Taliban resurgence in Afghanistan. For several years, Putin and other Russian officials have urged NATO to cooperate with the Russian-led CSTO on joint operations to counter Afghan narcotics trafficking. Since NATO is still having trouble ensuring security in that country, greater cooperation with Russia to curb terrorism and narcotics trafficking makes sense.

The Georgia War and Its Fallout: Demonstration for Ukraine?

Russia's 2008 war with Georgia had a lengthy prehistory in a long-unresolved ethnic conflict, and assignment of the burden of guilt depends on the start date of the chronology. Since the early 1990s, Georgia has wanted to restore control over Abkhazia and South Ossetia, which seceded during the Georgian civil war in 1991–92. More recently, Georgian President Saakashvili, first elected in January 2004, has sought close links to the United States and NATO and has sent 2,000 soldiers to Iraq. Since 2006, Russia has imposed an almost complete trade and transportation embargo against Georgia. Russia demanded that Georgia pledge not to apply for NATO membership, but in early 2008 the nation applied for a membership action plan (it was turned down at the NATO summit in Bucharest in April but the organization promised membership at an unspecified date). Russia demanded that Georgia not host US forces on its territory; Georgia has acquired both military training and small arms from

---

12. See for example the exchange in "Secretary's Remarks: Remarks with Secretary Gates, Russian Foreign Minister Sergey Lavrov and Russian Defense Minister Anatoly Serdyukov," March 18, 2008, www.state.gov/secretary.

the United States in addition to its purchases of arms from Israel, Turkey, and Ukraine.

In July 2008 Georgia held a military exercise in which 600 servicemen trained alongside about 1,000 US forces. In parallel to that exercise, across the border in the north Caucasus, a much larger Russian force trained and remained on high alert afterward. In early August, military activity began escalating in South Ossetia. The war itself began with Georgia's attack against Tskhinvali, the South Ossetian capital, during the night of August 7, but Russian troops were prepared and executed a massive counterattack, routing the Georgian forces. The fighting ceased on August 12 after French (and EU) President Nicolas Sarkozy negotiated a ceasefire between Moscow and Tbilisi.

This incident marked the first time in nearly 30 years (since the Soviet attack on Afghanistan in December 1979) that Russia sent its troops across the border to take on an enemy. The Russian action was limited in the sense that the army did not take Tbilisi, depose the Saakashvili government, or damage pipelines through Georgia. But it crippled the country's military infrastructure and deployed forces deep into Georgia to ensure that its people felt the consequences of their military defeat. The Russian hope was apparently that Saakashvili would be held responsible for the misadventure and be replaced by a politician ready to "accept realities" and make a "peace with deference" with Russia.

Just a few weeks later, on August 26, Russia took the unprecedented step of recognizing Abkhazia and South Ossetia as independent states. Although it referenced the Western recognition of the independence of Kosovo in February 2008, the two cases were very different. Both Abkhazia and South Ossetia are tiny and Abkhazia has only a small minority of Abkhaz. Russia based its decision on the large number of Russian citizens in the two territories, but most of them had become "citizens" through a recent Russian distribution of passports. In its unilateral recognition of these two tiny territories, Russia violated its long-standing principle of opposing any secession. Belarus and Kazakhstan refused to condone Russia's acts, although they did not protest publicly. Only one country, Nicaragua, followed Russia in its recognitions. Russia thus found itself in a new international isolation, but it refused to concede.

Although both Putin and Saakashvili had consistently demonstrated their enmity in public, the Russian-Georgian five-day war came as a shock to the international community. It also indicated that Russia's leaders had significantly lowered their threshold for international armed intervention. Through this war, Russia sent a warning to other post-Soviet states about what could happen if they become too close with Washington. Ukraine was the indirect target of the warning, but it was also of concern to Azerbaijan and other CIS countries.

Until 2008, Russian leaders had publicly upheld Ukraine's territorial integrity, including Crimea; but in his speech at the NATO summit in

Bucharest on April 4, President Putin discarded this position. He challenged Ukraine sharply and at length, effectively threatening to end its existence, with the following arguments: "one-third of the population are ethnic Russians," from "Russia the country obtained vast territories in what is now eastern and southern Ukraine," "Crimea was simply given to Ukraine by a CPSU Politburo's decision, which was not even supported with appropriate government procedures that are normally applicable to territory transfers," and an attempted NATO membership "may bring into question Ukraine's existence as a sovereign state."[13] To many listeners this sounded like a conditional declaration of war in case Ukraine tried to join NATO.

As with Georgia, Moscow's apparent hope is that Ukraine's pro-Western, pro-NATO President Viktor Yushchenko will be replaced in the 2010 election by someone who would chart a middle course between NATO and Russia—one who more explicitly accommodated Russia's wishes. But Moscow does not seem to oppose Ukraine's EU aspirations.

US-Russia Relations: Increasingly Strained

Practical and substantive changes in the US and Russian administrations over the past two decades have contributed to the increasingly strained relationship between the two countries. In the 1990s, the Bill Clinton administration organized a number of bilateral government meetings, notably through the Gore-Chernomyrdin Commission; President Bush, in contrast, focused on informal bilateral meetings with President Putin (although there were 27 of these compared with the 18 meetings between Presidents Clinton and Yeltsin) and minimized formal agreements between the two countries. The economic assistance agenda that was prominent in the 1990s ended with Russia's economic recovery in 1999, and democracy and human rights have fallen by the wayside as Russia has rejected any criticism in these spheres. The extensive discussions of energy cooperation in the 1990s have largely ceased. During the Bush administration, US-Russia relations were dominated by strategic military issues, such as nuclear nonproliferation, Iran, strategic arms reductions, and nuclear security. Trade was another subject of discussion, but the most important topic was Russia's accession to the WTO, which has been suspended. The US-Russian agenda has now narrowed to little more than arms control.

US-Russia relations are thus at their lowest point since 1986 before Gorbachev and Reagan's successful summit in Reykjavik. President Medvedev, in his annual address to the nation the day after Barack Obama's

---

13. "What Precisely Vladimir Putin Said at Bucharest," *Zerkalo nedeli*, April 19, 2008, www.mw.ua (accessed on December 1, 2008)

election, made clear that he did not foresee any improvement in relations between the two countries.

The United States and Russia have the largest nuclear arsenals in the world and they share a long and rich history of negotiated agreements in arms control and nonproliferation. But without deep cooperation between them, the nonproliferation regime will likely collapse, rendering the world a much more dangerous place. The good news is that the Russians want to return to this agenda; indeed, they would argue that they were more responsible in this regard than the Bush administration.

Even as its economy has rebounded, Russia remains in decline from a strategic military standpoint. The country has become more reliant on its nuclear deterrent since the deterioration of its conventional forces in the 1990s, but the aging of its nuclear arsenal leads Moscow to prefer deeper cuts in strategic weapons than Washington. Russian policymakers still believe that stabilizing the strategic competition with Washington is in Moscow's interests. When Prime Minister Putin, at a September 2008 meeting of the Valdai Discussion Club in the Russian Black Sea resort of Sochi, was asked whether he supported the proposal from US statesmen Henry Kissinger, Sam Nunn, William Perry, and George Shultz to make the world free of nuclear weapons,[14] he replied positively. But he added important caveats by noting recent major developments in conventional weapons technology (including the promise of nanotechnology) that are blurring the difference in power between nuclear and conventional weapons. He also expressed concern about missile defense and its potential to erode strategic stability.[15] Putin's remarks indicated that the Russians are prepared to engage with the Americans in deep nuclear cuts but only in a broader context of agreements on strategic stability that address missile defenses as well as conventional weapons. Russian strategists are worried that deep nuclear cuts plus US advances in defense may make the world "safe for American conventional weapons dominance." Despite the United States being mired in Iraq and Afghanistan, to Russia the United States still looks as though it is on the march—developing missile defense, outspending Moscow at about a 10:1 rate, enlarging NATO, and calling for new bases in former Warsaw Pact countries.

In their April 2008 meeting at Sochi, then presidents Putin and George W. Bush issued the Strategic Framework Declaration, aimed at "moving the US-Russia relationship from one of strategic competition to strategic partnership." This can be an excellent foundation for fundamentally changing

---

14. George P. Shultz, William J. Perry, Henry A. Kissinger, and Sam Nunn, "Toward a Nuclear-Free World," *Wall Street Journal*, January 15, 2008.

15. Putin made these comments on September 11, 2008 in Sochi, when he met with the Valdai Discussion Club. While there is no transcript of the meeting, one of the authors attended and took notes.

the negative momentum in the US-Russia relationship if the Obama administration shows some flexibility and ingenuity.

Since March 2007, Russian and American negotiators have been discussing the contours of a new bilateral arms control accord to replace the 1991 Strategic Arms Reduction Treaty (START), set to expire in December 2009. In the 2002 Russian-American Strategic Offensive Reductions Treaty (SORT), known as the Moscow Treaty, Washington and Moscow committed to reducing their nuclear arsenals to between 1,700 and 2,200 "operationally deployed strategic warheads" by December 31, 2012. This figure is lower than some of the limits imposed by START, but SORT's verification depends heavily on the extensive on-site inspections, data exchanges, and other compliance measures articulated in START. Thus, if START expires without a new agreement, both governments will, as of December 2009, be severely hampered in their ability to verify any strategic arms control.

Russian negotiators have pushed for a new legally binding treaty that would replace START and supersede SORT. The Kremlin wants the new accord to be more detailed than SORT, whose limits Moscow sees as insufficient to ensure predictability and parity in the Russian-American strategic balance. Russian representatives also seek to require the United States to destroy the warheads removed from its active stockpile rather than simply placing them in storage. Russian leaders are concerned that the earlier agreements enable the United States to simply "upload" these warheads back into US strategic systems and thereby quickly reconstitute its pre-START II force.

In the Strategic Framework Declaration, Moscow and Washington affirm that any reductions in their nuclear arsenals will represent "a further step in implementing our commitments" under the Nuclear Non-Proliferation Treaty (NPT). Yet, under NPT Article VI, "Each of the Parties to the Treaty undertakes to pursue negotiations in good faith . . . on a Treaty on general and complete disarmament under strict and effective international control." Given the NPT's call for nuclear weapons states to relinquish their arsenals, many NPT signatories believe that Russia and the United States must make more drastic reductions—possibly total elimination—to meet their NPT obligations.

Russian political and military leaders have stridently denounced American plans to erect a comprehensive ballistic missile defense network beyond US territory. In particular, Moscow objects to US steps to deploy ballistic missile defense systems in Poland and the Czech Republic by 2012–13. The Kremlin rejects the US explanation that these deployments are to counter threats from the South, notably Iran, claiming instead that they threaten Russia's strategic nuclear forces. Russian leaders fear that this deployment is part of a future global US system, a fear that drives their insecurity about their country's future strategic stability. Like NATO enlargement, the Russian anxiety about missile defense stems from the concern that the United States and its European allies are advancing unilaterally without Russia to alter European and global security arrangements to Moscow's detriment.

The tensions between Russia and the United States over Georgia have claimed, at least temporarily, a significant nonproliferation and economic casualty: the US-Russia Agreement for Peaceful Nuclear Cooperation (123 Agreement), which was signed on May 6, 2008, after nearly two years of negotiations. The proposed 30-year accord would facilitate the flow of technologies, materials, and equipment for nuclear research and nuclear energy.[16] But in early September President Bush withdrew the agreement from congressional consideration.

The Russian government and nuclear industry had sought the cooperation agreement to enhance their ability to expand the country's role as a provider of international nuclear fuel services, as Russia has considerable excess capacity to manufacture or reprocess uranium fuel for foreign customers. Yet most of the world's nuclear fuel originates in the United States. Until a 123 Agreement is in place, countries are prohibited from sending their nuclear fuel of US origin to Russia. Despite the possibility of increased competition, many representatives of the American nuclear industry endorsed the proposed Russia-US agreement. They wanted the option of importing Russian nuclear technology as well as selling American services and equipment directly to Russian buyers—provided the Russian government opened its nuclear market to foreign competition and established a comprehensive liability regime for commercial nuclear activities.[17] Arms control experts who backed the accord emphasized the importance of giving Moscow some financial incentives that might increase its cooperation with Western countries to constrain Iran's nuclear weapons program. They hoped that, by offering Russian nuclear energy companies new markets, the Russian government would find it more acceptable to reduce nuclear cooperation with Iran.[18]

Other than the United States, Russia possesses more nuclear material suitable for manufacturing weapons and relevant expertise than any

---

16. Section 123 of the US Atomic Energy Act of 1954 requires the United States to negotiate a separate bilateral accord with each country before they can cooperate on commercial nuclear projects. These accords obligate the recipient country to obtain Washington's approval to use any US nuclear material or equipment for uranium enrichment, reprocessing, or transfer to a third party. US Department of State, US-Russia Agreement for Peaceful Nuclear Cooperation (123 Agreement), May 15, 2008, www.state.gov (accessed on December 26, 2008).

17. Jack Spencer, "Russia 123 Agreement: Not Ready for Primetime," Heritage Foundation, May 15, 2008, www.heritage.org (accessed on December 1, 2008).

18. Richard Lugar and Sam Nunn, "Help Russia Help Us," *New York Times*, May 30, 2008. See also Miles A. Pomper, "Bush Sends Russia Nuclear Energy Pact to Hill," *Arms Control Today* (June 2008), www.armscontrol.org (accessed on January 10, 2009).

other country. For years, experts have considered the hundreds of tons of fissile material located in Russia to be the most vulnerable to falling into the wrong hands. The Strategic Framework Declaration commits both countries to "expand and strengthen" their joint Global Initiative to Combat Nuclear Terrorism, which aims to improve coordination of nonproliferation programs that contribute to averting nuclear terrorism. Although it began as a bilateral Russian-American initiative, the Global Initiative has gained widespread international support, and as of July 2008, 75 countries were full partners.

After the initial US-Russian Cooperative Threat Reduction (CTR) effort helped Russia and other former Soviet republics dismantle unwanted Soviet-era strategic weapons systems, focus shifted to enhancing the safety and security of residual weapons against illicit trafficking by terrorists and other nonstate actors. The CTR priority in recent years has been joint efforts to lessen third-party proliferation threats. This new focus holds the most promise for future Russian-American threat reduction cooperation because it moves from the donor-recipient dynamic of earlier CTR programs to one of joint partnership against common threats. Russian and American experts have already engaged in periodic discussions about applying CTR-like programs to other countries, especially in North Korea and Pakistan.[19]

Flourishing Friendship with China

In contrast to the deteriorating relationship between the United States and Russia, friendship has flourished between Russia and China as never before. Moscow's attitude toward China reflects its sense of identity as a uniquely Eurasian power, but its China policy during the past 15 years has been driven by pragmatic considerations. In 1996 Presidents Yeltsin and Jiang Zemin established a strategic partnership, which appeared long on rhetoric and short on substance, but since Putin assumed power in 2000 economic and political cooperation between Russia and China has deepened. Moscow may not wish to form an alliance with Beijing, but growing Russian irritation with the United States and Europe has benefited the China-Russia relationship.

A consistent thread running through Russian attitudes toward China from the Yeltsin era to the present is that China offers important leverage with the West. As President Yeltsin explained in 1995:

> China is a very important state for us. It is a neighbor, with which we share the longest border in the world and with which we are destined to live and work side by side forever. Russia's future depends on the success of cooperation with China. Relations with China are extremely important to us from the global politics per-

---

19. David E. Hoffman, "Lugar, Nunn Push Arms Security Program," *Washington Post*, August 28, 2007, www.washingtonpost.com (accessed on January 10, 2009).

spective as well. We can rest on the Chinese shoulder in our relations with the West. In that case the West will treat Russia more respectfully.[20]

In 2000 Vladimir Putin echoed Yeltsin's reasoning during his first tour of Asia: "Russia is both a European and an Asiatic state. It is like a bird and can fly well only if it uses both wings."[21] Yet Russia's perspective on China is based on the traditional *realpolitik* of the dynamics between rising and falling great powers; in this Darwinist framework, Russian appreciation of China has risen with the deterioration of US-Russia relations. When Moscow protested US support for NATO expansion in 1997, the 1999 war in Kosovo, and the development of national missile defense, the Yeltsin administration gravitated toward Beijing. More recently, US support for democracy promotion as well as increased US influence in the post-Soviet states drove the Putin administration even closer to China. Like Yeltsin before him, Putin repeatedly invoked an improvement in ties with China as an alternative to a more pro-Western foreign policy if Washington did not pay greater attention to Moscow's interests.

Tellingly, as new president in May 2008, Dmitri Medvedev chose Kazakhstan and China for his first foreign visits. He and China's president Hu Jintao signed a Sino-Russian joint declaration on foreign affairs, which claimed that Russia and China share nearly the same views on almost all major international issues—missile defense, opposition to expanding military alliances, rejection of the militarization of outer space, and support for China's position vis-à-vis Tibet and Taiwan. The two presidents also reaffirmed cooperation on bilateral energy projects and signed important economic and trade agreements. The rhetoric from Moscow and Beijing indicates that their relations have never been better, and the economic data support this claim: Trade between the two countries has grown exponentially, reaching $40 billion in 2007—a jump of more than 40 percent from the previous year.[22]

Yet Russia's trade with China contradicts the development goals set by Moscow in its Concept of Long-Term Socioeconomic Development of the Russian Federation to 2020 (Russia 2020), in which Russia aims to reduce its overreliance on exports of raw materials and encourage more innovation-based development to diversify its economy. (To that end, the 2020 plan suggests that Europe, Japan, and the United States will play a much greater role in Russian economic modernization.) Russian exports to China are overwhelmingly raw materials, such as crude oil and timber, especially as military technology exports fall, so greater economic ties

20. Boris Yeltsin, quoted in Alexander Lukin, *The Bear Watches the Dragon* (Armonk, NY: M.E. Sharpe, 2003, 305).

21. Vladimir Putin, introductory remarks at a meeting on the Development of the Urals Federal District, July 14, 2000, www.kremlin.ru (accessed February 17, 2009).

22. "Chinese Exports to Russia Expected to Increase," *China Daily*, March 3, 2008, www.chinadaily.com.cn (accessed on September 30, 2008).

with China do little to promote Russia's diversification. Moreover, Russian arms exports, a long-standing cornerstone of Sino-Russian economic cooperation, have become an unexpected bone of contention. After years of importing Russian military technology, the Chinese have replicated not only Russian automatic rifles and rocket launchers but also SU-27S fighters. China has, therefore, reduced its imports of Russian military technology and even exports its own versions to traditional Russian clients such as Angola, Ethiopia, and Syria.

China, the fastest-growing petroleum consumer in the world, has viewed Russia as an important alternative source of oil and gas. Russia, in turn, has used China to frighten its European customers who are nervous about diminishing supplies. Until recently, however, the Chinese have been frustrated by the slow development of the Sino-Russian energy relationship and by competition for Central Asian resources (notably in Turkmenistan, but also in Kazakhstan). Yet aside from growing demand, Chinese companies have little to offer in the development of Russian greenfields in eastern Siberia and the High North, projects that will entail large capital expenditures and great technical challenges. To the extent that foreign companies will be allowed to participate in the development of the Russian hydrocarbon sector, Western businesses have a significant advantage over Chinese firms.

Despite these advantages, however, the United States should keep in mind that during troughs in Russia's relations with the West, the Chinese have come to the financial aid of Russian oil giant Rosneft twice in the past four years: first in December 2004 when China National Petroleum Corporation (CNPC) lent Rosneft $6 billion to finance the purchase of former prime Yukos asset, Yuganskneftegaz, and again in February 2009 when CNPC completed a $25 billion loan package to the deeply indebted and leveraged Russian oil major ($15 billion to Rosneft) and the similarly leveraged pipeline monopoly Transneft ($10 billion).[23]

There are striking similarities, however, between the maturing ideological foundations that underpin Russia's and China's outlooks on the world and their global roles. The Putin administration began promoting an emerging ideology, described by Russians as "sovereign democracy," that presents Putin as the leader who restored stability and set Russia on the road to recovery by adapting democratic values and institutions to Russian values and traditions. Foreign Minister Sergey Lavrov described the foreign policy analogy to sovereign democracy in a January 2007 speech:

> The fundamental principles of Russia's foreign policy—pragmatism, multiple vectors, and consistent but nonconfrontational protection of national interests—

---

23. "China Offers $25 billion Oil Loan," *Moscow Times*, February 18, 2009. This deal may also reflect heightened Chinese leverage in the bilateral relationship resulting from the global financial crisis.

have gained broad international recognition. . . . Many countries have come to re-
alize that a new, safer, fair, and democratic world order, whose foundations we are
laying together, can only be multipolar, based on international law, and regulated
by the UN's unique legitimacy and central role.[24]

Lavrov's rhetoric has much in common with the rhetorical and opera-
tional foundations of Chinese foreign policy, called the Beijing Consensus,
which Joshua Cooper Ramo described as principally a socioeconomic development model that the Chinese have successfully implemented. Despite the similar name, it differs substantially from the so-called Washington Consensus promoted by the US government, the International
Monetary Fund, and the World Bank.[25]

Two major points of the Beijing Consensus resonate with the Kremlin's
sovereign democracy and have implications for Russia's foreign policy.
First, there is not just one correct path to development; a country must ex-
periment to find the path best suited to its culture and traditions. Most
Russians today view the advice of Western advisers and multilateral organizations as having failed and exacerbated Russia's socioeconomic
problems, so they are interested in exploring non-Western alternatives.

Second, global power is shifting from the unipolar model of the 1990s
to a genuinely multipolar world. The Russians consider themselves one of
several emerging powers and Putin is especially enamored with the idea
of the joint emergence of the BRICs (Brazil, Russia, India, and China);
Russian and Chinese cooperation on a number of issues seems to support
Putin's outlook. In the UN Security Council, for example, the Chinese
have consistently followed Russia's lead both in votes against sanctions
on Iran, Burma, and most recently Zimbabwe and on the importance of
the territorial integrity of Serbia when negotiating the status of Kosovo.

A more serious example of Sino-Russian coordination is the decision in
2005 by the Shanghai Cooperation Organization (SCO)—the intergovern-
mental group consisting of China, Kazakhstan, Kyrgyzstan, Russia, Tajikistan, and Uzbekistan—to request clarification from the United States about
its plans for withdrawing from military bases established in Central Asia
after September 11, 2001. The 2005 gathering of SCO foreign ministers in
Moscow also included representatives of states that had recently acquired
observer status—India, Iran, Mongolia, and Pakistan. In his opening remarks, Putin crowed about the fact that three billion people, virtually half
the global population, were represented at the gathering and noted that the
"SCO has gone far beyond the framework of the task originally set for it."

Yet Russian elites remain ambivalent about the emerging Chinese superpower. Russian public opinion about China tends to be quite positive

---

24. Russian Minister of Foreign Affairs Sergey Lavrov, speech at the Moscow State Institute
of International Relations, January 29, 2007, www.mid.ru (accessed on February 17, 2009).

25. Joshua Cooper Ramo, *The Beijing Consensus* (London: Foreign Policy Center, 2004).

but probably reflects Russian national television, which promotes Putin's sunny outlook on China. In April 2007 the VTsIOM public opinion research center reported that 63 percent of Russians viewed China as either a strategic partner or ally, yet at the same time 62 percent saw the involvement of Chinese companies and workers in the development of mineral resources in Siberia and the Russian Far East as dangerous for Russia.[26] Many Russians fear that China will eventually take over the almost unpopulated Russian Far East.

The Russia-Georgia war tested the Russian-Chinese friendship. China strongly opposes any secession because of its own predicaments in Taiwan, Tibet, and Sinkiang and refused to condone Russia's recognition of South Ossetia and Abkhazia. China thus demonstrated that it may value its relations with Russia but will be reluctant to fully align with Moscow.

Russia as Energy Superpower

The extraordinary rise in oil prices transformed Russia in less than 10 years from a case of near bankruptcy to one of the world's largest creditor nations. Yet Russia's role as a major player in global energy security—especially as a gas supplier in Europe—is a matter of debate. There are many areas of concern: the terms and extent of foreign investment in Russia, Moscow's dominance over pipelines in the Eurasian region, and the reliability of Russian supplies of gas and oil. The Russian government denies that its intentions are anything but commercial and maintains that it is a reliable supplier, but other governments in the region watch it with trepidation and justifiable distrust. After all, three of the most significant events of the Putin years pertained to oil and gas: the Yukos affair and the 2006 and 2009 gas disputes with Ukraine. The Yukos affair marked a dramatic power shift and the recentralization of political and economic authority back to the Kremlin. In Ukraine Moscow seemed to be punishing the nation for the Orange Revolution and for its rejection of the Kremlin's favored presidential candidate (from the Kremlin's point of view, Russia's political and economic/commercial interests coincided in the Ukrainian gas disputes). In addition, the coincidence that Russia took this step on the very day that it assumed chairmanship of the G-8, with energy security as its main theme, added to the fallout. US Secretary of State Condoleezza Rice was one of the first international figures to accuse Russia of using energy as a "political weapon." Regardless of the merits of Gazprom's negotiating position, cutting off gas supplies was a public relations fiasco for Moscow. In January 2007 Gazprom undertook a similar cut of its deliveries to and through Be-

---

26. "Rossiiane khotiat druzhit'siia s Kitaem, no na rasstoianii" ["Russians want to be friendly to China, but from a distance"], Vserosisiiskii Tsentr Izucheniia Obshestvennogo Mneniia Press Release no. 674, April 16, 2007, http://wciom.ru.

larus because of another pricing dispute. Concern in Europe about excessive dependence on Russia and the need to diversify supplies has been intensifying ever since, and the resonance is loud in Washington as well.

There are two important questions about Russia's contributions to regional and global energy security: (1) Will consumers of Russian oil and gas be vulnerable to Moscow's political whims, or are the Russian companies and state taking measures to ensure adequate supply to meet domestic and foreign demands?[27] (2) Will Europe be able to develop a common energy policy toward Russia? Russia naturally takes advantage of Europe's inability to act collectively on energy by providing attractive terms to politically favored clients such as France, Germany, and Italy, but the recent threats are enhancing the desire among EU members for common action.

Russia and the other countries in the region are competing to determine whether Russia will control the gas and oil pipelines from the former Soviet Union to Europe. The Kremlin has pursued a concerted strategy to augment Russian domination of pipeline infrastructure and views efforts to develop alternative pipeline routes that bypass Russia as hostile. It did accept the construction of the large private and foreign-owned Caspian Pipeline System from Kazakhstan to the Russian Black Sea port of Novorossiisk in the 1990s, but it was forced to accept the US-supported Baku-Tbilisi-Ceyhan pipeline from Azerbaijan to the Turkish Mediterranean coast.

The current big competition is whether European countries will build the Nabucco and Transcaspian pipelines to supply Central Europe with gas from the Caspian Basin or whether Gazprom's South Stream pipeline project through the Black Sea to Italy will outcompete it. Related disputes have prevented Russia and Europe from agreeing on the Energy Charter Treaty, which Moscow has refused to ratify principally because of Gazprom's refusal to renounce its monopoly of domestic gas pipelines.

The gas dispute with Ukraine in January 2006—Gazprom shut off gas supplies for two days to that country and, therefore, partially to eight European customers as well—raised questions about Moscow's reliability as a supplier. The complete and much longer supply disruption in January 2009 confirmed Gazprom's unreliability. Whether Russia is a responsible stakeholder on energy security depends on where you sit. Germans have had positive experiences, unlike residents of the Baltic States, Belarus, the Caucasus, Moldova, Poland, or Ukraine. However, Russian behavior is not so different from that of other large hydrocarbon suppliers when a high-price environment enhances their leverage. When prices are skyrocketing, Russian companies are not alone in revisiting contracts, production-sharing agreements, and equity stakes that were negotiated

27. Vladimir Milov, *Russia and the West: The Energy Factor* (Washington: Center for Strategic and International Studies, 2008).

when prices were much lower. The recent demonstration in Georgia, however, of Moscow's willingness to use force outside its constitutional borders marks a new development bound to affect the calculations of all neighboring states on a wide variety of issues, including energy.

The controversy surrounding the gas cutoffs to Ukraine has obscured two underlying problems: the growing strain between supply of and demand for Russian gas and the Kremlin's decision to end its subsidization of the CIS countries with cheap gas. Gazprom's production has been stagnant for years, while the demand for Russian gas both abroad and at home is steadily rising. All production growth after 2000 has come from independent Russian gas companies, and they are increasingly constrained or nationalized. This brings us back to the Yukos case and the push for greater state intervention in the energy sector. Is the Russian state killing the goose that lays the golden egg? Is the ruling elite interested in enlarging the country's energy-sector pie—or merely getting larger pieces for themselves?

Democracy and Human Rights

US and European support for democracy promotion in Russia has been increasingly controversial in Russian-Western relations and ultimately ineffective. When Russia started the first Chechnya war in December 1994, Western criticism was limited, as Russia was recognized as a democracy; most criticism was domestic. When Russia launched the second Chechnya war in September 1999, domestic criticism was contained, whereas the West was more critical, but the Kremlin simply ignored the criticism. Beginning in 2000, Putin systematically undermined political and civil freedoms, but gradually and always with some formal, legal excuse that minimized foreign criticism. In response to Western criticism of Russia's authoritarian drift and accusations of human rights violations, corruption, and other abuses, officials countered with a steady refrain of double standards.

More recently, Russian leaders were alarmed by the color revolutions in Georgia (2003), Ukraine (2004), and Kyrgyzstan (2005), especially after Ukraine's Orange Revolution inspired George W. Bush to speak eloquently about democracy and peace in his second inaugural address in 2005.[28] With support from China and other authoritarian governments in the region, Russian leaders sought to break this momentum. Putin condoned the massacre by Uzbek security forces in Andijan in May 2005, and the wave of democratization seemed to be over as the authoritarian capitalists mobilized. As Thomas Carothers observed in 2006, "The growing backlash [against

---

28. Much of the discussion on democracy promotion is derived from Andrew Kuchins, "État Terrible," *National Interest* (September/October 2007): 92–96.

democracy] has yet to coalesce into a formal or organized movement. But its proponents are clearly learning from and feeding off of one another."[29]

Russia's somewhat liberal approach to economic integration contrasts starkly with the Kremlin's posture in the debate between national sovereignty and international intervention to promote democracy and address human rights abuses. In these areas, Russia under Vladimir Putin developed what Sarah Mendelson called a sense of "hypersovereignty."[30]

Russia has also taken steps—in alliance with China and others—to systematically thwart the efforts of international organizations responsible for establishing and defending human rights. Russia's relationship with OSCE and the Council of Europe, which both address human rights concerns, has been tense for years as Moscow has aggressively sought to reduce their role in election monitoring and human rights protection.

For all these reasons, practitioners and academics working on democracy promotion and human rights increasingly view Russia more as a determined spoiler than a responsible stakeholder.[31] The West has largely accepted that it can do little about human rights in Russia and has toned down its criticism, which does not seem likely to lead to any concrete benefits and which the Kremlin simply ignores.

Conclusion

This review of selected major issues in Russia's foreign policy illustrates several points. First, the nature and goals of future Russian foreign policy will depend primarily on how the country develops domestically. The big contrasts between Russia's foreign policy in the 1990s and the 2000s are largely due to two factors: domestic political values and economic strength. The drastic downturn in Russia's economic situation at the end of 2008 and the uncertainty about its duration have radically altered the assumption of a relatively high oil price on which the Kremlin has operated for the last several years.

Second, the international oil price appears to be the most important determinant of Russian foreign policy. A high oil price has closely correlated with more assertive and aggressive Soviet and Russian foreign policy for the last 40 years. The first oil crisis in 1973 culminated in the invasion of Afghanistan in December 1979. Mikhail Gorbachev's and Boris Yeltsin's rapprochement with the West and retrenchment of Russian international

---

29. Thomas Carothers, "The Backlash against Democracy Promotion," *Foreign Affairs* 85, no. 2 (2006): 55–68.

30. Sarah Mendelson, "Russia Today: In Transition or Intransigent," testimony before the US Commission on Security and Cooperation in Europe, May 24, 2007, www.csis.org (accessed on February 1, 2009).

31. Mendelson, "Russia Today."

power coincided with low oil prices; Putin's "resurgent Russia" of the past five years has been facilitated by a massive inflow of gas and oil revenues. The two peaks of hydrocarbon revenues around 1980 and the summer of 2008 correspond to the last two instances of Russian military engagement in conflicts abroad.[32]

If the current low oil prices endure and history is a guide, there should be a change in the substance and tone of Russian foreign policy toward greater accommodation to the West. Foreign policy decisions will be constrained by their economic costs; for example, the recent foray of the Russian navy into Latin America may seem an unaffordable luxury in the next year. The Obama administration may thus find a more pliable partner in Russia in the coming year. The danger, however, is that the Kremlin will react to growing social and political unrest due to economic hardship with a brutal crackdown, which would naturally be accompanied by a more isolationist, prickly, and dangerous foreign policy, particularly toward its neighbors.

A third aspect of Russian foreign policy is that the Russians are ingrained practitioners of *realpolitik*. Their international outlook is pragmatic and realistic. That is why the oil price is so important for Russian foreign policy.

A fourth consideration is Russia's actual interests. In its attitude toward its near abroad, Russia behaves as any traditional great power—wanting to have influence—and its greatest sources of influence on the world stage are its nuclear arms and its energy assets. The nuclear arms are likely to have a positive influence, as they promote Russian partnership with the United States. The energy assets have a negative influence when prices are high, but should be a source of international cooperation in times of more moderate energy prices.

Finally, as a large open economy and a great power, Russia has a considerable interest in being a full-fledged participant in the international system and its governance. The overall challenges of reforming institutions of global governance weigh most heavily on the United States, since Americans played the lead role in creating the existing system. But the unipolar moment is fading, as is the broader historical dominance of the West that has lasted for nearly 300 years. Russia is not very different from other large emerging powers in that it will likely behave more responsibly to the extent that its leaders believe they participate in the shaping (and reshaping) of international political, security, and economic institutions. Russians appear eager to play a more leading and vocal role, including by championing the interests of other powers that were not involved in crafting the existing institutions.

---

32. For more on this argument, see Andrew C. Kuchins, *Alternative Futures of Russia* (Washington: Center for Strategic and International Studies, 2007) and Samuel Charap and Andrew Kuchins, *Economic Whiplash in Russia: An Opportunity to Bolster U.S.-Russia Commercial Ties?* (Washington: Center for Strategic and International Studies, February 2009).

9

Pressing the "Reset Button" on US-Russia Relations

Whither Russia? Russia's economic circumstances as well as its articulated goals hold the answer to this eternal question. In this concluding chapter, we outline a policy approach for the Barack Obama administration. We believe our views reflect to some degree an emerging consensus for the new administration's Russia policy.[1]

Russia is important for US foreign policy in many ways. The United States needs a more constructive relationship with Russia to address many core global security issues including nuclear security and nonproliferation, terrorism, energy, and climate change. The United States also needs to assume a stronger leadership role in reforming the institutions of global governance as the international system evolves in a more pluralistic direction. Assimilating the rapidly rising emerging powers—including

---

1. On the eve of the Obama administration, numerous papers were published on a new US policy on Russia. We tried to draw on them all, with particular attention to two: Steven Pifer, "Reversing the Decline: An Agenda for U.S.-Russian Relations in 2009," Brookings Policy Paper 10 (Washington: Brookings Institution, January 2009) and Stephen Sestanovich, "What Has Moscow Done? Rebuilding U.S.-Russian Relations," *Foreign Affairs* (November/December 2008). We also consulted Henry A. Kissinger and George P. Shultz, "Building on Common Ground with Russia," *Washington Post*, October 8, 2008, A19; Michael McFaul, "U.S.-Russia Relations in the Aftermath of the Georgia Crisis," testimony to the House Committee on Foreign Affairs, US Congress, Washington, September 9, 2008; and Rose Gottemoeller, "Russian-American Security Relations after Georgia," Carnegie Endowment for International Peace Policy Brief (Washington: Carnegie Endowment for International Peace, October 2008). Dmitri Trenin offers a useful Russian commentary; see "Thinking Strategically about Russia," Carnegie Endowment for International Peace Policy Brief (Washington: Carnegie Endowment for International Peace, December 2008).

Russia—will be easier if Russia is a constructive partner rather than an obstructionist outsider or, worse, a revanchist bully.

The global financial crisis and Russia's battered international reputation in the wake of the August 2008 war in Georgia and its January 2009 gas war compel Russian leaders to reconsider its foreign policy. At this critical juncture, the United States has a new opportunity to shape how Russia conceives of its interests, and we suggest steps the United States can take to improve its Russia policy.

Deterioration of US-Russia Relations

The hostilities between Russia and Georgia that began on August 8, 2008, brought the US-Russia relationship to a new post-Soviet nadir, its lowest point since before the Reykjavik summit between Ronald Reagan and Mikhail Gorbachev in 1986. The war in Georgia made clear that US policy toward Russia requires a fundamental reassessment and a new direction.

The war and its aftermath also confirmed that nearly 20 years after the fall of the Berlin Wall and the end of the Cold War, Russia has not successfully integrated into a European or broader Eurasian security framework. Yet, "To reach its full potential . . . Russia needs to be fully integrated into the international political and economic order," as former US Secretary of State Condoleezza Rice put it.[2] Neither Russia nor its neighbors will feel secure unless Russia is more committed to regional security arrangements.

Despite the new low in the US-Russia relationship, the United States undertook few concrete measures in response. It withdrew the completed US-Russia Agreement for Peaceful Nuclear Cooperation (123 Agreement) from consideration in the US Congress, but neither the United States nor the European Union imposed any sanctions against Russia. In anticipation of Western reactions, however, Moscow officially suspended its attempts to enter the World Trade Organization (WTO), and Russian anti-American propaganda reached a crescendo not heard since the Soviet period.

Before we discuss what the United States should do, however, it is important to establish why US-Russia relations have deteriorated to such an extent. Relations between the two countries seemed to enjoy a new beginning with the election of both George W. Bush and Vladimir Putin in 2000. Their mutual agenda had shrunk and become much less ambitious, no longer including economic assistance and Russian reforms. The Bush administration's primary aim was to abolish the bilateral Anti-Ballistic Missile (ABM) Treaty of 1972 in order to develop missile defense. A sec-

---

2. US Department of State, "Secretary Rice Addresses U.S.-Russia Relations at the German Marshall Fund," September 18, 2008, www.state.gov (accessed on December 15, 2008).

ondary American goal was to engage Russia against nuclear proliferation, especially with respect to Iran. The Bush administration paid less attention to issues of previous importance—the former Soviet republics, energy, democracy, human rights, and commerce. Its policy toward Russia followed a "minimalist-realist" agenda.

Chronology of Key Events

Putin's initial agenda focused on elevating Russia's international position. To that end, he undertook significant goodwill gestures toward the United States, closing a Russian intelligence-gathering facility in Cuba and a naval base in Vietnam. The high point of the Bush-Putin relationship came after 9/11 at the Moscow summit in May 2002. The United States needed bases in Central Asia for its war in Afghanistan and Putin accommodated this request. The two countries concluded the Strategic Offensive Reduction Treaty (SORT or Moscow Treaty) in 2002, and Russia accepted without protest the US abandonment of the ABM Treaty in December 2001. In return, the United States did little for Russia other than to discontinue its criticism of Russia's policy in Chechnya and, in 2002, recognize Russia as a market economy.

Before long, however, the US-Russia relationship began to deteriorate on a broad front. At the end of 2002 and in early 2003, the presidents of France, Germany, and Russia jointly protested US plans for a war in Iraq against Saddam Hussein, although the United States largely refrained from criticizing Russia for its opposition.

With the confiscation of the oil company Yukos, initiated in 2003, Russia began renationalizing its oil and gas assets, leaving less room for foreign oil companies. The losses of American shareholders probably amounted to as much as $12 billion, but the US government did not publicly protest.

In 2004 the deterioration in US-Russia relations became more obvious. In March, Bulgaria, Estonia, Latvia, Lithuania, Romania, Slovakia, and Slovenia became members of the North Atlantic Treaty Organization (NATO), which prompted sharp Russian protests, especially against the admission of the three Baltic countries. The Kremlin viewed this development as US intrusion in its sphere of influence and only grudgingly accepted the new countries' status. In July of that year the West was shocked by the murder in Moscow of the American *Forbes Russia* editor Paul Klebnikov. But with the Orange Revolution in Ukraine that fall, the deterioration became a rupture. Russia and Putin himself had heavy-handedly intervened in the Ukrainian presidential elections to direct the election results to their advantage. A united West protested, and although the United States carefully avoided taking the lead and instead ceded the diplomatic response to Europe, the Kremlin considered the protest a US-led conspiracy against its influence in its "near abroad."

In April 2005 Putin stunned Western observers when he asserted in his annual address that "the collapse of the Soviet Union was the biggest geopolitical disaster of the century."[3] Then in December of that year, Russia adopted a restrictive law on nongovernmental organizations despite both American and European protests.

In January 2006 Gazprom disrupted gas deliveries to Europe through Ukraine for two days, raising concerns about Russia's reliability as a supplier. In July, however, Bush proceeded as though nothing had happened and attended the St. Petersburg G-8 summit, which was held as a celebration of Putin's rule in Russia; the United States concluded bilateral WTO negotiations with Russia in November 2006. At about the same time the world learned of the murders of journalist Anna Politkovskaya in October and security police defector Aleksandr Litvinenko in London in November.

In February 2007 Putin dramatically escalated his rhetoric after the United States revealed plans to establish antimissile bases in Poland and the Czech Republic. He threatened to withdraw from two arms control agreements, the Treaty on Conventional Armed Forces in Europe (CFE) and the Intermediate-Range Nuclear Forces (INF) Treaty.[4] And in December Russia suspended its implementation of the CFE Treaty.

In 2008 both Georgia and Ukraine applied for membership action plans (MAPs) to NATO. In protest, Putin threatened them at the NATO Bucharest summit in April. If Ukraine was allowed to join NATO, he said, "this may bring into question Ukraine's existence as a sovereign state."[5]

After the NATO summit, Russia quickly strengthened its support for the two secessionist Georgian territories, Abkhazia and South Ossetia. But a rapid escalation of military incidents led to a full war that broke out between Georgia and Russia on the night of August 7, and the next day Russian troops invaded parts of Georgia. The war ended after just five days thanks to European mediation. Soon after, referencing the precedent of Western recognition of Kosovo's independence in February, Russia formally recognized Abkhazia and South Ossetia as independent states, but to date only Nicaragua has recognized these two statelets. Russia's recognition of Abkhazia and South Ossetia marked a sharp reversal of post-Soviet Russian foreign policy to respect the territorial integrity of its neighbors.

After the Georgia war, Russia has let up a little, but not much. On November 5, 2008, a few hours after the election of Barack Obama as US

---

3. Vladimir V. Putin, annual address to the Federal Assembly of the Russian Federation, April 25, 2005, www.kremlin.ru. (accessed on July 1, 2007).

4. Vladimir V. Putin, speech and the following discussion at the Munich Conference on Security Policy, February 10, 2007, www.kremlin.ru.

5. "What Precisely Vladimir Putin Said at Bucharest," *Zerkalo nedeli*, April 19, 2008.

president, President Dmitri Medvedev held his first annual address to the Russian parliament. Ignoring the newly elected US president, Medvedev announced that Russia would deploy nuclear missiles in the Kaliningrad exclave, targeting Poland and the Czech Republic since they had accepted American missile defense installations. Later in November, Medvedev toured Cuba and Venezuela as Russian bombers and naval ships toured the region. Yet in a positive gesture, Medvedev promised in January 2009 not to locate the missiles targeting Poland and the Czech Republic in the Kaliningrad region. Still, on February 3, Kyrgyz President Kurmanbek Bakiyev announced that he asked the United States to evacuate its Manas air base from his country. He did so during a visit to Moscow, because Russia had offered him better financing. Moscow did so although it has a clear security interest in the United States and its allies defeating the Taliban in Afghanistan. Then on February 6, to accentuate the mixed message, the Russian foreign minister announced that Russia had agreed to open itself as a transit corridor for nonlethal materials from the United States to reach Afghanistan. In sum, Russia's anti-American policies have become a little less pronounced but not softened much.

Differing Values and Problematic Policies

We hope that Russia and the United States have reached the end of the unfortunate trajectory of the past eight years. To reverse the destructive momentum, it is necessary to establish why things went so wrong.

Presidents Bush and Putin met no fewer than 27 times, far more than the 18 meetings between Presidents Clinton and Yeltsin. Meetings, however, do not necessarily solve problems. Moreover, President Bush repeatedly and publicly praised his Russian colleague and seemed to presume that the two of them shared democratic and legal values, despite Russia's record consistently suggesting the contrary. Indeed, in 2004, then US ambassador to Moscow Alexander Vershbow observed that the main hazard in the US-Russia relationship was the "values gap,"[6] which has persistently grown. As Ronald Asmus wrote, "The gap between Western and Russian values and our readings of recent history is greater today than at any time since communism's collapse."[7]

On the eve of the second Bush administration and in the wake of the Orange Revolution in Ukraine, many concerned Russian and American observers viewed the breakdown of trust between Washington and Moscow as more pernicious than the "values gap" and suggested that the two

---

6. Sestanovich, *Foreign Affairs*, 12.

7. Ronald D. Asmus, "Dealing with Revisionist Russia," *Washington Post*, December 13, 2008, A15.

countries focus on an agenda of common interests to restore trust.[8] Although Moscow was receptive to this approach, Washington was not. The Bush administration was riding the crest of the momentum of the color revolutions and placed democracy promotion and US values, at least rhetorically, near the top of its foreign policy agenda. This momentum would soon reverse, however, lending credence to Moscow's view of the Bush agenda as a cynical fig leaf for the expansion of American hegemony in Eurasia.

In the spring of 2006 the Council on Foreign Relations published a comprehensive report on the US-Russia relationship entitled *Russia's Wrong Direction*.[9] The report's assessment and recommendations concerning developments in Russia and its foreign policy were quite sensible and balanced. But the problem with the broader message of the report, beginning with the title, was the implication that most of the problems in the relationship were Russia's fault. Not surprisingly, the report received substantial criticism from Russian government officials and elites. It also became a lightning rod for debate over policy toward Russia, illustrating how difficult it was for Republicans and Democrats to agree on the contributions of the United States, and specifically the Clinton and Bush administration policies, to the deterioration of the relationship. As Henry Kissinger and George Shultz noted, "fairness requires some acknowledgment that the West has not always been sensitive to how the world looks from Moscow."[10]

US policy on Russia has suffered from many flaws. Most fundamentally, the Bush administration never had an explicit Russia policy, instead pursuing disparate policies such as those for arms control and energy security. Furthermore, the many Bush-Putin meetings were characterized as fly-by summits, mostly lasting no more than an hour or so; they accomplished little, and it is difficult to escape the impression that the resulting photos were more important than the substance of the discussion.

Since the United States did not have a Russia policy, it did not have a functioning interagency process either to ensure accountability or to follow up on promises made at the Bush-Putin summits, giving Putin the impression that Bush was an unreliable partner. The most obvious example is that Bush, like Clinton, promised his Russian colleague at least twice to have Congress repeal the anachronistic Jackson-Vanik Amendment but did not follow through with a serious attempt to do so. In con-

---

8. See, for example, Andrew C. Kuchins, Vyacheslav Nikonov, and Dmitri Trenin, *US-Russian Relations: The Case for an Upgrade* (Moscow and Washington: Carnegie Endowment for International Peace, 2005).

9. Council on Foreign Relations, *Russia's Wrong Direction: What the United States Can and Should Do*, Independent Task Force Report 57 (New York, 2006).

10. Henry A. Kissinger and George P. Shultz, "Building on Common Ground with Russia," *Washington Post*, October 8, 2008, A19.

trast, although there were significant conflicts during the Clinton-Yeltsin period, the Gore-Chernomyrdin Commission had ensured broad bilateral contacts between many government agencies from 1993 to 1999—a mechanism that the Bush-Putin relationship lacked.

The two new leaders never enjoyed any common understanding. The Bush administration assumed that Russia was a dwindling power of little significance, ignoring Russia's booming economy. Needless to say, this attitude did not go over well with the Russians. When Putin initially made substantial concessions to the United States—closing military facilities in Cuba and Vietnam—he received nothing in return. The Russian perception was that the Bush administration viewed these acts as signs of weakness rather than as gestures of goodwill.

Aside from the Putin government's preference for binding nuclear arms control agreements, both the Bush and Putin administrations aspired to reduce the number of international treaties and the influence of international organizations. The United States abrogated the ABM Treaty and Russia suspended the CFE Treaty. The United States bypassed the United Nations, and Russia undermined the Organization for Security and Cooperation in Europe (OSCE) and blocked UN Security Council sanctions against countries such as Iran, Zimbabwe, and Burma/Myanmar.

By the end of 2008, the balance sheet for the two countries did not look good. The US-Russia energy dialogue had all but ceased. Although the United States and Russia concluded a bilateral protocol on Russia's WTO entry in November 2006, Russia's accession stalled. The US-Russia bilateral investment treaty of 1992 remained unratified by the Russian parliament. Apart from the Moscow Treaty of 2002 and the 123 Agreement of 2008 on civilian nuclear cooperation, which has not been ratified, the United States and Russia under Putin and Bush concluded no significant bilateral agreements.

The Kremlin's perception is that the United States is encircling Russia through NATO enlargement and missile defense installations in Poland and the Czech Republic. The United States considers that Russia has abandoned its democratic trajectory and is growing more closed to foreign investment, notably in the important energy sector. The United States is also concerned that, although Russia ranks as one of the most corrupt countries in the world, the Kremlin does little to improve the situation.

Mutual distrust prevails between Washington and Moscow. The relations have not developed but shrunk in recent years. Because of the lack of strong ties and shared commitments, the cost for Moscow to act against the United States is low. But Henry Kissinger and George Shultz recently observed that "isolating Russia is not a sustainable long-range policy. It is neither feasible nor desirable to isolate a country adjoining Europe, Asia and the Middle East and possessing a stockpile of nuclear arms comparable to that of the United States."[11] If relations between the two countries

---

11. Ibid.

were more extensive, as between Russia and Germany, mutual understanding and confidence would be greater. The Obama administration will need to make a substantial and coordinated effort to improve the US-Russia relationship and generate mutual confidence. It is essential to halt and reverse the current steady deterioration of the relationship.

Alternative Scenarios for US-Russia Relations

For a decade until 2008, Russia's GDP in US dollars rose nine times from $200 billion to $1.8 trillion, but that is still only 2.5 percent of global GDP. Even so, the Kremlin presented Russia as a revanchist economic powerhouse. As oil prices plummeted from $147 in July 2008 to $35 at present, these pretenses have fallen in tatters. But Western engagement and integration present an opportunity to shape Russia's possible new course, both internally and externally.

Russia has reached the end of the road in resource-based development and catch-up growth, but it remains only semimodernized and highly vulnerable to external circumstances beyond its control, primarily the oil price. About 85 percent of its exports are based on energy and commodities such as metals and chemicals. With the exception of the arms industry, Russia's manufacturing has largely failed to develop because of an adverse business climate (widespread corruption and onerous state intervention) and a lack of comparative advantages outside of the commodity sector.

The global financial crisis has hit Russia hard. As commodity prices have fallen sharply, the status quo is not a viable option. Russia cannot continue to depend to such an extent on its resource wealth, which is prone to booms and busts. No other large emerging market or developed economy is so dependent on a single volatile factor (the oil price) as is Russia. Sustaining economic growth for the country's population will have a direct influence on popular support for the government. A recent study by Daniel Treisman found that the popularity of Russian presidents "closely followed perceptions of economic performance, which, in turn, reflected objective economic indicators." Thus the presidential approval rating depends on the Russian people's sense of material well-being; "most other factors"—such as the war in Chechnya, in the case of Putin in 1999—"had only marginal, temporary effects."[12]

Russia faces two starkly different choices for its economy. One option is to continue the current course toward increased state control and renationalization, which would result in economic domination by large monopolistic state corporations. In that case, the country would have little

---

12. Daniel Treisman, "The Popularity of Russian Presidents" (paper presented at the Frontiers of Political Economics conference, New Economic School, Moscow, May 30–31, 2008).

need for the WTO, and increasing isolationism would be the natural out-come. Russia's economic growth, however, would probably wither, be-cause such a system breeds stagnation.

The alternative would be to return to the liberal economic reform agenda that Putin abandoned in 2003. Indeed, then presidential candidate Dmitri Medvedev's February 15, 2008, speech in Krasnoyarsk called for the revival of such a program.[13] In his speech in Davos on January 28, 2009, Putin further stated: "The crisis has exposed the problems we have. They are an excessive orientation of exports, and of the economy, toward natural resources and a weak financial market. . . . There is a greater de-mand for the development of basic structures. . . ."[14] Major elements of such a policy would be the control of corruption, deregulation of the do-mestic economy, and reinforcement of private property rights. Such an economic choice would naturally accompany political liberalization and enhanced international integration.

Our view is that the second option is more likely because the growth motive is pervasive in the current Russian establishment, and so US pol-icy should be designed primarily for that option. Yet US policy must also prepare for less felicitous alternatives. We, therefore, consider three sce-narios of US-Russia relations.

The worst scenario would be a New Cold War[15] in which Russia and the United States would work against one another around the globe. Many ob-servers point to Putin's anti-American speech in Munich in February 2007 as proof of that intention on Moscow's part.[16] The August 2008 war in Geor-gia and the gas disruption in January 2009 also seem to point in this direc-tion. Yet an adversarial policy, with full-scale containment and abandon-ment of engagement, is neither useful nor desirable and must be avoided.

The second scenario is realistic engagement: an ambition to develop productive and constructive relations, with an understanding that Russia and the United States have different values as well as some common in-terests. In this scenario, the two countries promote and pursue their shared interests, while acknowledging and managing their contradictory interests. Secretary of State Condoleezza Rice's valedictory address on

---

13. Transcript of the speech of the first deputy chairman of the Government of Russia, Dmitri Medvedev, at the 5th Krasnoyarsk economic forum "Russia 2008–2020. Management of Growth," February 15, 2008 [Stenogramma vystupleniya Pervogo zamestitelia Predse-datelia Pravitelstva Rossiyi Dmitriya Medvedeva na V Krasnoyarskom economicheskom forume "Rossiya 2008–2020. Upravleniye rostom"], available at www.rost.ru (accessed on February 9, 2009).

14. "Putin's Speech at Davos World Economic Forum," *Russia Today*, January 28, 2009, avail-able at www.russiatoday.com (accessed on February 2, 2009).

15. Edward Lucas, *The New Cold War: Putin's Russia and the Threat to the West* (New York: Pal-grave Macmillan, 2008).

16. John R. Bolton, "Russia Unromanticized," *Washington Post*, October 20, 2008, A15.

Russia on September 18, 2008, sums up this policy.[17] In light of current Russian policies, this is the natural choice.

The third scenario is full-fledged engagement based on converging values. This was the aim of President Clinton and the initial assumption of President Bush. The precondition is that Russia truly transforms. Although such a development may not appear likely today, the United States should remain open to such a possibility.

US policy on Russia should aim for constructive engagement based on a realistic understanding of differences in values, interests, and goals. It should promote mutual confidence between the two countries and deepen and broaden the relationship so that it encourages the development of greater understanding and respect.[18]

Key Areas of US-Russia Cooperation

Our main recommendation for the US policy community is that integration, as opposed to isolation, is the best way to "manage Russia's rise," to borrow a phrase from US policy on China. From an American perspective, Russia and China are becoming increasingly similar as authoritarian polities with powerful interests in deeper economic integration, yet US policy on China has been considerably more successful than that on Russia in recent years, not least because it is so much more important for the US economy.

Vice President Joseph Biden set the line of the Obama administration on US-Russia relations in his speech in Munich on February 7, 2009, when he stated: "It is time to press the reset button and to revisit the many areas where we can and should work together." He also stated that "the United States and Russia can disagree and still work together where our interests coincide."[19] The new US policy cannot, however, be unconditional. Russia needs to comply with elementary rules of international conduct. Unfortunately, the last year witnessed several impermissible acts by Russia. Its war in Georgia and its recognition of the independence of Abkhazia and South Ossetia violated multiple commitments to sovereignty and territorial integrity. By cutting gas and oil supplies to numerous countries without warning for two weeks, Russia endangered energy security. By promising to deliver air defense missiles to Iran, Russia is undermining

---

17. US Department of State, "Secretary Rice Addresses U.S.-Russia Relations at the German Marshall Fund," September 18, 2008, available at www.state.gov (accessed on December 15, 2009).

18. Michael Mandelbaum, "Stop Baiting the Bear," *Newsweek*, December 31, 2008.

19. Joseph R. Biden, speech at the 45th Munich Security Conference, February 7, 2009, available at www.securityconference.de (accessed on February 9, 2009).

US attempts to persuade Iran's leadership to abstain from the development of nuclear arms. And the official Russian media's anti-American propaganda casts the United States as a convenient scapegoat that the Kremlin can blame for Russia's economic woes and geopolitical isolation. None of these acts is acceptable from a US point of view, and Russia must show some goodwill if the two countries are to engage in a constructive realpolitik.

There are six key areas of desired cooperation: Iran and missile defense, European and regional security including Afghanistan, arms control, commercial relations, energy policy, and democracy and human rights.

Iran and Missile Defense

The greatest security concern of the United States is Iranian access to intercontinental ballistic missiles with nuclear warheads that can threaten the United States. Both the Clinton and Bush administrations tried to work with Russia to reduce this threat. But Russia has completed a non-military nuclear power station in Bushehr in Iran and agreed to provide the Iranians with S-300 ground-to-air missiles, diminishing the threat to Iran of possible American or Israeli bombings. In the United Nations, Russia has persistently argued against sanctions on Iran and thus eased the international pressure on Iran.

The US assumption has been that Russia should be worried about nuclear proliferation to Iran, but Russia's actions suggest that its worries are limited. As Stephen Sestanovich writes, "Moscow is no more likely to support a drastic increase in U.S. pressure against Iran . . . than it did against Iraq in the lead-up to the 2003 war."[20] Russia can rightly point to Washington's relative equanimity when India and Pakistan acquired nuclear arms and missiles.

To counter the Iranian nuclear threat, the United States has concluded agreements with the Czech Republic and Poland about missile defense installations there. Moscow has reacted sharply, alleging that the real purpose is to intimidate Russia. It has threatened to target the Czech Republic and Poland with nuclear missiles, but it has also offered to cooperate with the United States in a missile defense installation in Azerbaijan, an offer that the United States has declined.

The Obama administration needs to break this logjam, ideally with a two-part solution. One part should initiate direct negotiations with Iran and encourage Moscow to put more pressure on Tehran. But Russia is clearly part of the Iranian issue, and it is important to transform its role from that of principal agent to one party among many.

The other part of the solution should tie the development of missile defense to progress in the containment of Iran's nuclear arms program. The

---

20. Sestanovich, *Foreign Affairs*, 15.

United States could undertake a couple of goodwill gestures to facilitate such progress. First, greater transparency—for example, through a return to the agreement to establish a joint data exchange center and cooperation on shared early warning data—will diminish Russian suspicions. Second, a review and delay of the plans for missile system deployments could permit needed progress in the containment of Iran's nuclear program. Third, an agreement in principle between the United States and Russia to work together to develop broader missile defense capabilities could ultimately provide for a global missile defense system that includes Russia. Still, the United States must not let down its loyal allies Poland and the Czech Republic. Deployment should be delayed but not canceled, pending more challenging testing to ensure that the system actually works. Biden has indicated that the new administration is choosing this road: "We will continue to develop missile defenses to counter a growing Iranian capability—provided the technology is proven to work and is cost-effective."[21]

Since the system deployments planned for Poland and the Czech Republic are designed to address threats from the south, the United States should also engage with the Russians on a joint threat assessment of the region that includes Iran but stretches more broadly throughout the Greater Middle East.

European Security, NATO, and the OSCE

Russia has a nearly symbiotic economic relationship with Europe, which serves as a powerful foundation for their interdependency, but it needs to be a full participant in European norms and rules. Russia should feel it is inside the tent rather than brooding outside in the cold. It must have a stake in peace in Europe. The war in Georgia showed how brittle security remains in Europe and made plain that the issue is much more important than at any time since 1991. Because the United States has broad global security responsibilities, the onus is on Washington to take the lead in recasting European security.

A prime goal of the United States must be to guarantee the sovereignty and territorial integrity of other states in Europe. Russia's recognition of the independence of Abkhazia and South Ossetia violates the generally accepted principle of sovereignty and territorial integrity of states, clearly set forth in the OSCE Convention.

The outstanding bone of contention is Ukraine—Russian pundits argued in 2008 that it represents 90 percent of Russia's foreign policy. It is, therefore, appropriate to carefully examine what Russian leaders say about Ukraine. The most salient comments are from President Putin's speech at the NATO summit in Bucharest in April 2008, when he sug-

---

21. Biden, speech at the 45th Munich Security Conference, February 7, 2009.

gested that Ukraine lacked legitimacy as a state and then threatened to end its existence:

- "As for Ukraine, one third of the population are ethnic Russians. According to official census statistics, there are 17 million ethnic Russians there, out of a population of 45 million. . . . Southern Ukraine is entirely populated with ethnic Russians."

- "Ukraine, in its current form, came to be in Soviet-era days. . . . From Russia the country obtained vast territories in what is now eastern and southern Ukraine."

- "Crimea was simply given to Ukraine by a CPSU Politburo's decision, which was not even supported with appropriate government procedures that are normally applicable to territory transfers."

- "If the NATO issue is added there, along with other problems, this may bring into question Ukraine's existence as a sovereign state."[22]

Putin appears to question the legitimacy of the breakup of the Soviet Union and the resulting borders. As Michael McFaul stresses, "The United States and Europe must act proactively to deter Russian hostile actions against the other post-Soviet democracy at risk, Ukraine."[23]

The United States has already guaranteed the sovereignty and territorial integrity of Ukraine and other post-Soviet countries in multiple agreements. The OSCE Convention applies to all of these states. In addition, the United States offered strong security guarantees to Belarus, Kazakhstan, and Ukraine when they agreed on denuclearization in 1994. The United States can and should persistently remind Moscow of the validity of these agreements to avoid any repeat of the war in Georgia.[24]

The critical issue is the application by Georgia and Ukraine for MAPs to NATO and the possibility of their eventual NATO membership. Their applications were rebuffed by the NATO summit in Bucharest, but its communiqué stated that

> NATO welcomes Ukraine's and Georgia's Euro-Atlantic aspirations for membership in NATO. We agreed today that these countries will become members of NATO. . . . MAP is the next step for Ukraine and Georgia on their direct way to membership. Today we make clear that we support these countries' applications for MAP.[25]

---

22. "What Precisely Vladimir Putin Said at Bucharest," *Zerkalo nedeli*, April 19, 2008.

23. McFaul, "U.S.-Russia Relations in the Aftermath of the Georgia Crisis."

24. Ibid.

25. Bucharest Summit Declaration, issued by the Heads of State and Government participating in the meeting of the North Atlantic Council, Bucharest, April 3, 2008, available at www.nato.int (accessed on July 1, 2008).

On the one hand, Ukraine and Georgia are sovereign states entitled to seek membership in NATO. On the other hand, they are not militarily and politically ready, key European allies oppose their MAP and membership (for now), and Russia objects vehemently. A middle way is needed. In December 2008 NATO foreign ministers seemed to have found a solution: Ukraine and Georgia will have national action plans (essentially the same as MAPs in all but name) that gradually bring them closer to NATO, but no MAP is being offered.

The NATO-Russia relationship also needs to improve. NATO's 60th anniversary in April 2009 offers a good opportunity to review the organization's future purpose, goals, and membership, including possible Russian membership if Moscow is genuinely interested. Russian leaders have never categorically rejected their potential membership, and on occasion Yeltsin and Putin expressed interest. Former Secretary of State James Baker made a powerful argument in 2002 about the importance of (eventually) bringing Russia into NATO.[26]

The enhancement of NATO's capabilities to successfully pursue its mission should be as high a priority for Washington as enlargement. The foremost task of NATO today is to succeed in Afghanistan; if the organization fails there, its future seems dubious. Because Russia also has a strong interest in stabilizing Afghanistan—from transit agreements to intelligence sharing to reconstruction efforts—fostering a closer relationship between NATO and Russia should be a much higher priority. Russian cooperation was essential in the allied defeat of the Taliban in 2001, but the United States did not solidify its partnership with Russia through further collaboration in stabilizing Afghanistan. Such a joint effort in an area of shared interest would be an opportunity to restore trust with Moscow.

In his speech in Berlin on June 5, 2008, President Medvedev proposed a conference on reforming the European security system,[27] and the idea has become a recurring refrain from Moscow, although with few details. Nonetheless, the Obama administration should accept Medvedev's proposal to begin discussions, which present an opportunity to engage the Russians as the Helsinki accords did in the 1970s. Precisely what Medvedev means by "privileged relations with neighbors" can be fleshed out and if necessary rejected if it implies traditional "spheres of interest" that have no place in modern conceptions of cooperative security. The West can also make its own proposals. A first step could be a nonaggression

---

26. James A. Baker III, "Russia in NATO?" *Washington Quarterly* 25, no. 1 (Winter 2002): 95–103. For a comprehensive history of the NATO-Russia relationship and ideas to advance it, see Julianne Smith, *The NATO-Russia Relationship: Defining Moment or Déjà vu?* CSIS Report (Washington: Center for Strategic and International Studies, November 14, 2008).

27. President of Russia, speech at Meeting with German Political, Parliamentary and Civic Leaders, Berlin, June 5, 2008, available at www.kremlin.ru (accessed on December 15, 2008).

treaty that further confirms national sovereignty and the inviolability of national borders.

Another question to explore at such a conference is how to revitalize the OSCE and strengthen its role in promoting cooperative security. The Russians profess to be interested in this topic, although their recent endeavors have aimed at weakening the OSCE. But even if the Russian proposals for the OSCE are a means of reducing the role of NATO in the region, the United States has no reason to worry because its position on most contentious issues in the OSCE is shared by all organization members except Russia. The proposed conference would offer the United States and its European allies an opportunity to demonstrate solidarity and force Russia to clarify its stands. It could also preserve and bolster the OSCE's promotion and defense of human rights among member countries.

A third topic is modification and ratification of the CFE Treaty. The great importance of the treaty is that it allows inspections and offers an early warning system crucial to European security. Russia suspended its compliance with the treaty in December 2007, and its disagreements were understandable. Several newly independent countries in the region that have refused to sign the treaty should sign it. Moscow also protested excessive control over military deployments on its territory, and these restrictions could be eased. These are important aspects of an updated review of cooperative security measures in Europe.

Finally, the solution of the "frozen conflicts" has become more urgent since the war in Georgia. In addition to Abkhazia and South Ossetia, this term refers to the breakaway Transnistria region in Moldova and the formerly Azerbaijani autonomous region of Nagorno-Karabakh, which is occupied by local ethnic Armenians. In both cases, there have been serious efforts to solve these conflicts since the war in Georgia, and the United States needs to actively support these efforts.

Arms Control

Arms control is the area where the United States and Russia have the longest history of cooperation, and it is the easiest place to renew the bilateral relationship. Both parties have an interest in new agreements, and the international arms control regime that contributed to the end of the Cold War is in grave danger.[28] The United States is the primary player on security issues, but in recent years has underused its leverage and influence with the Russians. It has withdrawn from the ABM Treaty, and Russia has suspended the CFE Treaty. The Strategic Arms Reduction Treaty (START I)

---

28. For an account of the essence of the arms control regime, see Michael Mandelbaum, *The Ideas that Conquered the World: Peace, Democracy, and Free Markets in the Twenty-First Century* (New York: Public Affairs, 2004).

is set to expire in December 2009, and without it the SORT (set to lapse in 2012) becomes nonverifiable. The Kremlin is critical of the INF Treaty, and the Nuclear Non-Proliferation Treaty (NPT) is up for review in 2010.

The danger here is not to be sufficiently ambitious. The United States should seize the initiative to pursue extensive negotiations to improve and thus save the arms control regime.

The first step is to return to the traditional nuclear arms control agenda that the Bush administration neglected for eight years and to renew START I, which is necessary for verification measures.

Second, the United States needs to engage with Russia in a new treaty that provides considerably deeper cuts in strategic offensive forces than the 2002 SORT, which allowed the two countries each to maintain 1,700 to 2,200 warheads. Neither side needs (or is interested in maintaining) so many warheads. Steven Pifer advocates that the Obama administration "should propose to the Russians a legally binding treaty under which each side would reduce and limit the number of its strategic nuclear missiles to no more than 1,000."[29] The reduced warheads should be destroyed, and the new SORT should incorporate standard verification procedures.

Third, the United States needs to lead in the recommitment to nuclear nonproliferation. More and more countries are acquiring nuclear arms, and there is a concern that if Iran, in particular, develops nuclear arms, the nonproliferation regime will have failed and no further controls will be feasible. If the United States is serious about achieving a nuclear-free world and thus fulfilling its Article 6 commitments to the NPT, there must be a substantial cut in the US nuclear arsenal. The Obama administration should also work closely with its Russian partners to promote a successful 2010 NPT review conference, in part by trying to ensure that Russia does not perceive any threats to its strategic stability.

As the two leading nuclear powers, the United States and Russia have shared interests in preventing the collapse of nonproliferation efforts. Cooperation on cuts as well as defenses will send the strongest message to Tehran and is the best way to encourage Moscow to move more aggressively on sanctions against Tehran if the latter does not transparently abandon its nuclear weapons program. US collaboration with Moscow in this area could persuade Russia to become a more constructive partner in dealings with Iran.

Because Russia harbors concerns about the INF treaty, it is up to Moscow to propose changes. Its objection is that the bilateral treaty prohibits the United States and Russia from having intermediary nuclear missiles even as other countries have or are developing such missiles. Russia may, therefore, propose that the INF Treaty become a multilateral treaty involving all nuclear powers. If so, the United States should be open to such a suggestion, especially if the alternative is Russia's withdrawal from the treaty.

---

29. Pifer, Brookings Policy Paper 10, 2009, 13.

Commercial Relations

US government engagement with Russia on economic integration presents an opportunity to broaden and deepen their bilateral relationship.[30] Economic cooperation will build goodwill and mutual confidence, which can facilitate discussion of other areas of interest such as cooperation on nonproliferation and dealing with Iran's nuclear program. Yet one of the most underdeveloped areas of the US-Russia relationship is commerce. The two countries' very limited mutual trade and investment—the United States accounts for only 4 percent of Russian trade and foreign direct investment—indicate a very significant potential to expand bilateral economic relations to the benefit of both Americans and Russians.

One reason direct US investment in the Russian economy is so small is that the United States does not have a ratified bilateral investment treaty (BIT) with Russia, unlike 38 other nations that represent most of the major global economies and most members of the European Union. As a consequence, Americans usually invest in Russia through a European subsidiary that enjoys better legal protection. Although Russia did not ratify the 1992 BIT, it has clearly indicated that it welcomes such an agreement—which became part of the bilateral April 2008 Sochi Declaration—but the Bush administration sought to negotiate a new, better BIT only in its final months.

A BIT would also encourage Russian investment in the United States. Foreign investment not only provides jobs for Americans but also, as Yale professor of economics Aleh Tsyvinski writes, "foster[s] economic interdependence." He continues: "By investing in U.S. and European assets, Russia's government and business elites are buying a stake in the global economy. This should bring better mutual understanding and a more rational and accountable foreign policy."[31] The United States must work with Russia to ensure that openness to foreign investment is reciprocal and that legal protections for investors are guaranteed.

A crucial issue in Russia's standing in world commerce is its WTO accession. Russia suspended its application to join the WTO in anticipation of Western sanctions against its war in Georgia, which never materialized. Hopefully, it will reinstate its application soon. It is the largest economy that remains outside the organization. The United States has consistently favored Russia's membership in the WTO as well as in other international economic institutions, as such integration would not only boost commerce but also promote rules-based international norms of economic behavior in Russia and thus influence Russian policy. The United States

---

30. See also Samuel Charap and Andrew C. Kuchins, *Economic Whiplash in Russia: An Opportunity to Bolster U.S.-Russia Commercial Ties?* (Washington: Center for Strategic and International Studies, February 2009).

31. Aleh Tsyvinski, "Turning Russia into a Global Citizen," *Moscow Times*, October 23, 2008.

should continue to support Russia's WTO accession and work with Russia and WTO members to overcome their objections.

Russia is already an active and responsible board member of the International Monetary Fund (IMF) and the World Bank. In 2007 Russia showed positive engagement by proposing its own, highly respected candidate for managing director of the IMF. Economic integration will provide additional opportunities for the Russian leadership to further develop its global engagement.

In addition, Russia has been a full member of the G-8 since 1997 (although the finance ministers group is still only G-7). The Obama administration should follow the lead of the Bush administration and devote more attention and resources to developing the G-20 (created by the Clinton administration in 1998) rather than the G-8, which seems increasingly unrepresentative and obsolete. Russia shares this view.

In his October 2008 speech in Evian, France, President Medvedev expressed a strong interest in reforming the anachronistic system of international financial governance.[32] Although Russian proposals have not been very concrete, such efforts should be welcomed in principle. Russia's interest in engaging in reform of the international financial architecture is a positive development, even if its views may sometimes conflict with those of the United States.

Russian accession to the Organization for Economic Cooperation and Development (OECD) is also important. Like the WTO, the OECD is a highly legalistic organization that requires new members to adopt many rules before they are granted entry. Membership carries with it obligations such as observance of international standards relating to rule of law, transparency, and property rights, all of which must be adopted in coordination with other members, in particular close European allies.

Another roadblock is the Jackson-Vanik Amendment to the Trade Act of 1974. It requires the executive branch to certify to Congress annually that there are no restrictions on the emigration of Jews from Russia; if it were invoked, prohibitive Smoot-Hawley tariffs would apply to all Russian imports to the United States. This Cold War holdover no longer serves any useful purpose and is routinely voided. Presidents Clinton and Bush both promised to graduate Russia from the amendment. The United States should fulfill its promise, which would facilitate Russia's entry into the WTO.

In May 2008 the United States and Russia signed the 123 Agreement on civilian nuclear cooperation, which should be of great commercial significance. It was ready for Senate ratification in the fall, but the administration withdrew it after Russia's war in Georgia. As soon as bilateral condi-

---

32. President of Russia, speech at World Policy Conference, Evian, October 8, 2008, available at www.kremlin.ru (accessed on December 15, 2008).

tions allow, this treaty should be reintroduced and ratified. It will offer the United States and Russia great commercial benefits in peaceful nuclear cooperation, in which both enjoy comparative advantages.

The United States should increase export support and trade facilitation for US companies interested in the Russian market. The Export-Import Bank and Overseas Private Investment Corporation (OPIC) exist for these purposes, but they should receive more support, especially during the current financial crisis. The United States should also reinvigorate and deepen bilateral economic dialogue involving government and business at all levels, building on the US-Russia Economic Dialogue launched in April 2008.

Energy Policy

The two-week disruption of gas supplies from Russia to Europe in January 2009 was a reminder of Russia's malfunctioning energy policy. The question for the United States is not what principles to support but how deeply to engage in European energy policy. The United States has limited regional interests, and even less leverage, but needs to carefully consider its policy stance vis-à-vis Russia, one of the world's two largest energy exporters.

If the United States is to engage on energy issues with Russia, it needs to do so in concert with the European Union to have any impact. The US-Russia Energy Dialogue should be reformulated as a US-EU-Russia dialogue to ensure that the United States and the European Union coordinate their energy policies toward Russia to mitigate the asymmetry between Washington and its European allies in their policy.

The United States has many significant interests in the energy resources of the Eurasian region and should support the evolution of market-based principles for trade in those resources. The Energy Charter was adopted by 54 countries in 1994, including Russia but not the United States. It forms a regional European and Eurasian trade agreement for energy, setting forth such principles. The United States could reconsider acceding to it and engage in discussions with member countries about how to modernize it so that Russia will also ratify it.

Russian oil and gas production from mature West Siberian fields are past their peak, and gas production is in decline. Maintaining, let alone increasing, current production levels will entail massive capital expenditures for complicated and risky projects. Russian companies and the government will have to determine how to develop these fields, but it would make sense for Russia to involve foreign companies and investors, and their technology and project management, to diversify risk exposure as well as to operate more efficiently. Because of the financial crisis, sharply falling energy prices, and contracting production, the Russian government is likely to be forced to reconsider its nationalistic energy policy.

Although American oil companies have been marginalized in Russia, they are still there and quite substantial, and they are even more important in Kazakhstan and Azerbaijan. The United States has an interest in supporting these companies and facilitating the independent energy policy of these two nations.

The United States should also continue its long-standing policy of supporting the development of alternative pipelines to avoid Russia's monopolization of energy transportation. It did so successfully with the Baku-Ceyhan pipeline, which brings oil from the Caspian basin to the Mediterranean. The most immediate project is the planned Nabucco gas pipeline from Turkey through the Balkans to Austria, which the United States sensibly has supported. A natural extension of Nabucco would be a Transcaspian pipeline, for which the Bush administration intermittently lobbied as well.

The United States, together with its European and Asian allies, should make cooperation with Russia for better energy efficiency a priority. In several ways, the United States and Russia are in similar situations: In comparison with Europe, they are highly inefficient consumers of energy and, with large carbon emissions, are likely to opt for a cap-and-trade regime of emissions control in multilateral negotiations. A recent World Bank study[33] concludes that Russia can save up to 45 percent (nearly 6 million barrels per day of oil equivalent) of its total primary energy consumption by adopting measures that could pay for themselves within four years. Russia will thus be a significant player in any multilateral solution to reduce emissions of greenhouse gases in the years ahead. Dramatically improving energy efficiency in Russia is the most cost-effective means to improve European energy security as well as reduce carbon emissions.

Last, the Obama administration needs to assume leadership in the adjudication of resource wealth and transportation rights in the High North. A first step entails Washington ratification of the Law of the Sea Treaty or renegotiation of it in light of the rapidly melting polar ice cap, which makes access to resources in the Arctic as well as transportation through the area a growing point of dispute for the surrounding countries.

Democracy and Human Rights

After the Rose Revolution in Georgia in 2003 and particularly the Orange Revolution in Ukraine in 2004, the relationship between the United States and Russia grew tense over democracy and human rights. The United

---

33. World Bank and International Finance Corporation, *Energy Efficiency in Russia: Untapped Reserves* (Washington, 2008).

States cannot pretend that it does not stand for freedom and democracy, as these are fundamental American values, but it must pursue policies in this area more consistently to be effective.

The Kremlin has long claimed that Russia is subject to double standards on democracy and human rights issues. We believe that its claim is, in fact, valid.[34] The United States rarely decries human rights violations in friendly dictatorships such as Saudi Arabia and Egypt; it says little about repression in Azerbaijan and Kazakhstan; and it complains less about human rights violations in China than those in Russia, despite the fact that Freedom House has assessed China's abuses as more extensive than Russia's. Clearly, the US policy on democracy and human rights needs greater consistency to be relevant. As Sestanovich notes, "The next U.S. administration, then, will have good reasons to make the issue of democracy a less contentious part of U.S.-Russian relations."[35]

Two organizations, the OSCE and the Council of Europe, have consistently promoted orderly elections in the postcommunist world. As a member of the OSCE, the United States should actively support this organization, which has done so much to promote democratic elections.

The United States has provided significant assistance to nongovernmental organizations for the development of civil society and democracy. While this assistance has done much good, many forms of assistance are no longer possible. When the Kremlin actively resists US assistance to nongovernmental organizations, the United States has little choice but to withdraw, as was the case with the Peace Corps.

But the United States can do much more to develop many kinds of people-to-people exchanges. These exchanges are mutually beneficial, nonintrusive, and not very expensive; they greatly help to develop the understanding between peoples; and the United States has abundant resources for and experience in such exchanges. These exchanges also enjoy Russian support. In Davos, Putin said, "We will expand the practice of student exchange and organize internships for our students in leading universities and most advanced companies. We will create conditions for the best scientists, professors and teachers—regardless of their ethnic background and nationality—to desire to work in Russia."[36] The United States should offer a large number of scholarships for Russian citizens at US universities; Russian students tend to return home after completing their studies because they have very good career opportunities there. In addition, any facilitation of the issuing of visas for Russian visitors would enhance the image of the United States among the Russian elite.

---

34. Stephen Sestanovich, "Putin's Double Standards," *Washington Post*, October 17, 2004, B7.

35. Sestanovich, *Foreign Affairs*, 23.

36. "Putin's Speech at Davos World Economic Forum," *Russia Today*.

Creating a New US-Russia Policy

The current situation has several advantages for US-Russia relations. One is that these relations have deteriorated so badly so that there is a strong feeling in both Washington and Moscow that something has to be done to improve them. Another advantage is that both the United States and Russia have new, young presidents who aspire to do better than their predecessors. A third precondition is that the global financial crisis offers all world leaders an opportunity to think big and reach out to international cooperation. In this situation, President Obama needs to enhance the credibility of the United States in the eyes of the world, including the Russians, reach out to US allies, and establish a positive interaction with President Medvedev based on an early formulation of a Russia policy.

Increasing Credibility

The Bush administration's highly selective approach to multilateral engagement, institutions, and treaties has greatly weakened US capacity to lead in global affairs, with a particularly pernicious impact on relations with Moscow and on Russian behavior. Russians have repeatedly pointed to US unilateralist tendencies and violations of international law and human rights as justification for their own selective approach to multilateralism.

During the 1990s, the United States benefited from a total peace dividend of no less than $1.4 trillion at current prices, as the collapse of the Soviet Union permitted a reduction in US defense expenditures from 6 percent of GDP in the 1980s to 3 percent in 1999.[37] Yet regardless of this windfall, American assistance to Russia during its time of hardship was trifling and late in coming. Nor has the United States delivered on its actual promises, such as the revocation of the Jackson-Vanik Amendment. Regardless of Bush's many friendly words, the Russian leadership under Putin effectively made the case to the Russian public that the United States regarded and treated Russia as an enemy. Now the United States must consistently and unambiguously show the Russian people that such a perspective is invalid.

The Obama administration needs to restore the credibility of American values and resurrect mutual confidence and trust around the world. Coupled with strained transatlantic ties and cleavages in Europe, the loss of US credibility enhances Moscow's leverage to play US European allies against themselves as well as against the United States. McFaul rightly argues that the "first element of a new strategy must be to reestablish unity with our European allies."[38]

---

37. Anders Åslund, *Building Capitalism: The Transformation of the Former Soviet Bloc* (New York: Cambridge University Press, 2001).

38. McFaul, "U.S.-Russia Relations in the Aftermath of the Georgia Crisis."

Working with Allies

The Obama administration should rebalance US interaction with Russia away from bilateralism to multilateralism. Despite President Bush's 27 meetings with President Putin (more than with any foreign leader except British Prime Minister Tony Blair), his administration could point to few accomplishments as a result. Of course bilateral summitry has its place, but it has been overemphasized and underdelivered with Moscow. Efforts to achieve consensus in and with the European Union regarding Russia have been made more difficult by US overreliance on its bilateral links with Moscow. While it is important to promote greater US-EU solidarity on Russia, the United States must also avoid the trap of eurocentricity and keep the door open to cooperation with East Asian allies.

Moscow may reject the comprehensive effort we suggest in order to more effectively accommodate its interests and concerns. If so—and this should be clear by the end of 2009—then the Obama administration must be prepared to quickly adjust its policies. However, we do not advocate a hedging strategy from the outset, as that would undermine the administration's ability to convince the deeply skeptical leadership in Moscow of US sincerity.

Timeline for US Actions

The Obama administration must seize the initiative to define both its policy toward Russia and the agenda for the many multilateral meetings already planned, especially as unanticipated events will inevitably affect any agenda. As Pifer writes: "The Obama administration needs to have an explicit Russia policy—one that is carefully considered, focused and sustained—if it wishes to get Russia right."[39] President Obama has selected his key policymakers and his intention is to lead Russian policy from the National Security Council (NSC). An interagency group for Russia has been created under the leadership of the NSC's senior director for Russia.

We propose the following steps:

- It is imperative that the Obama administration establish an explicit Russia policy rather than subordinating it to other issues in order to enable the administration to make necessary tradeoffs and follow up on promises. Determination of the policy should be the task of the interagency group for Russia and should take the form of an NSC directive.

- Since START I expires in December 2009, a prime task of the Obama administration is to launch negotiations on replacement of the treaty,

---

39. Pifer, Brookings Policy Paper 10, 2009, 21.

further cuts in ballistic nuclear missiles, and reconciliation of the different approaches in the START and SORT treaties.

- At the G-20 meeting in London on April 2, 2009 President Obama will have his first occasion to meet with President Medvedev. This will only be a brief getting-to-know-one-another meeting.

- At the subsequent NATO summit in early April, President Obama will have the occasion to consult with European leaders on the future role of NATO. He should also discuss policy toward Russia, with the security of Ukraine and Georgia as major goals.

- Sometime in May–June 2009, the new Russia policy should be ready and an NSC directive on Russia adopted. At this time, President Obama himself should make a public statement on his policy on Russia. If the circumstances are appropriate, the president should have something positive to offer. Ideally, President Obama would declare his determination to finally persuade the US Congress to graduate Russia from the Jackson-Vanik Amendment and really do so. Another offer could be to have the mutually beneficial 123 Agreement on civilian nuclear cooperation reintroduced in the US Senate.

- The first full-scale summit between Presidents Obama and Medvedev could take place in connection with the G-8 meeting in Italy in July 2009. The two presidents should recommit to fulfilling the April 2008 Sochi Declaration and to reestablishing a broader organized cooperation mechanism between the two countries, like that of the Gore-Chernomyrdin Commission, to promote action and accountability. However, this must not be done mechanically. It is important to appeal to the parts of the Russian administration that are positively inclined to further cooperation with the United States and the West.

Conclusion

We believe President Obama has an important opportunity to dramatically turn around US-Russia relations. Despite lingering concerns about the resurgence of a revanchist Russia, Moscow harbors powerful motivations to improve its ties with the United States and the West to both enhance its security and facilitate its economic development. Russian leaders wish to be seen in public on an equal footing with global leaders, especially the US president. Furthermore, and more importantly, they understand that Russia cannot afford to fall back into another long-term confrontation with the West: Integration with the West remains Russia's best chance to develop and reach its ambitious target of becoming the fifth largest economy in the world by 2020.

For the United States, the motivation for closer cooperation with Russia is grounded in the reality that the world's most pressing energy and security challenges cannot be addressed effectively without Moscow's cooperation and trust. This is most obvious in the realm of nuclear nonproliferation and European security. A Russia that is more interdependent with the West for both its economy and its security is a Russia that will have the best chance to develop in a more democratic direction.

The US approach to Russia should, therefore, foster an environment of mutual trust in which Russians are likely to make choices that will both promote global security and enhance their own prosperity. We firmly believe that a Russia with a mature market economy and robust democratic institutions will be the most constructive and effective partner for the United States.

Appendix

Appendix Key Facts on Russia, 2000–2008(p)

Indicator	2000	2001	2002	2003	2004	2005	2006	2007	2008(p)
Output and expenditure (percent change in real terms)									
GDP	10.0	5.1	4.7	7.3	7.1	6.4	7.4	8.1	5.6
Private consumption	7.3	9.5	8.5	7.5	12.1	11.8	11.2	12.8	n.a.
Public consumption	1.9	–0.8	2.6	2.2	2.1	1.3	2.5	5.0	n.a.
Gross fixed capital formation	21.5	10.2	2.8	12.8	12.6	10.6	17.7	20.8	9.1
Exports of goods and services	9.4	4.2	10.3	12.5	11.8	6.5	7.3	6.4	n.a.
Imports of goods and services	31.5	18.7	14.6	17.7	23.3	16.6	21.9	27.3	n.a.
Industrial gross output	11.9	4.9	3.7	7.0	7.3	4.0	6.3	6.3	2.1
Agricultural gross output	7.7	7.5	1.5	5.5	3.0	1.1	3.6	3.1	10.8
Unemployment (percent of labor force, end-year)	10.2	8.9	8.5	7.8	7.9	7.1	6.7	4.8	7.7
Prices and wages (percent change)									
Consumer prices (end-year)	20.1	18.6	15.0	12.0	11.7	10.9	9.0	9.0	13.3
Gross average monthly earnings in economy (annual average)	39.2	47.3	36.7	24.4	24.0	25.3	25.4	25.0	25.2
Government sector (percent of GDP)									
General government balance	3.2	2.7	0.6	1.4	4.9	8.1	8.4	5.1	4.1
General government expenditure	33.7	34.6	37.1	35.7	33.6	31.5	31.2	33.0	n.a.
General government debt	62.5	48.2	41.4	32.4	25.9	16.5	10.6	9.5	n.a.

(continued on next page)

Appendix   Key Facts on Russia, 2000–2008(p) *(continued)*

Indicator	2000	2001	2002	2003	2004	2005	2006	2007	2008(p)
Monetary sector (percent change)									
Broad money (M2, end-year)	63.8	39.7	32.4	50.5	35.8	38.5	48.8	47.5	n.a.
Interest and exchange rates (percent per annum, end-year)									
Central bank refinance rate (uncompounded)	25.0	25.0	21.0	16.0	13.0	12.8	11.7	10.3	13.0
Deposit rate	4.2	5.2	4.3	4.4	3.8	3.6	4.1	5.1	7.0
Lending rate	18.2	16.5	15.0	13.0	11.4	10.7	10.5	10.0	15.5
Exchange rate (rubles per US dollar, end-year)	28.2	30.1	31.8	29.5	27.9	28.8	26.3	24.5	29.4
External sector (billions of US dollars)									
Current account balance	46.8	33.9	29.1	35.4	59.5	84.4	94.3	78.3	98.9
Merchandise trade balance	60.2	48.1	46.3	60.5	85.8	118.5	139.2	132.0	179.8
Merchandise exports	105.0	101.9	107.3	135.9	183.2	243.8	303.9	355.5	471.8
Merchandise imports	44.9	53.8	61.0	75.4	97.4	125.3	164.7	223.4	292.0
Inward foreign direct investment	2.7	4.0	4.0	6.7	9.4	13.2	28.7	52.3	67.0
International reserves, excluding gold (end-year)	24.3	32.5	44.1	73.2	120.8	175.9	295.6	465.9	412.5
External debt stock	160.0	151.1	169.9	199.4	225.0	257.2	310.6	464.0	498.0
Debt service (percent of exports of goods and services)	10.3	15.2	16.8	20.1	22.2	26.0	25.1	n.a.	n.a.

Memorandum items:

Population (millions, end-year)	145.2	144.4	145.0	144.2	143.5	142.8	142.2	142.2	142.0
GDP (trillions of rubles)	7.3	8.9	10.8	13.2	16.8	21.7	26.9	33.0	41.6
GDP per capita (US dollars)	1,789.0	2,123.0	2,380.0	2,983.0	4,059.0	5,361.0	6,978.0	9,062.0	12,579.0
Share of industry in GDP (percent)	n.a.	n.a.	24.9	24.1	27.5	28.8	27.9	28.0	n.a.
Share of agriculture in GDP (percent)	6.4	6.8	6.0	6.0	5.4	4.8	4.3	4.1	n.a.
Current account/GDP (percent)	18.0	11.1	8.4	8.2	10.2	11.0	9.5	6.1	5.9
External debt—reserves (billions of US dollars)	135.8	118.6	125.8	126.2	104.2	81.3	15.0	-1.9	n.a.
External debt/GDP (percent)	61.6	49.3	49.2	46.4	38.6	33.6	31.3	36.0	29.8
External debt/exports of goods and services (percent)	139.6	133.4	140.5	131.2	110.6	95.7	92.8	118.5	n.a.

n.a. = not available
(p) = preliminary

Sources: European Bank for Reconstruction and Development (EBRD) online statistics (accessed on December 19, 2008); Goskomstat, www.gks.ru (accessed on February 11, 2009); Central Bank of the Russian Federation, www.cbr.ru (accessed on March 16, 2009); JP Morgan, "The Convergence of CEEMEA Countries Amid a Synchronized Global Recession," February 24, 2009.

Bibliography

Amalrik, Andrei. 1980. *Will the Soviet Union Survive until 1984?* London: Harper Collins.

Anderson, James H., and Cheryl W. Gray. 2006. *Anticorruption in Transition 3: Who Is Succeeding . . . and Why?* Washington: World Bank.

Aron, Leon. 2000. *Yeltsin: A Revolutionary Life.* New York: St. Martin's Press.

Åslund, Anders. 1989. *Gorbachev's Struggle for Economic Reform.* Ithaca, NY: Cornell University Press.

Åslund, Anders. 2001. *Building Capitalism: The Transformation of the Former Soviet Bloc.* New York: Cambridge University Press.

Åslund, Anders. 2007. *Russia's Capitalist Revolution: Why Market Reform Succeeded and Democracy Failed.* Washington: Peterson Institute for International Economics.

Baker, Peter, and Susan Glasser. 2005. *Kremlin Rising: Vladimir Putin's Russia and the End of Revolution.* New York: Scribner.

Berdyaev, Nikolai. 1992. *The Russian Idea.* Hudson, NY: Lindisfarne Press.

Bialer, Seweryn. 1986. *The Soviet Paradox: External Expansion, Internal Decline.* London: I.B. Tauris.

Charap, Samuel, and Andrew Kuchins. 2009. *Economic Whiplash in Russia: An Opportunity to Bolster U.S.-Russia Commercial Ties?* Washington: Center for Strategic and International Studies.

Colton, Timothy. 2008. *Yeltsin: A Life.* New York: Basic Books.

Fortescue, Stephen. 2006. *Russia's Oil Barons and Metal Magnates: Oligarchs and the State in Transition.* London: Palgrave Macmillan.

Freeland, Chrystia. 2000. *Sale of the Century: Russia's Wild Ride from Communism to Capitalism.* New York: Crown Business.

Gaddy, Clifford G. 1996. *The Price of the Past: Russia's Struggle with the Legacy of a Militarized Economy.* Washington: Brookings Institution Press.

Gaidar, Yegor T. 2005. *Dolgoe vremya [The Long Term].* Moscow: Delo.

Gaidar, Yegor T. 2007. *The Collapse of the Empire: Lessons for Modern Russia.* Washington: Brookings Institution.

Hill, Fiona, and Clifford G. Gaddy. 2003. *The Siberian Curse: How Communist Planners Left Russia Out in the Cold.* Washington: Brookings Institution Press.

Hoffman, David E. 2002. *The Oligarchs: Wealth and Power in the New Russia.* New York: Public Affairs.

Holloway, David. 1994. *Stalin and the Bomb: The Soviet Union and Atomic Energy, 1939–1956.* New Haven: Yale University Press.

Kalb, Judith E. 2008. *Russia's Rome: Imperial Visions, Messianic Dreams, 1890–1940.* Madison: University of Wisconsin Press.

George F. Kennan, *Memoirs 1925–1950* (New York: Pantheon Books, 1967).

Kuchins, Andrew C., ed. 2002. *Russia after the Fall.* Washington: Carnegie Endowment for International Peace.

Kuchins, Andrew C. 2007. *Alternative Futures of Russia.* Washington: Center for Strategic and International Studies.

Kuchins, Andrew C., Vyacheslav Nikonov, and Dmitri Trenin. 2005. *US-Russian Relations: The Case for an Upgrade.* Moscow and Washington: Carnegie Endowment for International Peace.

Lieven, Dominic. 2000. *Empire: The Russian Empire and Its Rivals.* New Haven: Yale University Press.

Lukin, Alexander. 2003. *The Bear Watches the Dragon.* Armonk, NY: M.E. Sharpe.

Lucas, Edward. 2008. *The New Cold War: Putin's Russia and the Threat to the West.* New York: Palgrave Macmillan.

Malia, Martin. 1999. *Russia under Western Eyes.* Cambridge, MA: Harvard University Press.

Mandelbaum, Michael. 2004. *The Ideas that Conquered the World: Peace, Democracy, and Free Markets in the Twenty-First Century.* New York: Public Affairs.

McFaul, Michael. 2001. *Russia's Unfinished Revolution: Political Change from Gorbachev to Putin.* Ithaca, NY: Cornell University Press.

Milov, Vladimir. 2008. *Russia and the West: the Energy Factor.* Washington: Center for Strategic and International Studies.

Neumann, Iver B. 1996. *Russia and the Idea of Europe.* New York: Routledge.

Olcott, Martha Brill, Anders Åslund, and Sherman Garnett. 1999. *Getting It Wrong: Regional Cooperation and the Commonwealth of Independent States.* Washington: Carnegie Endowment for International Peace.

Pipes, Richard. 1974. *Russia under the Old Regime.* London: Weidenfeld & Nicholson.

Putin, Vladimir V. 2000. *First Person*. New York: Public Affairs.

Remington, Thomas F. 2006. *Politics in Russia*. New York: Pearson Longman.

Riasanovsky, Nicholas V. 1969. *A History of Russia*, 2d ed. New York: Oxford University Press.

Ulam, Adam B. 1973. *Stalin: The Man and His Era*. Boston: Beacon Press.

Vernadsky, George. 1944. *A History of Russia*, 3d ed. Philadelphia: The Blakiston Company.

Volkov, Vadim. 2002. *Violent Entrepreneurs: The Use of Force in the Making of Russian Capitalism*. Ithaca, NY: Cornell University Press.

Yelizarov, Valery. *Demographic Policy in Russia: From Reflection to Action*. Moscow: United Nations in Russia.

Yeltsin, Boris. 1994. *The Struggle for Russia*. New York: Crown.

Yeltsin, Boris. 2000. *Midnight Diaries*. New York: Public Affairs.

Yergin, Daniel, and Thane Gustafson. 1993. *Russia 2010 and What It Means for the World*. New York: Random House.

Zubok, Vladislav, and Constantine Pleshakov. 1996. *Inside the Kremlin's Cold War: From Stalin to Khrushchev*. Cambridge, MA: Harvard University Press.

Timeline of Major Events

Date	Event
1985	
March 11	Mikhail Gorbachev is elected general secretary of the Central Committee of the Communist Party of the Soviet Union (CPSU)
1986	
April 26	Meltdown at the Chernobyl nuclear power plant
October 11–12	Summit between Gorbachev and President Ronald Reagan in Reykjavik, Iceland
November	Law on Individual Labor Activity adopted
1987	
January 27–28	Central Committee plenum on democratization
June 25–26	Central Committee plenum on economic reform
December 8	Intermediate-Range Nuclear Forces (INF) Treaty between the United States and the Soviet Union is signed
1988	
January 1	The Law on State Enterprises comes into force

(continued on next page)

Date	Event
May 15	The Soviet Union starts withdrawing troops from Afghanistan
May	The Law on Cooperatives is enacted
June 28–July 1	The 19th Party Conference reforms party and introduces elections
December 7	Gorbachev's speech at the United Nations declares freedom for Eastern Europe
1989	
March 26	First elections to the Congress of People's Deputies of the USSR
May–June	First session of the USSR Congress of People's Deputies brings freedom of speech
November 9	The fall of the Berlin Wall
1990	
March 4	First elections to the Russian Congress of People's Deputies
March 15	Gorbachev is elected president of the USSR by the USSR Congress of People's Deputies
May 29	Yeltsin is elected chairman of the new Russian Congress of People's Deputies
June 12	The Russian Congress of People's Deputies declares Russia a sovereign state
August	Shatalin 500-day program is written
October	Gorbachev dismisses the 500-day program
November 19	Multilateral Treaty on Conventional Armed Forces in Europe (CFE) is signed in Paris
1991	
March 17	Referendum on the future of the USSR
June 12	Boris Yeltsin becomes Russia's first popularly elected president
July 31	Treaty on the Reduction and Limitation of Strategic Offensive Arms (START I) is signed

Date	Event
August 19–21	Abortive coup against Gorbachev
August 24	Russia recognizes the independence of Estonia, Latvia, and Lithuania
October 28	Yeltsin's speech to the Congress of People's Deputies
November 6–8	Formation of Yegor Gaidar's reform government
December 1	Ukrainian referendum on independence
December 8	Belovezhsky agreement between Belarus, Russia, and Ukraine on the dissolution of the USSR and the foundation of the Commonwealth of Independent States (CIS)
December 21	The CIS broadens to 11 countries at meeting in Alma-Ata
December 25	Gorbachev resigns as president of the USSR; the USSR ceases to exist
1992	
January 2	Comprehensive liberalization of prices and imports
May–June	Yeltsin appoints three industrialists as deputy prime ministers, including Viktor Chernomyrdin, signaling end of radical reform
June 11	Russian parliament adopts privatization program
July 17	Viktor Gerashchenko is appointed chairman of the Central Bank of Russia, expanding the money supply
August 19	Yeltsin announces voucher privatization
December 14	Chernomyrdin is nominated prime minister
1993	
April 25	Yeltsin wins referendum
June 30	International Monetary Fund (IMF) agreement on Systemic Transformation Facility

(continued on next page)

Date	Event
July 24	Cancellation of Soviet ruble banknotes: end of ruble zone
September 21	Yeltsin dissolves parliament and orders new elections
October 3–4	Armed uprising in Moscow, storming of the White House
December 12	Elections to the State Duma and the Federation Council; national referendum backs Yeltsin's draft constitution
1994	
January 5	Agreement on monetary union with Belarus is signed
January 14	Presidents Yeltsin, Bill Clinton, and Leonid Kravchuk sign Trilateral Accord on Ukraine's denuclearization
March 22	IMF agreement on Systemic Transformation Facility
April 15	Formation of free trade area of all 12 CIS countries
October 11	"Black Tuesday": exchange rate of the ruble collapses; Yeltsin sacks the economic policy team
December 11	First Chechen War starts
1995	
January 20	Customs union between Russia, Belarus, and Kazakhstan is established
April 11	IMF approves stand-by credit for Russia
November–December	Loans-for-shares privatizations
December 17	Elections to the State Duma
1996	
Spring	Oligarchs and reformers unite to support Yeltsin in presidential campaign

Date	Event
March 26	IMF approves three-year credit for Russia under the Extended Fund Facility
June 16	First round of presidential elections: Yeltsin wins
July 3	Second round of presidential elections: Yeltsin wins
August 31	Khasavyurt armistice between Russia and Chechnya
Fall	Yeltsin is absent for several months for heart surgery
1997	
May 27	NATO-Russia Founding Act concluded
June 22	Russia becomes a full member of the G-8
July 8	Poland, the Czech Republic, and Hungary join the North Atlantic Treaty Organization (NATO)
July 27	Privatization of one-quarter of Svyazinvest; "bankers' war" erupts
1998	
March 23	Yeltsin sacks Prime Minister Chernomyrdin
April 24	Sergei Kirienko is confirmed as prime minister
July 13	IMF and World Bank emergency package is agreed
July 16	Duma refutes IMF conditions
August 17	Russian financial crisis; default on domestic debt and ruble devaluation
September 11	Duma confirms Yevgeny Primakov as Russia's new prime minister
1999	
January	First part of the Russian tax code comes into force
March 20	Kosovo crisis erupts

(continued on next page)

Date	Event
August 7	Chechen incursion into Dagestan starts
August 9	Vladimir Putin is nominated as prime minister
September 4–16	Four Russian apartment buildings bombed
September 24	Second Chechen War starts
December 19	Elections to the State Duma
December 31	Yeltsin resigns in surprise TV announcement and Prime Minister Putin becomes acting president
2000	
March 26	Presidential elections: Putin wins
May 7	Putin's presidential inauguration; he presents the concept of "managed democracy"
May 13	Putin's decree changes Russia's federal order
May 17	Mikhail Kasyanov is confirmed as prime minister
June 13	Media magnate Vladimir Gusinsky is arrested
July	The Gref program is adopted as the government's economic reform program
July 28	Putin meets with 21 oligarchs in the Kremlin
August 12	Russian nuclear submarine Kursk sinks in Barents Sea
2001	
May 30	Putin sacks Rem Vyakhirev as CEO of Gazprom and appoints Dmitri Medvedev as chairman, Aleksei Miller as CEO
July	Duma passes laws on deregulation of small and medium-sized enterprises
September 11	Terrorist attacks in the United States; Putin first to reach President George W. Bush by phone
December	A package of new laws on judicial reform is adopted

Date	Event
December 13	The United States abrogates the Anti-Ballistic Missile Treaty of 1972
2002	
February	A new labor code is adopted
May 29	Presidents Bush and Putin sign the Moscow Treaty on Strategic Offensive Reductions
July 24	Duma legalizes the sale of agricultural land
December 5	Slavneft is privatized (last big privatization)
2003	
February 23	Russia, Ukraine, Kazakhstan, and Belarus agree to form Common Economic Space
June	St. Petersburg tercentenary celebrations
October 25	Yukos owner Mikhail Khodorkovsky is arrested
November 2	Parliamentary elections in Georgia: Rose Revolution starts
December 7	Elections to the State Duma
2004	
January	Customs code comes into force
February 24	Putin sacks Prime Minister Kasyanov
March 5	Mikhail Fradkov is nominated as prime minister
March 14	Presidential elections: Putin wins
March 29	Bulgaria, Estonia, Latvia, Lithuania, Romania, Slovakia, and Slovenia join NATO
May 1	Poland, Hungary, the Czech Republic, Slovakia, Slovenia, and the three Baltic states become members of the European Union
May 21	Russia concludes World Trade Organization (WTO) bilateral negotiations with the European Union
September 1–3	Beslan hostage crisis

(continued on next page)

Date	Event
September 13	Putin proposes to eliminate direct elections of regional governors
November–December	Ukrainian presidential elections: Orange Revolution
December 19	Yuganskneftegaz is sold in a restricted fire sale
2005	
January	Unsuccessful attempt to reform Russia's social benefit system
March 24	Kyrgyzstan's president Askar Akaev is overthrown
May 13	Uzbekistan's Andijan uprising is stopped by massacre
September 29	Gazprom buys Roman Abramovich's oil company Sibneft
2006	
January 1–2	Gazprom cuts gas deliveries to Ukraine
January	Gazprom's domestic stocks become freely tradable
January 10	Putin signs restrictive bill on nongovernmental organizations into law
March	Russia embargoes import of wine from Georgia and Moldova
July 15–17	G-8 summit is held in St. Petersburg
July 19	Rosneft carries out international initial public offering
November 19	Russia concludes WTO bilateral negotiations with the United States
2007	
January 1	Bulgaria and Romania join the European Union
January 8	Russia cuts oil supply to Belarus
February 10	Putin's Munich speech

Date	Event
April 27	Estonia removes Soviet war memorial; cyber war against Estonia
May 11	Vneshtorgbank's (VTB) initial public offering
June	Last pieces of Yukos are auctioned off
December 2	Duma elections; United Russia wins a large majority
December 24	Russia suspends its application of the CFE Treaty
2008	
March 2	Presidential elections: Dmitri Medvedev wins
April 3–4	NATO summit in Bucharest does not offer membership action plan to Georgia and Ukraine (though both countries are guaranteed eventual membership)
April	Presidents Putin and Bush adopt their Sochi Declaration
May 6	US-Russia Agreement for Peaceful Nuclear Cooperation (123 Agreement) signed
May 7	Inauguration of Medvedev as president
	Law on Foreign Investment in Strategic Industries adopted
May 8	Putin becomes prime minister
May 16	Ukraine becomes 152nd member of the WTO
May 19	Russian stock market reaches an all-time high
Mid-July	Oil and other commodity prices reach an all-time high
August 8–12	Russia-Georgia War in South Ossetia
August 26	Russia recognizes the independence of Abkhazia and South Ossetia
August	Russia imposes select trade sanctions on the United States and Turkey; suspends its WTO accession; and threatens to revoke its bilateral free trade agreement with Ukraine

(continued on next page)

Date	Event
September 8	President Bush withdraws 123 Agreement from congressional consideration
October	Russian stock market plummets to one-fifth of the May peak
November 5	President Medvedev announces intention to amend 1993 constitution
November 15	G-20 meeting in Washington
December	Constitutional amendments adopted: presidential term prolonged to six years and Duma term extended to five years
2009	
January	Russian gas supplies to Ukraine and Europe disrupted for two weeks
February 7	US Vice President Joseph Biden sets the line of the Barack Obama administration on US-Russia relations in a speech in Munich
April 2	G-20 meeting in London; first meeting between Presidents Obama and Medvedev
December 5	START I set to expire

Abbreviations

ABM	Anti-Ballistic Missile Treaty
ASEAN	Association of Southeast Asian Nations
BIT	bilateral investment treaty
BMD	ballistic missile defense
CFE	Treaty on Conventional Armed Forces in Europe
CIS	Commonwealth of Independent States
CNPC	China National Petroleum Corporation
CSTO	Collective Security Treaty Organization
CTR	cooperative threat reduction
EBRD	European Bank for Reconstruction and Development
ESS	European Social Survey
EurAsEC	EurAsian Economic Community
FCTC	Framework Convention on Tobacco Control
FDI	foreign direct investment
FSB	Federal Security Service
FTA	free trade agreement
GATT	General Agreement on Tariffs and Trade
GDP	gross domestic product
Gosplan	State Planning Committee
HIV/AIDS	human immunodeficiency virus/acquired immunodeficiency syndrome
IMF	International Monetary Fund
INF	Intermediate-Range Nuclear Forces Treaty
ITC	International Trade Commission

KGB	Committee for State Security
MAP	membership action plan
NATO	North Atlantic Treaty Organization
NPT	Nuclear Non-Proliferation Treaty
NRC	NATO-Russia Council
OECD	Organization for Economic Cooperation and Development
OSCE	Organization for Security and Cooperation in Europe
PfP	Partnership for Peace
PNTR	permanent normal trade relations
SALT	Strategic Arms Limitation Talks Treaty
SCO	Shanghai Cooperation Organization
SORT	Strategic Offensive Reductions Treaty
START	Treaty on the Reduction and Limitation of Strategic Offensive Arms
UNCTAD	United Nations Conference on Trade and Development
UNESCO	United Nations Educational, Scientific and Cultural Organization
UNICEF	United Nations Children's Fund
USSR	Union of Soviet Socialist Republics
VAT	value-added tax
WTO	World Trade Organization

About the Authors

Anders Åslund is a leading specialist on Russia and postcommunist economic transformation with more than 30 years of experience in the field. In the mid-1980s, he worked as a Swedish diplomat in Moscow, which led him to boldly predict the fall of the Soviet communist system in his book *Gorbachev's Struggle for Economic Reform* (1989). He was one of the chief economic advisers to President Boris Yeltsin's reform government (1991–94) and concluded in *How Russia Became a Market Economy* (1995) that Russia had made its market choice. In *Russia's Capitalist Revolution* (2007) he explained why Russia's market reform succeeded and democracy failed.

He has written a total of nine books, also including *How Capitalism Was Built: The Transformation of Central and Eastern Europe, Russia, and Central Asia* (2007) and *How Ukraine Became a Market Economy and Democracy* (2009). He is the editor or coeditor of 13 books.

Åslund joined the Peterson Institute for International Economics as senior fellow in 2006. He also teaches at Georgetown University. He was the director of the Russian and Eurasian Program at the Carnegie Endowment for International Peace (2003–05) and codirector of the Carnegie Moscow Center's project on Post-Soviet Economies. He was founding director of the Stockholm Institute of Transition Economics and professor at the Stockholm School of Economics (1989–94). He earned his doctorate from the University of Oxford.

Andrew C. Kuchins is a senior fellow and director of the Russia and Eurasia Program at the Center for Strategic and International Studies (CSIS). He is an internationally renowned expert on Russian foreign and domestic policies who publishes widely and is frequently called on by business, government, media, and academic leaders for comment and consulting on Russian and Eurasian affairs.

Recently published books, articles, and reports include *Economic Whiplash in Russia: An Opportunity to Bolster U.S.-Russia Commercial Ties?* (2009); "Putin's Plan," *Washington Quarterly* (Spring 2008); *Alternative Futures for Russia to 2017* (2007); *Russia: The Next Ten Years* (2004); and *Russia after the Fall* (2002).

From 2000 to 2006, he was a senior associate at the Carnegie Endowment for International Peace, where he was also director of its Russian and Eurasian Program in Washington (2000–2003 and again in 2006) and director of the Carnegie Moscow Center in Russia (2003–05). He has also held senior management and research positions at the John D. and Catherine T. MacArthur Foundation, Stanford University, and the University of California at Berkeley.

Kuchins currently teaches at Johns Hopkins School of Advanced International Studies (SAIS) and has also taught at Georgetown and Stanford Universities. He holds a BA from Amherst College and an MA and PhD from Johns Hopkins SAIS.

About the Organizations

Center for Strategic and International Studies

At a time of new global opportunities and challenges, the Center for Strategic and International Studies (CSIS) provides strategic insights and policy solutions to decision makers in government, international institutions, the private sector, and civil society. A bipartisan, nonprofit organization headquartered in Washington, DC, CSIS conducts research and analysis and develops policy initiatives that look into the future and anticipate change.

Founded in 1962 by David M. Abshire and Admiral Arleigh Burke, at the height of the Cold War, CSIS was dedicated to finding ways for America to sustain its prominence and prosperity as a force for good in the world.

Since 1962, CSIS has grown to become one of the world's preeminent international policy institutions, with more than 220 full-time staff and a large network of affiliated scholars focused on defense and security, regional stability, and transnational challenges ranging from energy and climate to global development and economic integration.

Former US senator Sam Nunn became chairman of the CSIS Board of Trustees in 1999, and John J. Hamre has led CSIS as its president and chief executive officer since April 2000.

Peter G. Peterson Institute for International Economics

The Peter G. Peterson Institute for International Economics is a private, nonprofit, nonpartisan research institution devoted to the study of international economic policy. Since 1981 the Institute has provided timely and objective analysis of, and concrete solutions to, a wide range of international economic problems. It is one of the very few economics think tanks that are widely regarded as "nonpartisan" by the press and "neutral" by the US Congress, it is cited by the quality media more than any other such institution, and it was recently selected as Top Think Tank in the World in the first comprehensive survey of over 5,000 such institutions.

The Institute, which has been directed by C. Fred Bergsten throughout its existence, attempts to anticipate emerging issues and to be ready with practical ideas, presented in user-friendly formats, to inform and shape public debate. Its audience includes government officials and legislators, business and labor leaders, management and staff at international organizations, university-based scholars and their students, other research institutions and nongovernmental organizations, the media, and the public at large. It addresses these groups both in the United States and around the world.

The Institute's staff of about 50 includes more than two dozen experts, who are conducting about 30 studies at any given time and are widely viewed as one of the top group of economists at any research center. Its agenda emphasizes global macroeconomic topics, international money and finance, trade and related social issues, energy and the environment, investment, and domestic adjustment measures. Current priority is attached to the worldwide financial and economic crisis, globalization (including its financial aspects) and the backlash against it, global trade imbalances and currency relationships, the creation of an international regime to address global warming and especially its international trade dimension, the competitiveness of the United States and other major countries, reform of the international economic and financial architecture and particularly sovereign wealth funds, and trade negotiations at the multilateral, regional, and bilateral levels. Institute staff and research cover all key regions—especially Asia, Europe, Latin America, and the Middle East, as well as the United States itself and with special reference to China, India, and Russia.

Institute studies have helped provide the intellectual foundation for many of the major international financial initiatives of the past two decades: reform of the International Monetary Fund (IMF), adoption of international banking standards, exchange rate systems in the G-7 and emerging-market economies, policies toward the dollar, the euro, and other important currencies, and responses to debt and currency crises. The Institute has made important contributions to key trade policy decisions including the Doha Round, the restoration and then the extension of both trade promotion authority and trade adjustment assistance in the United States, the Uruguay Round and the development of the World Trade Organization, the North American Free Trade Agreement (NAFTA) and other US trade pacts (notably including Korea), the Asia Pacific Economic Cooperation (APEC) forum and East Asian regionalism, initiation of the Strategic Economic Dialogue between the United States and China and the related "G-2" concept, a series of United States–Japan negotiations, reform of sanctions policy, liberalization of US export controls and export credits, and specific measures such as permanent normal trade relations (PNTR) for China in 2000, import protection for steel, and Buy American legislation in 2009.

Other influential analyses have addressed economic reform in Europe, Japan, the former communist countries, and Latin America (including the Washington Consensus), the economic and social impact of globalization and policy responses to it, outsourcing, electronic commerce, corruption, foreign direct investment both into and out of the United States, global warming and international environmental policy, and key sectors such as agriculture, financial services, steel, telecommunications, and textiles.

The Institute celebrated its 25th anniversary in 2006 and adopted its new name at that time, having previously been the Institute for International Economics. It moved into its award-winning new building in 2001.

The Russia Balance Sheet Advisory Committee

Leon Aron, American Enterprise Institute
Anders Åslund, Peterson Institute for International Economics
David Bailey, ExxonMobil
William Beddow, Caterpillar
C. Fred Bergsten, Peterson Institute for International Economics
Steve Biegun, Ford Motor Company
Zbigniew Brzezinski, Center for Strategic and International Studies
Michael Calvey, Baring Vostok Capital Partners
Sarah Carey, Squire, Sanders & Dempsey
Edward Chow, Center for Strategic and International Studies
Ariel Cohen, Heritage Foundation
Keith Crane, Rand Corporation
Dorothy Dwoskin, Microsoft Corporation
Toby Gati, Akin, Gump, Strauss, Hauer & Feld
Thomas Graham, Kissinger Associates
Michael Green, Center for Strategic and International Studies
John Hamre, Center for Strategic and International Studies
Fiona Hill, NIC
Carla Hills, Hills & Company
Gary Clyde Hufbauer, Peterson Institute for International Economics
Andrei Illarionov, Cato Institute
Neville Isdell, Coca-Cola
Bruce Jackson, Project on Transitional Democracies
Oakley Johnson, AIG
Steven Kehoe, PepsiCo
Henry Kissinger, Center for Strategic and International Studies
Andrew C. Kuchins, Center for Strategic and International Studies

Cliff Kupchan, Eurasia Group
Eugene Lawson, US-Russia Business Council
Randi Levinas, US-Russia Business Council
Michael Mandelbaum, Johns Hopkins University, School of Advanced International Studies
Michael McFaul, Stanford University
Sarah Mendelson, Center for Strategic and International Studies
Scott Miller, Procter & Gamble
Sam Nunn, US Senate (ret.) and Nuclear Threat Initiative
Thomas Pickering, Hills & Company
Steven Pifer, Brookings Institution
Charles Ryan, Deutsche Bank
Diana Sedney, Chevron
Stephen Sestanovich, Council on Foreign Relations
Andrew Somers, American Chamber of Commerce in Moscow
Angela Stent, Georgetown University
John Sullivan, CIPE
Dmitri Trenin, Carnegie Moscow Center
Judyth Twigg, Virginia Commonwealth University
Edward Verona, US-Russia Business Council
Ann Wrobleski, International Paper

Index

Abkhazia, 2, 75, 124, 153
  Russian recognition of, 54, 125, 142,
    148, 150
ABM (Anti-Ballistic Missile) Treaty, 19,
  116, 140–41, 145, 153
absenteeism, 89
"achievement," attitude toward, 109
"administrative resources," election
    outcomes controlled via, 33
Afghanistan
  NATO involvement in, 123–24, 152
  Soviet invasion of, 119, 125, 137
  US involvement in, 127, 141, 143
age factors, in attitudes toward US,
    102–103, 103f
aging population, 83
123 Agreement (US-Russia Agreement for
    Peaceful Nuclear Cooperation), 129,
    140, 145, 156–57, 162
agricultural sector, 36, 81
AIDS, 89, 96
alcohol abuse, 83, 86, 88, 92–93, 97
Andijan massacre, 123, 136
Angola, 61
Anti-Ballistic Missile (ABM) Treaty, 19,
  116, 140–41, 145, 153
Anti-Corruption Council, 38
Arctic resources, 158
Armenia, 47, 122, 123
arms control
  agreements, 19, 127–30, 140–42, 145,
    153–54, 161
  policy recommendations, 153–55,
    161–62
arms trade, 132, 148
Asia. See also Central Asia; specific country
  orientation between Europe and, 14–15
  trade with, 72, 73f

Atomic Energy Act of 1954 (US), Section
    123, 129n
August coup (1991), 26, 27
authoritarianism, 7, 25–26, 110, 136–37
automotive industry, 46, 82
Azerbaijan, 47, 123, 149, 153, 158, 159

Baker, James, 152
Bakiyev, Kurmanbek, 143
Baku-Ceyhan pipeline, 158
Baku-Tbilisi-Ceyhan pipeline, 135
banking system, 51–52
Bank Moskvy, 51
Bashkortostan, 27
Beijing Consensus, 133
Belarus, 64, 107, 121, 122, 125, 151
Berdyaev, Nikolai, 14
Beslan terrorist attack, 31
Biden, Joseph, 148
bilateral investment treaty (BIT), 78–79,
    155
birth rate, 83, 83f, 86, 88, 95–96
Blair, Tony, 161
Bolshevik revolution, 16–17
BP, 63n, 64, 78
Brazil. See BRICs
Brezhnev, Leonid, 18, 19
Brezhnev Constitution, 27
bribery, 35, 48
BRICs
  consumer good imports, 72
  economic growth prediction, 40, 116,
    133
  FDI to GDP ratio, 77
  life expectancy in, 86
  population growth in, 83
budget
  deficit, 44

budget—*continued*
    oil prices and, 60
    surplus, 44–45, 50
Bulgaria, 141
Burma, 133
Bush, George W.
    arms control agreements and, 154
    on democracy, 136
    energy policy, 158
    "gentleman's agreement" with
        Gorbachev, 117
    investment treaty and, 155
    nuclear cooperation agreement and, 129
    Putin meetings with, 2, 126, 141, 143,
        144, 161
    Russian attitude toward, 115, 144
    US credibility weakened by, 160
    US-Russia relations under, 6, 23, 123,
        126–28, 140–41, 144–45
business, globalization of, 80–81
business environment, 48, 146
    foreign direct investment and, 77–78, 81

Cambodia, 75
capital flight, 53
capital investment, 53
capitalism, state, 115
capitalist transformation, 44–45, 99–100
    attitude toward, 108–109, 133
carbon emissions, 65, 66f, 67, 158
"caring about others," attitude toward,
    109
Caspian Pipeline System, 135
Catherine the Great, 13, 15
Central Asia. *See also specific country*
    gas supply from, 62
    NATO membership and, 124
    US military bases in, 123, 133, 141, 149
centralization
    conflict between economic
        modernization and, 57
    of energy sector, 58, 60–61
    under Putin, 30–32, 34–35
CFE (Treaty on Conventional Armed
    Forces in Europe), 142, 145, 153
Chaadaev, Pyotr, 13
Chechnya War, 27, 30, 31, 119, 136, 141
chemical industry, 36
Chernomyrdin, Viktor, 29
Chevron, 33
China. *See also* BRICs
    energy intensity, 65, 66f
    energy sector bridge loan, 64, 132, 132n
    FDI to GDP ratio, 77

gas pipelines to, 64
human rights violations, 159
public opinion of, 133–34
Russian boundary with, 15
Russian relations with, 130–34
trade with, 131–32
US policy on, 148
China National Petroleum Corporation
    (CNPC), 132, 132n
Christianity, 14–15, 16, 37, 113
chudo (miracle) scenario, 5
Churchill, Winston, 3–4
CIS. *See* Commonwealth of Independent
    States
Civil War (Russian), 16, 119
climate change, 65–67, 158
Clinton, Bill
    G-20 creation by, 156
    US-Russia relations under, 6, 115, 126,
        143–45, 148
CNPC (China National Petroleum
    Corporation), 132, 132n
Cold War, 17–21
    end of, 20
    lasting effects of, 7
    "New," 147
Collective Security Treaty Organization
    (CSTO), 121–22, 124
"color revolutions," 116, 136, 144, 158. *See
    also specific revolution*
command-administrative system (Soviet),
    18
commercial relations, 155–57
Committee to Protect Journalists, 35n
commodity prices, sensitivity to, 55
Commonwealth of Independent States
    (CIS), 121–22. *See also specific state*
    Collective Security Treaty, 122
    Customs Union, 122
    gas subsidies for, 136
    Russian interests in, 120, 122
    trade with, 72, 73f
Communist Party of the Soviet Union,
    12–13, 27
comparative advantage, 72–74, 146
competitiveness of exports, 72–74
Concept for the Development of
    Healthcare in the Russian Federation
    through 2020, 96
Concept of Long-Term Socioeconomic
    Development to 2020. *See* Russia 2020
Congress of People's Deputies (Soviet),
    19, 26, 27
Conoco-Lukoil, 64

conscription, military, 92
Constantinople, 14, 113
constitution
    Soviet Russian (1978), 27
    Yeltsin (December 1993), 28–29
constructive engagement policy, 148
consumer goods, imports of, 72
Cooperative Threat Reduction (CTR), 130
corporate foreign debt, 53
corporate governance, 81
corruption, 38, 48, 97, 146
corruption perceptions index
    (Transparency International), 35, 36f
Council of Europe, 79, 137, 159
coup (August 1991), 26, 27
credit volume, 46
crime, 28, 37, 38
Crimea, 125–26, 151
Crimean War, 15
crisis scenario, 55
CSTO (Collective Security Treaty
    Organization), 121–22, 124
CTR (Cooperative Threat Reduction), 130
Cuba, 141, 143, 145
current account surplus, 45, 50, 52
Czech Republic
    NATO membership, 122
    natural gas pipeline to, 64
    US antimissile base in, 128–29, 142–43,
        145, 149–50

Darwinist perspective, 115, 131
death rate. *See also* life expectancy
    causes of, 86, 97
    gender gap, 89, 90f
    infant, 83, 85f
    reducing, 93
death-to-birth ratio, 83, 83f, 88
demilitarization (Soviet), 20
democracy
    attitude toward, 106–108, 107f, 112
    "sovereign," 132–33
    "special," 108
    US-Russia relations and, 136–37, 158–59
democratization (Soviet), 20
demographic challenge, 50–51, 86–89
    economic effects of, 89–92
    limited improvements, 95–97
    remedies, 92–95
deregulation, economic effects of, 44
détente, 18, 19
Doing Business index (World Bank), 48,
    49f
Dutch disease, 47

East versus West question, 14–15
EBRD. *See* European Bank for
    Reconstruction and Development
economic behavior, 108–109
economic growth
    conflict between centralization and, 57
    factors causing, 40
    forecasts of, 37, 40–41
    rate of, 40, 41f
economic growth plan, 8, 42–44. *See also*
    Russia 2020
    balance between foreign policy and,
        8–9
    global financial crisis and, 48–50
    healthcare reform and, 96
    labor force and, 91
    national sovereignty issues and, 118–19
    Russian values and, 112–13
economic performance, government
    popularity linked to, 25–26, 146
economic policy, problems with, Russian
    denial of, 52–53
economic recovery, 1, 4–5, 8, 39
    causes of, 44–48, 60, 134, 138, 146
economic reforms
    public opinion of, 110
    US failure to support, 23, 160
    Soviet, 18–21
education, 42
    demand for, 88
    improvement in, 93–95
    public expenditure on, 43
Egypt, 159
elections
    democratic, 27–29
    government control over, 31, 33, 34, 141
    monitoring of, 137
    proportional, 29, 29n, 35
energy and raw materials scenario, 43
Energy Charter, 78, 135, 157
energy curse, 47–48
energy intensity of production, 43, 65, 66f,
    67, 158
energy prices, 65, 67. *See also* oil prices
energy rents, 47–48
energy sector, 57–68
    exports and, 45, 60, 69–72, 72f, 82, 132,
        146
    as focus of economic plan, 43
    foreign investment in, 63–65, 158
    as foreign policy tool, 63–64, 119,
        134–35, 137–38, 142, 157
    global financial crisis and, 59–60, 146
    importance of, 57, 59, 82, 146

energy sector—*continued*
  investment in, 58, 158
  labor force, 91
  reliability of, 134–36, 142, 148, 157
  renationalization of, 58, 60–61, 110, 134,
    136, 141
  risk management approaches, 59–60
  taxation of, 58, 61
  trade with China and, 132
  US-Russian relations and, 65, 68, 145,
    157–58
energy superpower, 57, 119, 134–36
ENI, 64
E.ON, 64
Esmark, 80
ESS (European Social Survey), 100n, 109
Estonia, 47, 50n, 141
ethnic nationalism, 37
EurAsian Economic Community
    (EurAsEC), 121–22
Europe
  disruption of gas supply to, 63–64, 119,
    134–36, 142, 148, 157
  orientation between Asia and, 14–15
European Bank for Reconstruction and
    Development (EBRD)
  bribe frequency survey, 35
  Life in Transition Survey, 100n, 102,
    106–108, 107f
  transition index, 44
European Court of Human Rights, 79
European security framework
  failure to integrate Russia into, 2–3, 140
  Russian attitude toward, 117–18, 150–53
  US role in, 150–53
European Social Survey (ESS), 100n, 109
European Union. *See also specific country*
  conflict with US policy, 3, 161
  democracy and, 136–37
  energy policy, 157–58
  former Soviet states as members in, 123
  Russian WTO accession and, 75
  trade with, 72, 73f
Evraz Holding, 80
exchange rate, managed, 52–53
export(s), 45, 55, 69
  arms, 132
  to China, 131–32
  competitiveness of, 72–74
  energy, 57, 60, 69–72, 72f, 82, 132, 146
  merchandise, 45, 70f, 70–71, 71f
  sensitivity to protectionism, 76–77, 82
Export-Import Bank, 157

export partners, 72, 73f
export tariffs, 70, 75
ExxonMobil, 33, 63

fairness of Western society, attitude
    toward, 106, 106t
FCTC (Framework Convention on
    Tobacco Control), 92
FDI. *See* foreign direct investment
federal districts, creation of, 31
Federation Council, 28, 29, 31, 35
Federation Treaty, 27
Fedorov, Boris, 22
fertility rate, 86
Filofey, 14
financial crash (August 1998), 30, 44, 47,
    59, 71, 88, 119
financial governance, international,
    reform of, 156
financial market, domestic, 51–52
financial stabilization, economic effects of,
    44
Finland, 75
flag, 37
food prices, 81
foreign currency reserves, 3, 4, 45, 50, 53
foreign direct investment (FDI), 69, 77–80
  in energy sector, 63–65, 158
  geographic distance and, 80n
  outward, 80–81, 155
  ratio of GDP to, 77
  from US, 79–80, 80n
  WTO accession and, 79–80
foreign expropriation, remedies to, 78–79
foreign policy
  balance between economic growth
    goals and, 8–9
  energy sector as tool in, 63–64, 119,
    134–35, 137–38, 142, 157
  Russian attitude toward, 115–16, 133,
    137
forestry industry, 46
formation of Russia, 21–22
Founding Act on NATO Cooperation
    with Russia, 122
free capacity, 45–47
Freedom House ranking, 26, 33, 34f, 110n,
    159
free market economy
  attitude toward, 106–108, 107f, 110, 133
  transition to, 44–45, 99–100
free trade agreements, 76, 78
"frozen conflicts," 153

FSB, 32
full-fledged engagement scenario, 148
functionality of political system, 37–38
FY2006 Russia Country Commercial Guide, 77*n*

Gaidar, Yegor, 22, 23, 59, 110
gas. *See* energy sector; natural gas
Gazprom
   foreign direct investment and, 63, 63*n*, 78
   government energy policy and, 33, 58, 59, 62
   market value, 64
   unreliability of, 134–36, 142
Gazprombank, 51
GDP, 1, 40, 41*f*, 50, 146
   per capita, 40, 43, 110, 111*f*
   ration of FDI to, 77
   share of energy sector in, 57, 69
   share of exports in, 70, 70*f*
   share of heavy industry in, 67
gender gap, in life expectancy, 83, 86, 87*f*, 89, 90*f*
geographical size, 11–12, 15
Georating survey, 100*n*, 101, 102, 108–109
Georgia
   NATO membership, 123, 124, 142, 151–52
   Rose Revolution, 136, 158
   Russian attitude toward, 120
   trade sanctions against, 124
   US assistance to, 124–25
Georgia War, 124–26, 142
   China-Russia relations and, 134
   European security and, 118–19, 150
   nuclear cooperation agreement and, 129
   Putin-Bush meeting on, 2
   trade sanctions after, 69 70, 76, 155
   US-Russia relations and, 140, 142, 148–49, 153
   WTO accession and, 75
German reunification, 20, 117
glasnost, 20
global financial crisis, 2–3
   energy sector and, 59–60, 146
   foreign direct investment and, 69
   impact on Russia, 25–26, 38, 39, 48–54, 146
   Russian government response to, 54–55
   US-Russia relations and, 6, 140, 160
global governance, changes in, 116–18, 120, 133, 138–40, 160

Global Initiative to Combat Nuclear Terrorism, 130
globalization, of Russian business, 80–81
global security issues, 4, 139
Goldman Sachs, 40, 42
Gorbachev, Mikhail
   anti-alcohol campaign, 86, 88, 93
   economic reforms, 18–21
   "gentleman's agreement" with Bush, 117
   indirect elections under, 29
   "new political thinking," 117
   oil prices and, 137–38
   Reykjavik summit meeting, 126, 140
Gore-Chernomyrdin Commission, 126, 145, 162
Gosplan, 48
government intervention
   in elections, 31, 33, 34, 141
   for foreign investment, 79
gravity model equations, 74
Group of Six (G-6), 40
Group of Seven (G-7), 115, 156
Group of Eight (G-8), 54, 65, 134, 142, 156, 162
Group of Twenty (G-20), 2, 54, 81, 162
gulag system, 17
Gulf War (1991), 20
Gusinsky, Vladimir, 31, 79

hate crimes, 37
health, poor, economic effects of, 89–92
health services
   demand for, 88
   limited improvements in, 95–97
   public expenditure on, 43, 88
   remedies, 92–95
healthy lifestyles, promotion of, 93
heavy industry, 36, 67
Hegel, 15
Helsinki accords, 152
historical roots, 11–23
Hitler, Adolf, 18
HIV/AIDS, 89, 96
housing construction, 36
Hu Jintao, 131
human capital, 48
   investment in, 93–95, 112–13
human rights, 136–37, 158–59
Hungary, 122
Hussein, Saddam, 141
hypersovereignty, 132, 137

IMF (International Monetary Fund), 40, 96, 133, 156
immigrants, 37
immigration policy, 93–95, 156
import(s)
  diversification of, 71–72
  merchandise, 69, 70*f*, 71
import partners, 72, 73*f*
import tariffs, 70, 82
income
  attitudes toward democracy by, 107–108
  attitudes toward West by, 103–105, 104*f*, 105*t*
  life satisfaction by, 110, 111*f*
  real disposable, 50, 53–54
India, 133, 149. *See also* BRICs
industrialization, 16–17
industrial sector, 45–46, 50, 53, 67
inertia scenario, 43, 48, 54–55
infant mortality, 83, 85*f*
infectious disease, 89
inflation, 52–53
infrastructure, investment in, 43, 47, 51, 55
INF (Intermediate-Range Nuclear Forces) Treaty, 142, 154
innovation scenario, 8, 43, 112–13
Institute for the Economy in Transition, 91
interest rates, 52–53
Intermediate-Range Nuclear Forces (INF) Treaty, 142, 154
international economic integration, 45, 51, 69–72, 77, 118–19
International Energy Agency, 62
international financial governance, reform of, 156
International Monetary Fund (IMF), 40, 96, 133, 156
international security issues, 4, 139
investment
  capital, 53
  energy sector, 58, 158
  foreign (*See* foreign direct investment)
  human capital, 93–95, 112–13
  infrastructure, 43, 47, 51, 55
investment ratio, 51
investment treaty, US-Russia, 78–79, 155
Iran
  nuclear weapons program, 129, 141, 149–50, 154
  Obama policy toward, 149–50
  oil production, 61, 65

Russian arms sales to, 148
Russian position toward, 117, 133, 149–50
Iraq War, 6, 101, 127, 141
Ivan III, Prince, 14
Ivan IV, Tsar, 14

Jackson-Vanik Amendment, 75, 144, 156, 160, 162
Jewish emigration, 156
Jiang Zemin, 130
journalists
  murders of, 35, 141, 142
  protection of, 38
judicial reform, 32, 38, 45
"A Just Russia" party, 35

Kaliningrad exclave, 143
Karshi-Khanabad air base (Uzbekistan), 123
Kazakhstan, 47, 122, 123, 125, 131, 151, 158, 159
KGB, 31, 32, 35
Khasbulatov, Ruslan, 27
Khodorkovsky, Mikhail, 26, 32–33, 60–61
Khrushchev, Nikita, 18
Kievan period, 15
Kissinger, Henry, 127, 139*n*, 144, 145
Klebnikov, Paul, 141
Korea, North, 130
Kosovo, 116, 118, 122, 125, 133, 142
Kovykta gasfield, 63, 63*n*, 78
Kozyrev, Andrei, 22, 23
Kudrin, Alexei, 59
Kyoto Protocol, 67
Kyrgyzstan, 122, 136

labor force, 50, 90–95
labor productivity, 43, 93
land code, adoption of, 45
land redistribution, 46
Latin America, 138
Latvia, 47, 50*n*, 141
Lavrov, Sergey, 124, 132–33
law enforcement, 28, 38
Law of the Sea Treaty, 158
Law on Foreign Investments in Strategic Industries, 63, 79, 81
legal protection, foreign direct investment and, 77–78
legitimacy of political system, 37
Lenin, Vladimir, 16–17, 17*n*
Levada Center, 33, 106–108
liberal tax system, 45

Libya, 61
life expectancy, 43, 83, 87*f*, 90*f*
  economic plan goals for, 50, 86, 88
  gender gap in, 83, 86, 87*f*, 89, 90*f*
Life in Transition Survey, 100*n*, 102,
  106–108, 107*f*
life satisfaction index, 110, 111*f*
Lithuania, 141
"loans-for-shares" privatizations, 30
longevity. *See* life expectancy
Long-Term Development Concept, 86
Lukoil, 64
lumber industry, 75, 82

Manas air base (Kyrgyzstan), 123
Marxism-Leninism, 16–17
mass purges, 17
maternity incentives, 96
Mechel, 52
media control, 26, 31, 110, 110*n*
media coverage (US), 7–8
mediating capacity of political system,
  37–38
Medvedev, Dmitri
  China-Russia relations under, 131
  economic conditions under, 1, 8
  economic development plan, 112–13,
    147
  European security treaty proposed by,
    118, 152–53
  on financial governance reform, 156
  megalomaniacal ambitions, 120
  nuclear missile deployment, 143
  Obama meeting with, 162
  prospects, 38
  tandemocracy with Putin, 1, 36–38
  US-Russia relations under, 6, 126–27,
    160, 162
Medvedev Doctrine, 117*n*, 117–18
men, life expectancy for, 83, 86, 87*f*, 89, 90*f*
merchandise trade surplus, 45, 70*f*, 70–71,
  71*f*
messianism, 14–15, 16, 113
metals industry, 46
Mexico, 67
middle class, growth of, 42, 43, 86
militarization, 12, 18
military bases
  Russian, 141, 145
  US, 123, 128, 133, 141, 142, 149–50
military expenditures, 160
military-industrial complex, 3, 18, 20
military service conscription, 92
military technology, trade in, 132, 148

Milosevic, Slobodan, 122
mining, 36
ministerial appointments, 28–29
Ministry of Economic Development
  scenarios, 43, 54–55
  on WTO membership, 51, 76–77
Ministry of Health and Social
  Development, 93, 96
missile defense
  agreements on, 19, 116, 140–41
  Iran and, 148–50
  Medvedev on, 118
  Putin on, 127–28
  US installations for, 128–29, 142–43, 143,
    145, 149–50
Moldova, 153
Mongolia, 133
Mongol invasion, 15
Monroe Doctrine, 120
mortality. *See* death rate
Moscow Treaty, 128, 141, 145
multipolarity, 116, 133, 138
Muscovite principality, 12, 14
Muslim population, 37, 120

Nabucco pipeline, 135, 158
Nagorno-Karabakh, 153
Nashi (Ours) movement, 35
national anthem, 37
national health insurance, 96–97
national identity, 14–15, 35, 37, 113
nationalization, 52, 55
  of energy sector, 58, 60–61, 110, 134,
    136, 141
National Priority Health Project, 86, 95–97
National Security Council (NSC), 161
national sovereignty, 117, 132, 137
NATO
  Bush-Gorbachev agreement on, 117
  enlargement of, 116, 118, 122–24, 141,
    151–52
  Obama policy on, 162
  Russian attitude toward, 101, 117–18,
    123–24, 141, 150–53, 152
NATO-Russia Council, 123
natural gas. *See also* energy sector
  flaring of, 62
  government policy toward, 62–63,
    135–36
  production of, 57–58, 58*f*, 62, 157–58
  reserves of, 57
natural gas pipelines, 51, 64, 158
  to Europe, 63–64, 119, 134–36
"near abroad" concept, 120, 141

"negative value added," Soviet economy
as, 22
neoimperialism, 119–20
"New Cold War" scenario, 147
Nicaragua, 2, 125, 142
Nicholas II, Tsar, 15–16
nongovernmental organizations
restrictive law on, 34, 142
US assistance to, 159
nonproliferation agreements. *See* arms
control; nuclear weapons; *specific
agreement*
Nord Stream pipeline, 64
North Atlantic Treaty Organization. *See*
NATO
North Korea, 130
North Ossetia terrorist attack, 31
NPT (Nuclear Non-Proliferation Treaty),
128, 154
NSC (National Security Council), 161
NTV, 31
Nuclear Non-Proliferation Treaty (NPT),
128, 154
nuclear power
civilian cooperation agreement on, 140,
145, 156–57, 162
Russian support for, 67, 129
nuclear weapons
foreign policy and, 138
Iranian program, 129, 141, 149–50, 154
Medvedev's deployment of, 143
nonproliferation agreements, 127–30,
145, 154
Soviet development of, 18–19

Obama, Barack
energy policy, 158
G-20 development policy, 156, 162
Medvedev meeting with, 162
NATO policy, 162
negotiations with Iran, 149–50
US credibility and, 160
US-Russia relations under, 6, 127, 128,
138
policy recommendations, 139–63
OECD (Organization for Economic
Cooperation and Development), 156
oil. *See also* energy sector
government policy toward, 60–62
production of, 57–58, 58f, 59, 157–58
reserves of, 57
oil pipelines, 51, 60
oil prices
as determinant of foreign policy, 137–38

economic boom caused by, 5, 8, 47–48,
134, 138, 146
effect of global financial crisis on, 48,
146
exports and, 45, 82
peak, 1, 48, 59
volatility of, 59–60
oligarchy
energy sector and, 60–61
Putin's attacks on, 31–33
rise of, 29–30
Olympic Games, 1–2
OPEC (Organization of Petroleum-
Exporting Countries), 63, 65
open economy, 69–70
openness to change, attitude toward, 109
OPIC (Overseas Private Investment
Corporation), 157
opinion polls
of attitudes toward West, 100*n*,
100–103, 101*t*, 103*f*, 104*f*
organizations conducting, 34
Orange Revolution (Ukraine), 26, 136, 158
centralization after, 34–35
gas cutoff after, 63–64, 119, 134
Oregon Steel Mills, 80
Organization for Economic Cooperation
and Development (OECD), 156
Organization for Security and
Cooperation in Europe (OSCE), 118,
137, 145, 150–53, 159
Organization of Petroleum-Exporting
Countries (OPEC), 63, 65
ORT, 31
Orthodox Christianity, 14–15, 16, 37, 113
OSCE (Organization for Security and
Cooperation in Europe), 118, 137,
145, 150–53
Our Home is Russia party, 29
Overseas Private Investment Corporation
(OPIC), 157

Pakistan, 130, 133, 149
Partnership for Peace, 122, 123
path dependencies, 11
patrimonial authoritarianism, 25, 136–37
patriotism, 37
Peace Corps, 159
pension reform, 88, 91
people-to-people exchanges, 159
per capita income, 40, 110, 111*f*
perestroika, 19–20
permanent normal trade relations
(PNTR), 75

Peter I, Tsar, 15
petroleum industry. *See* energy sector; oil
petrostates, 43
Pew Global Attitudes Survey, 100*n*,
    101–102, 106–108
PNTR (permanent normal trade
    relations), 75
Poland
    NATO membership, 123
    US antimissile base in, 128–29, 142–43,
        145, 149–50
    political development, 25–38
    political system, challenges facing,
        37–38
Politkovskaya, Anna, 142
Polity IV, 110*n*
population decline. *See* demographic
    challenge
post-imperialism, 115–38
poultry industry, 76
poverty, 39, 86, 110
power ministers, 28–29
"power-wealth" index, 109
presidential elections, 29, 30, 141. *See also
    specific president*
presidential term, extension of, 38
price liberalization, economic effects of,
    44
prime minister. *See also specific minister*
    role of, 29
Priority National Health Project, 86, 95–97
private sector, strength of, 29–30, 44, 52
privatization, economic effects of, 44
production, energy intensity of, 43, 65,
    66*f*, 67, 158
propaganda, anti-American, 149
property rights, 55, 77–78
proportional elections, 29, 29*n*, 35
prosperity, 110, 112
protectionism, 69–70, 76–77, 81–82
pro-Western parties, 112*n*
Public Chamber, 35
public foreign debt, 45
public opinion
    of China, 133–34
    of economic reforms, 110
    of Western values, 99–114, 133, 160
Public Opinion Foundation, 100*n*
public sector, inefficient, 48
purchasing power parity, 40
Putin, Vladimir
    anti-American sentiments, 147, 160
    appointment as prime minister, 26, 30,
        36

attacks on oligarchy, 31–33
authoritarianism under, 7, 25–26, 110,
    136–37
Bush meetings with, 2, 126, 141, 143,
    144, 161
centralization under, 30–32, 34–35
China-Russia relations under, 134
on collapse of Soviet Union, 142, 151
economic plan, 36, 42–44, 48–50, 95–96,
    112–13, 147
economic recovery under, 1, 4–5, 8
election as president, 30, 33
electoral rules changed by, 34–35
energy sector and, 59, 60, 138
foreign policy, 115–16, 132–33
legacy of, 38
megalomaniacal ambitions, 120
on multipolarity, 116
nationalism under, 37, 132, 137
on nuclear weapons, 127
popularity of, 25, 33, 38, 146
resignation as president, 36
on student exchanges, 159
tandemocracy with Medvedev, 1,
    36–38
Ukraine independence and, 126,
    150–51
US investment treaty and, 78
US-Russia relations under, 6, 123,
    126–28, 140–41, 144–45
"Putin's Plan," 36

Qatar, 65

Reagan, Ronald, 126, 140
real disposable income, 50, 53–54
real estate prices, 54
real interest rates, 52–53
"realist" foreign policy *(realpolitik)*,
    116–20, 131, 138
realistic engagement scenario, 147–48
real wages, 91
reform scenario, 55
regional governors, 31
regional migration, 95
regional power, devolution of, 27, 31
registered enterprises, number of, 46
regulatory environment, 48, 146
    foreign direct investment and, 77–78, 81
religion, 14–15, 16, 37, 113
remonetization, 47
renationalization, 52, 55
    of energy sector, 58, 60–61, 110, 134,
        136, 141

rent seeking, 48
research and development spending, 43
retirement age, 91
revealed comparative advantage, 72–74
Reykjavik summit (Gorbachev-Reagan),
    126, 140
Rice, Condoleezza, 134, 140, 147
risk management, in energy sector, 59–60
risk taking, attitude toward, 109
road network, 38, 51
Romania, 141
Rose Revolution (Georgia), 158
Rosneft, 33, 52, 61, 63, 64, 132, 132n
Royal Dutch Shell, 63, 63n, 78
ruble
    devaluation of, 3, 53, 60, 71
    fixed exchange rate, 52–53
Rus civilization, 15
Rusia (Kovykta), 52
Russia 2020, 42–44
    global financial crisis and, 48–50
    for healthcare reform, 96
    national sovereignty issues and, 118–19
    trade with China and, 131–32
Russia at the Turn of the Millennium, 31
Russia-Belarus Union State, 121
Russian Empire, 14–16, 113
Russian expansion, 12–13, 16, 119–20
Russian identity, 14–15, 35, 37, 113
Russian Orthodox Church, 14–15, 16, 37,
    113
Russian values, 109–14, 115, 137
    gap between US values and, 143–46
Russia's Choice party, 29
Russo-Japanese war, 15–16

Saakashvili, Mikheil, 2, 120, 124, 125
Sakhalin Energy, 52
Sakhalin I project, 63
Sakhalin II project, 63, 63n, 78
SALT (Strategic Arms Limitation
    Treaties), 19
Sarkozy, Nicolas, 2, 125
Saudi Arabia, 63, 75, 159
Sberbank, 51
SCO (Shanghai Cooperation
    Organization), 133
seat belt promotion campaign, 97
security issues
    European
        failure to integrate Russia into, 2–3,
        140
        Russian attitude toward, 117–18,
        150–53

global, 4, 139
    Soviet, 16–18, 20
September 11 terrorist attacks, 123, 133,
    141
service sector, 45
Severstal, 80
Shanghai Cooperation Organization
    (SCO), 133
Shtokman offshore gasfield, 63, 64
Shultz, George, 127, 139n, 144, 145
Sibneft, 52
Slavophiles, 14–15, 113
Slovakia, 141
Slovenia, 141
small and medium-sized enterprises, 46
smoking, 83, 88–89, 92–93, 97
Smoot-Hawley tariffs, 156
Smutnoe Vremya (Time of Troubles), 119
Sochi Declaration, 79, 127–28, 155
social expenditures, 43, 88
social indicators, 42
social justice, attitude toward, 106, 106t
social shock, of global financial crisis, 50
socioeconomic factors, in attitudes toward
    West, 103–105, 104f, 105t
SORT (Strategic Offensive Reductions
    Treaty), 128, 141, 154, 162
Southern Druzhba pipeline, 64
South Ossetia, 2, 75, 120, 124, 153
    Russian recognition of, 54, 125, 142,
    148, 150
South Stream pipeline, 64, 135
sovereign democracy, 132–33
Soviet Russian Constitution (1978), 27
Soviet Union
    arms control agreements, 19
    collapse of, 18, 21–22, 27, 99, 112, 119,
        121, 142, 151, 160
    democratization in, 20
    economic development, 18, 19, 23, 39
    expansion of, 18
    foreign policy approach, 19–20
    formation of, 16–17
    oil production, 59
    resource misallocation in, 22, 22n
    security issues, 16–18, 20
    US relations with, 18–19
"special democracy," 108
sphere of influence, 120, 141, 152
SPS (Union of Right-Wing Forces) party,
    112n
Stalin, Joseph, 16–18
START (Strategic Arms Reduction Treaty),
    128, 153–54, 161–62

state banks, 51–52
state capitalism, 115
State Council, 35
State Duma, 29
  anti-smoking legislation, 93
  elections to, 28–29, 33, 35
StatoilHydro, 63
steel industry, 80–81
stock exchange, 1, 48
stock-market capitalization, 44–45
Strategic Arms Limitation Treaties
  (SALT), 19
Strategic Arms Reduction Treaty (START),
  128, 153–54, 161–62
2020 Strategic Economic Development
  Plan, 112–13
Strategic Framework Declaration, 127–28,
  130
Strategic Offensive Reductions Treaty
  (SORT), 128, 141, 154, 162
structural reforms, 45–47, 55, 96–97
student exchanges, 159
subprime mortgage crisis. *See* global
  financial crisis
superpresidential powers, 28
Sweden, 75

Tajikistan, 119, 122
Taliban, 124, 143, 152
tandemocracy (Putin-Medvedev), 1, 36–38
tariffs, 70, 75, 82, 156
Tartars, 15
Tatarstan, 27
taxation, 45, 58, 61
television networks, 31
territorial expansion, 12–13, 16, 119–20
terrorism, 5, 31, 123, 130, 133, 141
"Third Rome," Russia as, 14–15, 113
Time of Troubles *(Smutnoe Vremya),* 119
TNK-BP, 63, 64
tobacco use, 83, 88–89, 97
Total, 63, 64
trade
  policy recommendations, 155–57
  regional orientation of, 72, 73*f*
Trade Act of 1974 (US), Jackson-Vanik
  Amendment, 75, 144, 156, 160, 162
trade liberalization, economic effects of,
  44
trade protectionism, 69–70, 76–77, 81–82
trade sanctions, 69, 76, 81, 124, 155
trade surplus, 45, 69–71, 70*f*, 71*f*
trading partners, 72, 73*f*
Transcaspian pipeline, 135, 158

Transneft, 33, 60, 61
Transnistria region (Moldova), 153
transparency, emphasis on, 81
Transparency International corruption
  perceptions index, 35, 36*f*
Treaty on Conventional Armed Forces in
  Europe (CFE), 142, 145, 153
tsarist Russia, 12–15
Tskhinvali (South Ossetia), 125
tuberculosis, 89
Turkey, 70, 76, 81
Turkmenistan, 62

Ukraine
  free trade agreement with, 76
  gas pipelines through, cutoff of, 63–64,
    119, 134–36, 142, 148, 157
  independence, 21, 125–26
  NATO membership, 123, 126, 142,
    151–52
  Orange Revolution (*See* Orange
    Revolution)
  presidential elections, 141
  Russian policy toward, 150–51
  trade sanctions against, 70, 81
  trade with, 75
  US assistance to, 151
  WTO membership, 75
UN Conference on Trade and
  Development (UNCTAD), 77
unemployment, 90–91, 110
UNESCO, 42
UNICEF, 42
Union of Right-Wing Forces (SPS) party,
  112*n*
United Arab Emirates, 75
United Heavy Machineries, 52
United Russia party, 33, 35, 36
United States
  assistance to Georgia, 124–25
  bilateral investment treaty, 78–79
  China policy, 148
  credibility of, 160
  democracy and human rights policy,
    159
  failure to support Russian economic
    reform, 23, 160
  foreign investment from, 79–80, 80*n*
  global governance and, 138–40, 160
  military bases, 123, 128, 133, 141, 142,
    149–50
  perception of Russia, 7–8
  role in European security framework,
    150–53

United States—*continued*
  Russian investment in, 79, 155
  Russian policy flaws, 144–45
  Russian public opinion of, 100–103,
    101*t*, 103*f*, 104*f*
  Russian WTO accession and, 75
  trade sanctions against, 69, 76, 81
  trade with, 72, 73*f*, 155
US Atomic Energy Act of 1954, Section
    123, 129*n*
US-Russia Agreement for Peaceful
    Nuclear Cooperation (123
    Agreement), 129, 140, 145, 156–57, 162
US-Russia Economic Dialogue, 157
US-Russia Energy Dialogue, 157
US-Russia relations, 6, 22–23
  alternative scenarios, 146–48
  arms control, 153–55
  chronology of key events, 141–43
  commercial relations, 155–57
  democracy and, 136–37, 158–59
  deterioration of, 126–30, 140–46
  economic growth plans and, 118–19
  energy sector and, 65, 68, 145, 157–58
  Georgia War and, 140, 148–49
  global financial crisis and, 6, 140, 160
  human rights and, 136–37, 158–59
  importance of, 139–40, 163
  key areas of cooperation, 148–59
  policy recommendations, 139–63
  implementation of, 160–62
  values gap, 143–46
US Surgeon General's report on smoking
    (1964), 97
US Trade Act of 1974, Jackson-Vanik
    Amendment, 75, 144, 156, 160, 162
United Steelworkers, 81
unpredictability and complexity of
    Russia, 3–5
UN Security Council, 133, 145
Uralkali, 52
uranium fuel, 129
USSR. *See* Soviet Union
Uzbekistan, 122

Valdai Discussion Club, 127, 127*n*
values, Russian, 109–14, 115, 137
values gap, between US and Russia,
    143–46
Vankor, 52
VEB (Vneshekonombank), 51, 53
Venezuela, 61, 65, 143
vice presidential post, abolition of, 29*n*
Vietnam, 75, 141, 145

VSMPO-Avisma, 52
VTB, 51, 52
VTsIOM public opinion research center,
    134

wages, real, 91
Warsaw Pact, demise of, 119
Washington Consensus, 133
Wehrkunde Security Conference, 115–16
Westernization, 19–20, 23, 99–100, 113
Western values, attitudes toward, 99–114,
    133
women
  in labor market, 91
  life expectancy for, 83, 86, 87*f*, 89, 90*f*
World Bank
  bribe frequency survey, 35
  Doing Business index, 48, 49*f*
  energy consumption study, 158
  health surveys, 88–89
  Life in Transition Survey, 100*n*, 102,
    106–108, 107*f*
  poverty estimates, 39
  on Russian gas flaring, 62
  Russian membership, 156
  social expenditure forecasts, 88
  Washington Consensus, 133
  on WTO membership, 51, 76*n*, 76–77
world economy, integration into, 45, 51,
    69–72, 77, 118–19
World Health Organization Framework
    Convention on Tobacco Control
    (FCTC), 92
world merchandise trade, Russia's share
    of, 45, 70–71, 71*f*
World Trade Organization (WTO)
    accession, 51, 55, 69, 74–77
  commercial relations and, 155–56
  economic impact of, 74, 76–77
  foreign investment and, 79–80
  obstacles to, 74–76
  suspended attempt at, 69, 81, 140, 145,
    155
World Values Survey, 100*n*
World War I, 15–16
World War II, 17, 18
WTO. *See* World Trade Organization
    accession

xenophobia, 94

Yabloko party, 112*n*
Yeltsin, Boris, 21–22
  China-Russia relations under, 130–31

conflict between parliament and, 26, 27
democratization under, 28–30
domestic reforms under, 30
economic reforms under, 23
election of, 27, 30
oil prices and, 137–38
political power of, 29
popularity of, 25
resignation of, 26, 30
US investment treaty and, 78
US-Russia relations under, 6, 22–23, 115, 143, 145

vice presidential post abolished by, 29n
Yeltsin Constitution (December 1993), 28–29
youth movements, 35
Yuganskneftegaz, 64, 132, 132n
Yugoslavia, 116, 122
Yukos oil company, 26, 32–33, 52, 60–61, 110, 134, 136, 141
Yushchenko, Viktor, 120, 126

Zimbabwe, 54, 133
Ziuganov, Gennady, 29

Other Publications from the Peterson Institute for International Economics

WORKING PAPERS

94-1 APEC and Regional Trading Arrangements in the Pacific
Jeffrey A. Frankel with Shang-Jin Wei and Ernesto Stein

94-2 Towards an Asia Pacific Investment Code Edward M. Graham

94-3 Merchandise Trade in the APEC Region: Is There Scope for Liberalization on an MFN Basis?
Paul Wonnacott

94-4 The Automotive Industry in Southeast Asia: Can Protection Be Made Less Costly? Paul Wonnacott

94-5 Implications of Asian Economic Growth Marcus Noland

95-1 APEC: The Bogor Declaration and the Path Ahead C. Fred Bergsten

95-2 From Bogor to Miami . . . and Beyond: Regionalism in the Asia Pacific and the Western Hemisphere
Jeffrey J. Schott

95-3 Has Asian Export Performance Been Unique? Marcus Noland

95-4 Association of Southeast Asian Nations (ASEAN) and ASEAN Free Trade Area (AFTA): Chronology and Statistics Gautam Jaggi

95-5 The North Korean Economy
Marcus Noland

95-6 China and the International Economic System Marcus Noland

96-1 APEC after Osaka: Toward Free Trade by 2010/2020 C. Fred Bergsten

96-2 Public Policy, Private Preferences, and the Japanese Trade Pattern
Marcus Noland

96-3 German Lessons for Korea: The Economics of Unification
Marcus Noland

96-4 Research and Development Activities and Trade Specialization in Japan
Marcus Noland

96-5 China's Economic Reforms: Chronology and Statistics
Gautam Jaggi, Mary Rundle, Daniel Rosen, and Yuichi Takahashi

96-6 US-China Economic Relations
Marcus Noland

96-7 The Market Structure Benefits of Trade and Investment Liberalization
Raymond Atje and Gary Hufbauer

96-8 The Future of US-Korea Economic Relations Marcus Noland

96-9 Competition Policies in the Dynamic Industrializing Economies: The Case of China, Korea, and Chinese Taipei
Edward M. Graham

96-10 Modeling Economic Reform in North Korea Marcus Noland, Sherman Robinson, and Monica Scatasta

96-11 Trade, Investment, and Economic Conflict Between the United States and Asia Marcus Noland

96-12 APEC in 1996 and Beyond: The Subic Summit C. Fred Bergsten

96-13 Some Unpleasant Arithmetic Concerning Unification
Marcus Noland

96-14 Restructuring Korea's Financial Sector for Greater Competitiveness
Marcus Noland

96-15 Competitive Liberalization and Global Free Trade: A Vision for the 21st Century C. Fred Bergsten

97-1 Chasing Phantoms: The Political Economy of USTR Marcus Noland

97-2 US-Japan Civil Aviation: Prospects Open Regionalism C. Fred Bergsten

97-4 Lessons from the Bundesbank on the Occasion of Its 40th (and Second to Last?) Birthday Adam S. Posen

97-5 The Economics of Korean Unification
Marcus Noland, Sherman Robinson, and Li-Gang Liu

98-1 The Costs and Benefits of Korean Unification Marcus Noland, Sherman Robinson, and Li-Gang Liu

98-2 Asian Competitive Devaluations
Li-Gang Liu, Marcus Noland, Sherman Robinson, and Zhi Wang

98-3 Fifty Years of the GATT/WTO: Lessons from the Past for Strategies or the Future C. Fred Bergsten

98-4 NAFTA Supplemental Agreements: Four Year Review
Jacqueline McFadyen

98-5 Local Government Spending: Solving the Mystery of Japanese Fiscal Packages Hiroko Ishii and Erika Wada

98-6 The Global Economic Effects of the Japanese Crisis Marcus Noland, Sherman Robinson, and Zhi Wang

99-1 Rigorous Speculation: The Collapse and Revival of the North Korean Economy Marcus Noland, Sherman Robinson, and Tao Wang

99-2 Famine in North Korea: Causes and Cures Marcus Noland, Sherman Robinson, and Tao Wang

99-3 Competition Policy and FDI: A Solution in Search of a Problem?
Marcus Noland

99-4 **The Continuing Asian Financial Crisis: Global Adjustment and Trade** Marcus Noland, Sherman Robinson, and Zhi Wang

99-5 **Why EMU Is Irrelevant for the German Economy** Adam S. Posen

99-6 **The Global Trading System and the Developing Countries in 2000** C. Fred Bergsten

99-7 **Modeling Korean Unification** Marcus Noland, Sherman Robinson, and Tao Wang

99-8 **Sovereign Liquidity Crisis: The Strategic Case for a Payments Standstill** Marcus Miller and Lei Zhang

99-9 **The Case for Joint Management of Exchange Rate Flexibility** C. Fred Bergsten, Olivier Davanne, and Pierre Jacquet

99-10 **Does Talk Matter After All? Inflation Targeting and Central Bank Behavior** Kenneth N. Kuttner and Adam S. Posen

99-11 **Hazards and Precautions: Tales of International Finance** Gary Clyde Hufbauer and Erika Wada

99-12 **The Globalization of Services: What Has Happened? What Are the Implications?** Gary C. Hufbauer and Tony Warren

00-1 **Regulatory Standards in the WTO: Comparing Intellectual Property Rights with Competition Policy, Environmental Protection, and Core Labor Standards** Keith Maskus

00-2 **International Economic Agreements and the Constitution** Richard M. Goodman and John M. Frost

00-3 **Electronic Commerce in Developing Countries: Issues for Domestic Policy and WTO Negotiations** Catherine L. Mann

00-4 **The New Asian Challenge** C. Fred Bergsten

00-5 **How the Sick Man Avoided Pneumonia: The Philippines in the Asian Financial Crisis** Marcus Noland

00-6 **Inflation, Monetary Transparency, and G-3 Exchange Rate Volatility** Kenneth N. Kuttner and Adam S. Posen

00-7 **Transatlantic Issues in Electronic Commerce** Catherine L. Mann

00-8 **Strengthening the International Financial Architecture: Where Do We Stand?** Morris Goldstein

00-9 **On Currency Crises and Contagion** Marcel Fratzscher

01-1 **Price Level Convergence and Inflation in Europe** John H. Rogers, Gary Clyde Hufbauer, and Erika Wada

01-2 **Subsidies, Market Closure, Cross-Border Investment, and Effects on Competition: The Case of FDI on the Telecommunications Sector** Edward M. Graham

01-3 **Foreign Direct Investment in China: Effects on Growth and Economic Performance** Edward M. Graham and Erika Wada

01-4 **IMF Structural Conditionality: How Much Is Too Much?** Morris Goldstein

01-5 **Unchanging Innovation and Changing Economic Performance in Japan** Adam S. Posen

01-6 **Rating Banks in Emerging Markets: What Credit Rating Agencies Should Learn from Financial Indicators** Liliana Rojas-Suarez

01-7 **Beyond Bipolar: A Three-Dimensional Assessment of Monetary Frameworks** Kenneth N. Kuttner and Adam S. Posen

01-8 **Finance and Changing US-Japan Relations: Convergence Without Leverage—Until Now** Adam S. Posen

01-9 **Macroeconomic Implications of the New Economy** Martin Neil Baily

01-10 **Can International Capital Standards Strengthen Banks in Emerging Markets?** Liliana Rojas-Suarez

02-1 **Moral Hazard and the US Stock Market: Analyzing the "Greenspan Put"?** Marcus Miller, Paul Weller, and Lei Zhang

02-2 **Passive Savers and Fiscal Policy Effectiveness in Japan** Kenneth N. Kuttner and Adam S. Posen

02-3 **Home Bias, Transaction Costs, and Prospects for the Euro: A More Detailed Analysis** Catherine L. Mann and Ellen E. Meade

02-4 **Toward a Sustainable FTAA: Does Latin America Meet the Necessary Financial Preconditions?** Liliana Rojas-Suarez

02-5 **Assessing Globalization's Critics: "Talkers Are No Good Doers???"** Kimberly Ann Elliott, Debayani Kar, and J. David Richardson

02-6 **Economic Issues Raised by Treatment of Takings under NAFTA Chapter 11** Edward M. Graham

03-1 **Debt Sustainability, Brazil, and the IMF** Morris Goldstein

03-2 **Is Germany Turning Japanese?** Adam S. Posen

03-3 **Survival of the Best Fit: Exposure to Low-Wage Countries and the (Uneven) Growth of US Manufacturing Plants** Andrew B. Bernard, J. Bradford Jensen, and Peter K. Schott

03-4 **Falling Trade Costs, Heterogeneous Firms, and Industry Dynamics**
Andrew B. Bernard, J. Bradford Jensen, and Peter K. Schott

03-5 **Famine and Reform in North Korea**
Marcus Noland

03-6 **Empirical Investigations in Inflation Targeting** Yifan Hu

03-7 **Labor Standards and the Free Trade Area of the Americas**
Kimberly Ann Elliott

03-8 **Religion, Culture, and Economic Performance** Marcus Noland

03-9 **It Takes More than a Bubble to Become Japan** Adam S. Posen

03-10 **The Difficulty of Discerning What's Too Tight: Taylor Rules and Japanese Monetary Policy** Adam S. Posen/ Kenneth N. Kuttner

04-1 **Adjusting China's Exchange Rate Policies** Morris Goldstein

04-2 **Popular Attitudes, Globalization, and Risk** Marcus Noland

04-3 **Selective Intervention and Growth: The Case of Korea** Marcus Noland

05-1 **Outsourcing and Offshoring: Pushing the European Model Over the Hill, Rather Than Off the Cliff!**
Jacob Funk Kirkegaard

05-2 **China's Role in the Revived Bretton Woods System: A Case of Mistaken Identity** Morris Goldstein and Nicholas Lardy

05-3 **Affinity and International Trade**
Marcus Noland

05-4 **South Korea's Experience with International Capital Flows**
Marcus Noland

05-5 **Explaining Middle Eastern Authoritarianism** Marcus Noland

05-6 **Postponing Global Adjustment: An Analysis of the Pending Adjustment of Global Imbalances**
Edwin Truman

05-7 **What Might the Next Emerging Market Financial Crisis Look Like?**
Morris Goldstein, assisted by Anna Wong

05-8 **Egypt after the Multi-Fiber Arrangement** Dan Magder

05-9 **Tradable Services: Understanding the Scope and Impact of Services Offshoring** J. Bradford Jensen and Lori G. Kletzer

05-10 **Importers, Exporters, and Multinationals: A Portrait of Firms in the US that Trade Goods**
Andrew B. Bernard, J. Bradford Jensen, and Peter K. Schott

05-11 **The US Trade Deficit: A Disaggregated Perspective** Catherine L. Mann and Katharina Plück

05-12 **Prospects for Regional Free Trade in Asia** Gary C. Hufbauer/Yee Wong

05-13 **Predicting Trade Expansion under FTAs and Multilateral Agreements**
Dean A. DeRosa and John P. Gilbert

05-14 **The East Asian Industrial Policy Experience: Implications for the Middle East** Marcus Noland and Howard Pack

05-15 **Outsourcing and Skill Imports: Foreign High-Skilled Workers on H-1B and L-1 Visas in the United States**
Jacob Funk Kirkegaard

06-1 **Why Central Banks Should Not Burst Bubbles** Adam S. Posen

06-2 **The Case for an International Reserve Diversification Standard**
Edwin M. Truman and Anna Wong

06-3 **Offshoring in Europe—Evidence of a Two-Way Street from Denmark**
Peter Ørberg Jensen, Jacob F. Kirkegaard, Nicolai Søndergaard Laugesen

06-4 **The External Policy of the Euro Area: Organizing for Foreign Exchange Intervention** C. Randall Henning

06-5 **The Eurasian Growth Paradox**
Anders Åslund and Nazgul Jenish

06-6 **Has EMU Had Any Impact on the Degree of Wage Restraint?**
Adam S. Posen and Daniel Popov Gould

06-7 **Firm Structure, Multinationals, and Manufacturing Plant Deaths**
Andrew B. Bernard and J. Bradford Jensen

07-1 **The Trade Effects of Preferential Arrangements: New Evidence from the Australia Productivity Commission**
Dean A. DeRosa

07-2 **Offshoring, Outsourcing, and Production Relocation—Labor-Market Effects in the OECD Countries and Developing Asia**
Jacob Funk Kirkegaard

07-3 **Do Markets Care Who Chairs the Central Bank?** Kenneth N. Kuttner/ Adam S. Posen

07-4 **From Industrial Policy to Innovative Policy: Japan's Pursuit of Competitive Advantage** Marcus Noland

07-5 **A (Lack of) Progress Report on China's Exchange Rate Policies**
Morris Goldstein

07-6 **Measurement and Inference in International Reserve Diversification**
Anna Wong

07-7 **North Korea's External Economic Relations** Stephan Haggard and Marcus Noland

07-8 **Congress, Treasury, and the Accountability of Exchange Rate Policy: How the 1988 Trade Act Should Be Reformed**
C. Randall Henning

08-1 Exit Polls: Refugee Assessments of
      North Korea's Transitions
      Yoonok Chang, Stephan Haggard,
      Marcus Noland
08-2 Currency Undervaluation and
      Sovereign Wealth Funds: A New Role
      for the WTO   Aaditya Mattoo
      and Arvind Subramanian
08-3 Exchange Rate Economics
      John Williamson
08-4 Migration Experiences of North Korean
      Refugees: Survey Evidence from China
      Yoonok Chang, Stephan Haggard, and
      Marcus Noland
08-5 Korean Institutional Reform in
      Comparative Perspective Marcus Noland
      and Erik Weeks
08-6 Estimating Consistent Fundamental
      Equilibrium Exchange Rates
      William R. Cline
08-7 Policy Liberalization and FDI Growth,
      1982 to 2006
      Matthew Adler and Gary Clyde Hufbauer
08-8 Multilateralism Beyond Doha
      Aaditya Mattoo and Arvind Subramanian
08-9 Famine in North Korea Redux?
      Stephan Haggard and Marcus Noland
08-10 Distance Isn't Quite Dead: Recent
      Trade Patterns and Modes of Supply in
      Computer and Information Services in
      the United States and NAFTA Partners
      Jacob Funk Kirkegaard
08-11 On What Terms Is the IMF Worth
      Funding?
      Edwin M. Truman
08-12 The (Non) Impact of UN Sanctions on
      North Korea
      Marcus Noland

POLICY BRIEFS

98-1 The Asian Financial Crisis
      Morris Goldstein
98-2 The New Agenda with China
      C. Fred Bergsten
98-3 Exchange Rates for the Dollar, Yen, and
      Euro   Simon Wren-Lewis
98-4 Sanctions-Happy USA
      Gary Clyde Hufbauer
98-5 The Depressing News from Asia
      Marcus Noland, Sherman Robinson, and
      Zhi Wang
98-6 The Transatlantic Economic Partnership
      Ellen L. Frost
98-7 A New Strategy for the Global Crisis
      C. Fred Bergsten
98-8 Reviving the "Asian Monetary Fund"
      C. Fred Bergsten
99-1 Implementing Japanese Recovery
      Adam S. Posen

99-2 A Radical but Workable Restructuring
      Plan for South Korea
      Edward M. Graham
99-3 Crawling Bands or Monitoring Bands:
      How to Manage Exchange Rates in a
      World of Capital Mobility
      John Williamson
99-4 Market Mechanisms to Reduce the Need
      for IMF Bailouts
      Catherine L. Mann
99-5 Steel Quotas: A Rigged Lottery
      Gary C. Hufbauer and Erika Wada
99-6 China and the World Trade
      Organization: An Economic Balance
      Sheet   Daniel H. Rosen
99-7 Trade and Income Distribution: The
      Debate and New Evidence
      William R. Cline
99-8 Preserve the Exchange Stabilization
      Fund   C. Randall Henning
99-9 Nothing to Fear but Fear (of Inflation)
      Itself   Adam S. Posen
99-10 World Trade after Seattle: Implications
      for the United States
      Gary Clyde Hufbauer
00-1 The Next Trade Policy Battle
      C. Fred Bergsten
00-2 Decision-making in the WTO
      Jeffrey J. Schott and Jayashree Watal
00-3 American Access to China's Market:
      The Congressional Vote on PNTR
      Gary C. Hufbauer and Daniel Rosen
00-4 Third Oil Shock: Real or Imaginary?
      Consequences and Policy Alternatives
      Philip K. Verleger Jr.
00-5 The Role of the IMF: A Guide to the
      Reports   John Williamson
00-6 The ILO and Enforcement of Core Labor
      Standards   Kimberly Ann Elliott
00-7 "No" to Foreign Telecoms Equals "No"
      to the New Economy!
      Gary C. Hufbauer/Edward M. Graham
01-1 Brunei: A Turning Point for APEC?
      C. Fred Bergsten
01-2 A Prescription to Relieve Worker
      Anxiety   Lori Kletzer/Robert E. Litan
01-3 The US Export-Import Bank: Time for
      an Overhaul   Gary C. Hufbauer
01-4 Japan 2001—Decisive Action or
      Financial Panic   Adam S. Posen
01-5 Fin(d)ing Our Way on Trade and Labor
      Standards?   Kimberly A. Elliott
01-6 Prospects for Transatlantic Competition
      Policy   Mario Monti
01-7 The International Implications of
      Paying Down the Debt Edwin Truman
01-8 Dealing with Labor and Environment
      Issues in Trade Promotion Legislation
      Kimberly Ann Elliott
01-9 Steel: Big Problems, Better Solutions
      Gary Clyde Hufbauer/Ben Goodrich

01-10 Economic Policy Following the Terrorist Attacks   Martin Neil Baily

01-11 Using Sanctions to Fight Terrorism Gary Clyde Hufbauer, Jeffrey J. Schott, and Barbara Oegg

02-1 Time for a Grand Bargain in Steel? Gary C. Hufbauer and Ben Goodrich

02-2 Prospects for the World Economy: From Global Recession to Global Recovery Michael Mussa

02-3 Sovereign Debt Restructuring: New Articles, New Contracts—or No Change? Marcus Miller

02-4 Support the Ex-Im Bank: It Has Work to Do!   Gary Clyde Hufbauer and Ben Goodrich

02-5 The Looming Japanese Crisis Adam S. Posen

02-6 Capital-Market Access: New Frontier in the Sanctions Debate   Gary C. Hufbauer and Barbara Oegg

02-7 Is Brazil Next?   John Williamson

02-8 Further Financial Services Liberalization in the Doha Round? Wendy Dobson

02-9 Global Economic Prospects Michael Mussa

02-10 The Foreign Sales Corporation: Reaching the Last Act? Gary Clyde Hufbauer

03-1 Steel Policy: The Good, the Bad, and the Ugly   Gary Clyde Hufbauer and Ben Goodrich

03-2 Global Economic Prospects: Through the Fog of Uncertainty   Michael Mussa

03-3 Economic Leverage and the North Korean Nuclear Crisis Kimberly Ann Elliott

03-4 The Impact of Economic Sanctions on US Trade: Andrew Rose's Gravity Model   Gary Clyde Hufbauer and Barbara Oegg

03-5 Reforming OPIC for the 21st Century Theodore H. Moran/C. Fred Bergsten

03-6 The Strategic Importance of US-Korea Economic Relations   Marcus Noland

03-7 Rules Against Earnings Stripping: Wrong Answer to Corporate Inversions Gary C. Hufbauer and Ariel Assa

03-8 More Pain, More Gain: Politics and Economics of Eliminating Tariffs Gary C. Hufbauer and Ben Goodrich

03-9 EU Accession and the Euro: Close Together or Far Apart?   Peter B. Kenen and Ellen E. Meade

03-10 Next Move in Steel: Revocation or Retaliation?   Gary Clyde Hufbauer and Ben Goodrich

03-11 Globalization of IT Services and White Collar Jobs: The Next Wave of Productivity Growth   Catherine L. Mann

04-1 This Far and No Farther? Nudging Agricultural Reform Forward   Tim Josling and Dale Hathaway

04-2 Labor Standards, Development, and CAFTA   Kimberly Ann Elliott

04-3 Senator Kerry on Corporate Tax Reform: Right Diagnosis, Wrong Prescription Gary Clyde Hufbauer and Paul Grieco

04-4 Islam, Globalization, and Economic Performance in the Middle East Marcus Noland and Howard Pack

04-5 China Bashing 2004 Gary Clyde Hufbauer and Yee Wong

04-6 What Went Right in Japan Adam S. Posen

04-7 What Kind of Landing for the Chinese Economy?   Morris Goldstein and Nicholas R. Lardy

05-1 A Currency Basket for East Asia, Not Just China   John Williamson

05-2 After Argentina   Anna Gelpern

05-3 Living with Global Imbalances: A Contrarian View   Richard N. Cooper

05-4 The Case for a New Plaza Agreement William R. Cline

06-1 The United States Needs German Economic Leadership   Adam S. Posen

06-2 The Doha Round after Hong Kong Gary C. Hufbauer and Jeffrey J. Schott

06-3 Russia's Challenges as Chair of the G-8 Anders Åslund

06-4 Negotiating the Korea–United States Free Trade Agreement   Jeffrey J. Schott, Scott C. Bradford, and Thomas Moll

06-5 Can Doha Still Deliver on the Development Agenda? Kimberly Ann Elliott

06-6 China: Toward a Consumption Driven Growth Path   Nicholas R. Lardy

06-7 Completing the Doha Round Jeffrey J. Schott

06-8 Choosing Monetary Arrangements for the 21st Century: Problems of a Small Economy   John Williamson

06-9 Can America Still Compete or Does It Need a New Trade Paradigm? Martin N. Baily and Robert Z. Lawrence

07-1 The IMF Quota Formula: Linchpin of Fund Reform   Richard N. Cooper and Edwin M. Truman

07-2 Toward a Free Trade Area of the Asia Pacific   C. Fred Bergsten

07-3 China and Economic Integration in East Asia: Implications for the United States C. Fred Bergsten

07-4 Global Imbalances: Time for Action Alan Ahearne, William R. Cline, Kyung Tae Lee, Yung Chul Park, Jean Pisani-Ferry, and John Williamson

07-5 American Trade Politics in 2007: Building Bipartisan Compromise I. M. Destler

07-6 Sovereign Wealth Funds: The Need for Greater Transparency and Accountability   Edwin M. Truman

07-7 The Korea-US Free Trade Agreement: A Summary Assessment   Jeffrey J. Schott

07-8 The Case for Exchange Rate Flexibility in Oil-Exporting Economies   Brad Setser

08-1 "Fear" and Offshoring: The Scope and Potential Impact of Imports and Exports   J. Bradford Jensen and Lori G. Kletzer

08-2 Strengthening Trade Adjustment Assistance   Howard F. Rosen

08-3 A Blueprint for Sovereign Wealth Fund Best Practices   Edwin M. Truman

08-4 A Security and Peace Mechanism for Northeast Asia: The Economic Dimension   Stephan Haggard/Marcus Noland

08-5 World Trade at Risk   C. Fred Bergsten

08-6 North Korea on the Precipice of Famine   Stephan Haggard, Marcus Noland, and Erik Weeks

08-7 New Estimates of Fundamental Equilibrium Exchange Rates   William R. Cline and John Williamson

08-8 Financial Repression in China   Nicholas R. Lardy

09-1 Did Reagan Rule In Vain? A Closer Look at True Expenditure Levels in the United States and Europe   Jacob Funk Kirkegaard

09-2 Buy American: Bad for Jobs, Worse for Reputation   Gary Clyde Hufbauer and Jeffrey J. Schott

09-3 A Green Global Recovery? Assessing US Economic Stimulus and the Prospects for International Coordination   Trevor Houser, Shashank Mohan, and Robert Heilmayr

09-4 Money for the Auto Industry: Consistent with WTO Rules?   Claire Brunel and Gary Clyde Hufbauer

09-5 The Future of the Chiang Mai Initiative: An Asian Monetary Fund?   C. Randall Henning

09-6 Pressing the "Reset Button" on US-Russia Relations   Anders Åslund and Andrew Kuchins

09-7 US Taxation of Multinational Corporations: What Makes Sense, What Doesn't   Gary Clyde Hufbauer and Jisun Kim

* = out of print

POLICY ANALYSES IN INTERNATIONAL ECONOMICS Series

1 The Lending Policies of the International Monetary Fund*   John Williamson
August 1982   ISBN 0-88132-000-5

2 "Reciprocity": A New Approach to World Trade Policy?*   William R. Cline
September 1982   ISBN 0-88132-001-3

3 Trade Policy in the 1980s*
C. Fred Bergsten and William R. Cline
November 1982   ISBN 0-88132-002-1

4 International Debt and the Stability of the World Economy*   William R. Cline
September 1983   ISBN 0-88132-010-2

5 The Exchange Rate System,* 2d ed.
John Williamson
Sept. 1983, rev. June 1985   ISBN 0-88132-034-X

6 Economic Sanctions in Support of Foreign Policy Goals*
Gary Clyde Hufbauer and Jeffrey J. Schott
October 1983   ISBN 0-88132-014-5

7 A New SDR Allocation?*   John Williamson
March 1984   ISBN 0-88132-028-5

8 An International Standard for Monetary Stabilization*   Ronald L. McKinnon
March 1984   ISBN 0-88132-018-8

9 The Yen/Dollar Agreement: Liberalizing Japanese Capital Markets*
Jeffrey Frankel
December 1984   ISBN 0-88132-035-8

10 Bank Lending to Developing Countries: The Policy Alternatives*   C. Fred Bergsten, William R. Cline, and John Williamson
April 1985   ISBN 0-88132-032-3

11 Trading for Growth: The Next Round of Trade Negotiations*   Gary Clyde Hufbauer and Jeffrey J. Schott
September 1985   ISBN 0-88132-033-1

12 Financial Intermediation Beyond the Debt Crisis*   Donald R. Lessard, John Williamson
September 1985   ISBN 0-88132-021-8

13 The United States-Japan Economic Problem*   C. Fred Bergsten and William R. Cline
October 1985, 2d ed. January 1987
ISBN 0-88132-060-9

14 Deficits and the Dollar: The World Economy at Risk*   Stephen Marris
December 1985, 2d ed. November 1987
ISBN 0-88132-067-6

15 Trade Policy for Troubled Industries*
Gary Clyde Hufbauer and Howard R. Rosen
March 1986   ISBN 0-88132-020-X

16 The United States and Canada: The Quest for Free Trade*   Paul Wonnacott, with an appendix by John Williamson
March 1987   ISBN 0-88132-056-0

17 Adjusting to Success: Balance of Payments Policy in the East Asian NICs*
Bela Balassa and John Williamson
June 1987, rev. April 1990   ISBN 0-88132-101-X

18 Mobilizing Bank Lending to Debtor Countries*   William R. Cline
June 1987   ISBN 0-88132-062-5

19 Auction Quotas and United States Trade Policy*   C. Fred Bergsten,

Kimberly Ann Elliott, Jeffrey J. Schott, and
Wendy E. Takacs
September 1987   ISBN 0-88132-050-1

20 **Agriculture and the GATT: Rewriting the
Rules***   Dale E. Hathaway
September 1987   ISBN 0-88132-052-8

21 **Anti-Protection: Changing Forces in United
States Trade Politics***   I. M. Destler
and John S. Odell
September 1987   ISBN 0-88132-043-9

22 **Targets and Indicators: A Blueprint for the
International Coordination of Economic
Policy**   John Williamson/
Marcus H. Miller
September 1987   ISBN 0-88132-051-X

23 **Capital Flight: The Problem and Policy
Responses***   Donald R. Lessard
and John Williamson
December 1987   ISBN 0-88132-059-5

24 **United States-Canada Free Trade: An
Evaluation of the Agreement***
Jeffrey J. Schott
April 1988   ISBN 0-88132-072-2

25 **Voluntary Approaches to Debt Relief***
John Williamson
Sept.1988, rev. May 1   ISBN 0-88132-098-6

26 **American Trade Adjustment: The Global
Impact***   William R. Cline
March 1989   ISBN 0-88132-095-1

27 **More Free Trade Areas?***   Jeffrey J. Schott
May 1989   ISBN 0-88132-085-4

28 **The Progress of Policy Reform in Latin
America***   John Williamson
January 1990   ISBN 0-88132-100-1

29 **The Global Trade Negotiations: What Can
Be Achieved?***   Jeffrey J. Schott
September 1990   ISBN 0-88132-137-0

30 **Economic Policy Coordination: Requiem for
Prologue?***   Wendy Dobson
April 1991   ISBN 0-88132-102-8

31 **The Economic Opening of Eastern Europe***
John Williamson
May 1991   ISBN 0-88132-186-9

32 **Eastern Europe and the Soviet Union in the
World Economy***   Susan Collins/
Dani Rodrik
May 1991   ISBN 0-88132-157-5

33 **African Economic Reform: The External
Dimension***   Carol Lancaster
June 1991   ISBN 0-88132-096-X

34 **Has the Adjustment Process Worked?***
Paul R. Krugman
October 1991   ISBN 0-88132-116-8

35 **From Soviet DisUnion to Eastern Economic
Community?***
Oleh Havrylyshyn and John Williamson
October 1991   ISBN 0-88132-192-3

36 **Global Warming: The Economic Stakes***
William R. Cline
May 1992   ISBN 0-88132-172-9

37 **Trade and Payments after Soviet
Disintegration***   John Williamson
June 1992   ISBN 0-88132-173-7

38 **Trade and Migration: NAFTA and
Agriculture***   Philip L. Martin
October 1993   ISBN 0-88132-201-6

39 **The Exchange Rate System and the IMF: A
Modest Agenda**   Morris Goldstein
June 1995   ISBN 0-88132-219-9

40 **What Role for Currency Boards?**
John Williamson
September 1995   ISBN 0-88132-222-9

41 **Predicting External Imbalances for the
United States and Japan***   William R. Cline
September 1995   ISBN 0-88132-220-2

42 **Standards and APEC: An Action Agenda***
John S. Wilson
October 1995   ISBN 0-88132-223-7

43 **Fundamental Tax Reform and Border Tax
Adjustments***   Gary Clyde Hufbauer
January 1996   ISBN 0-88132-225-3

44 **Global Telecom Talks: A Trillion Dollar
Deal***   Ben A. Petrazzini
June 1996   ISBN 0-88132-230-X

45 **WTO 2000: Setting the Course for World
Trade**   Jeffrey J. Schott
September 1996   ISBN 0-88132-234-2

46 **The National Economic Council: A Work in
Progress***   I. M. Destler
November 1996   ISBN 0-88132-239-3

47 **The Case for an International Banking
Standard**   Morris Goldstein
April 1997   ISBN 0-88132-244-X

48 **Transatlantic Trade: A Strategic Agenda***
Ellen L. Frost
May 1997   ISBN 0-88132-228-8

49 **Cooperating with Europe's Monetary Union**
C. Randall Henning
May 1997   ISBN 0-88132-245-8

50 **Renewing Fast Track Legislation***
I. M. Destler
September 1997   ISBN 0-88132-252-0

51 **Competition Policies for the Global
Economy**   Edward M. Graham
and J. David Richardson
November 1997   ISBN 0-88132-249-0

52 **Improving Trade Policy Reviews in the
World Trade Organization**
Donald Keesing
April 1998   ISBN 0-88132-251-2

53 **Agricultural Trade Policy: Completing the
Reform**   Timothy Josling
April 1998   ISBN 0-88132-256-3

54 **Real Exchange Rates for the Year 2000**
Simon Wren Lewis and Rebecca Driver
April 1998   ISBN 0-88132-253-9

55 **The Asian Financial Crisis: Causes, Cures,
and Systemic Implications**
Morris Goldstein
June 1998   ISBN 0-88132-261-X

56 Global Economic Effects of the Asian Currency Devaluations
Marcus Noland, LiGang Liu, Sherman Robinson, and Zhi Wang
July 1998   ISBN 0-88132-260-1

57 The Exchange Stabilization Fund: Slush Money or War Chest?   C. Randall Henning
May 1999   ISBN 0-88132-271-7

58 The New Politics of American Trade: Trade, Labor, and the Environment
I. M. Destler and Peter J. Balint
October 1999   ISBN 0-88132-269-5

59 Congressional Trade Votes: From NAFTA Approval to Fast Track Defeat
Robert E. Baldwin/Christopher S. Magee
February 2000   ISBN 0-88132-267-9

60 Exchange Rate Regimes for Emerging Markets: Reviving the Intermediate Option
John Williamson
September 2000   ISBN 0-88132-293-8

61 NAFTA and the Environment: Seven Years Later   Gary Clyde Hufbauer, Daniel Esty, Diana Orejas, Luis Rubio & Jeffrey J. Schott
October 2000   ISBN 0-88132-299-7

62 Free Trade between Korea and the United States?   Inbom Choi and Jeffrey J. Schott
April 2001   ISBN 0-88132-311-X

63 New Regional Trading Arrangements in the Asia Pacific?   Robert Scollay and John P. Gilbert
May 2001   ISBN 0-88132-302-0

64 Parental Supervision: The New Paradigm for Foreign Direct Investment and Development   Theodore H. Moran
August 2001   *ISBN 0-88132-313-6*

65 The Benefits of Price Convergence: Speculative Calculations
Gary C. Hufbauer, Erika Wada, and Tony Warren
December 2001   ISBN 0-88132-333-0

66 Managed Floating Plus   Morris Goldstein
March 2002   ISBN 0-88132-336-5

67 Argentina and the Fund: From Triumph to Tragedy   Michael Mussa
July 2002   ISBN 0-88132-339-X

68 East Asian Financial Cooperation
C. Randall Henning
September 2002   ISBN 0-88132-338-1

69 Reforming OPIC for the 21st Century
Theodore H. Moran
May 2003   ISBN 0-88132-342-X

70 Awakening Monster: The Alien Tort Statute of 1789   Gary C. Hufbauer/ Nicholas Mitrokostas
July 2003   ISBN 0-88132-366-7

71 Korea after Kim Jong-il
Marcus Noland
January 2004   ISBN 0-88132-373-X

72 Roots of Competitiveness: China's Evolving Agriculture Interests
Daniel H. Rosen, Scott Rozelle, and Jikun Huang
July 2004   ISBN 0-88132-376-4

73 Prospects for a US-Taiwan FTA
Nicholas R. Lardy and Daniel H. Rosen
December 2004   ISBN 0-88132-367-5

74 Anchoring Reform with a US-Egypt Free Trade Agreement   Ahmed Galal and Robert Z. Lawrence
April 2005   ISBN 0-88132-368-3

75 Curbing the Boom-Bust Cycle: Stabilizing Capital Flows to Emerging Markets
John Williamson
July 2005   ISBN 0-88132-330-6

76 The Shape of a Swiss-US Free Trade Agreement   Gary Clyde Hufbauer/ Richard E. Baldwin
February 2006   ISBN 978-0-88132-385-6

77 A Strategy for IMF Reform
Edwin M. Truman
February 2006   ISBN 978-0-88132-398-6

78 US-China Trade Disputes: Rising Tide, Rising Stakes   Gary Clyde Hufbauer, Yee Wong, and Ketki Sheth
August 2006   ISBN 978-0-88132-394-8

79 Trade Relations Between Colombia and the United States   Jeffrey J. Schott, ed.
August 2006   ISBN 978-0-88132-389-4

80 Sustaining Reform with a US-Pakistan Free Trade Agreement   Gary C. Hufbauer and Shahid Javed Burki
November 2006   ISBN 978-0-88132-395-5

81 A US–Middle East Trade Agreement: A Circle of Opportunity?   Robert Z. Lawrence
November 2006   ISBN 978-0-88132-396-2

82 Reference Rates and the International Monetary System   John Williamson
January 2007   ISBN 978-0-88132-401-3

83 Toward a US-Indonesia Free Trade Agreement   Gary Clyde Hufbauer and Sjamsu Rahardja
June 2007   ISBN 978-0-88132-402-0

84 The Accelerating Decline in America's High-Skilled Workforce
Jacob Funk Kirkegaard
December 2007   ISBN 978-0-88132-413-6

85 Blue-Collar Blues: Is Trade to Blame for Rising US Income Inequality?
Robert Z. Lawrence
January 2008   ISBN 978-0-88132-414-3

86 Maghreb Regional and Global Integration: A Dream to Be Fulfilled
Gary Clyde Hufbauer and Claire Brunel, eds.
October 2008   ISBN 978-0-88132-426-6

BOOKS

IMF Conditionality*   John Williamson, editor
1983   ISBN 0-88132-006-4

Trade Policy in the 1980s*   William R. Cline, ed.
1983   ISBN 0-88132-031-5

Subsidies in International Trade*
Gary Clyde Hufbauer and Joanna Shelton Erb
1984   ISBN 0-88132-004-8

International Debt: Systemic Risk and Policy
Response*   William R. Cline
1984   ISBN 0-88132-015-3
Trade Protection in the United States: 31 Case
Studies*   Gary Clyde Hufbauer, Diane E.
Berliner, and Kimberly Ann Elliott
1986   ISBN 0-88132-040-4
Toward Renewed Economic Growth in Latin
America*   Bela Balassa, Gerardo M. Bueno,
Pedro Pablo Kuczynski, and Mario Henrique
Simonsen
1986   ISBN 0-88132-045-5
Capital Flight and Third World Debt*
Donald R. Lessard and John Williamson, editors
1987   ISBN 0-88132-053-6
The Canada-United States Free Trade
Agreement: The Global Impact*
Jeffrey J. Schott and Murray G. Smith, editors
1988   ISBN 0-88132-073-0
World Agricultural Trade: Building a
Consensus*
William M. Miner and Dale E. Hathaway, editors
1988   ISBN 0-88132-071-3
Japan in the World Economy*
Bela Balassa and Marcus Noland
1988   ISBN 0-88132-041-2
America in the World Economy: A Strategy
for the 1990s*   C. Fred Bergsten
1988   ISBN 0-88132-089-7
Managing the Dollar: From the Plaza to the
Louvre*   Yoichi Funabashi
1988, 2d. ed. 1989   ISBN 0-88132-097-8
United States External Adjustment
and the World Economy*   William R. Cline
May 1989   ISBN 0-88132-048-X
Free Trade Areas and U.S. Trade Policy*
Jeffrey J. Schott, editor
May *1989*   ISBN 0-88132-094-3
Dollar Politics: Exchange Rate Policymaking
in the United States*
I. M. Destler and C. Randall Henning
September 1989   ISBN 0-88132-079-X
Latin American Adjustment: How Much Has
Happened?*   John Williamson, editor
April 1990   ISBN 0-88132-125-7
The Future of World Trade in Textiles and
Apparel*   William R. Cline
1987, 2d ed. June *1999*   ISBN 0-88132-110-9
Completing the Uruguay Round: A Results-
Oriented Approach to the GATT Trade
Negotiations*   Jeffrey J. Schott, editor
September 1990   ISBN 0-88132-130-3
Economic Sanctions Reconsidered (2 volumes)
Economic Sanctions Reconsidered:
Supplemental Case Histories
Gary Clyde Hufbauer, Jeffrey J. Schott, and
Kimberly Ann Elliott
1985, 2d ed. Dec. 1990   ISBN cloth 0-88132-115-X
                         ISBN paper 0-88132-105-2

Economic Sanctions Reconsidered: History
and Current Policy   Gary Clyde Hufbauer,
Jeffrey J. Schott, and Kimberly Ann Elliott
December 1990   ISBN cloth 0-88132-140-0
                         ISBN paper 0-88132-136-2
Pacific Basin Developing Countries: Prospects
for Economic Sanctions Reconsidered: History
and Current Policy   Gary Clyde Hufbauer,
Jeffrey J. Schott, and Kimberly Ann Elliott
December 1990   ISBN cloth 0-88132-140-0
                         ISBN paper 0-88132-136-2
Pacific Basin Developing Countries: Prospects
for the Future*   Marcus Noland
January 1991   ISBN cloth 0-88132-141-9
                         ISBN paper 0-88132-081-1
Currency Convertibility in Eastern Europe*
John Williamson, editor
October 1991   ISBN 0-88132-128-1
International Adjustment and Financing: The
Lessons of 1985-1991*   C. Fred Bergsten, editor
January 1992   ISBN 0-88132-112-5
North American Free Trade: Issues and
Recommendations*
Gary Clyde Hufbauer and Jeffrey J. Schott
April 1992   ISBN 0-88132-120-6
Narrowing the U.S. Current Account Deficit*
Alan J. Lenz/*June 1992*   ISBN 0-88132-103-6
The Economics of Global Warming
William R. Cline/*June 1992*   ISBN 0-88132-132-X
US Taxation of International Income:
Blueprint for Reform   Gary Clyde Hufbauer,
assisted by Joanna M. van Rooij
October 1992   ISBN 0-88132-134-6
Who's Bashing Whom? Trade Conflict
in High-Technology Industries
Laura D'Andrea Tyson
November 1992   ISBN 0-88132-106-0
Korea in the World Economy*   Il SaKong
January 1993   ISBN 0-88132-183-4
Pacific Dynamism and the International
Economic System*
C. Fred Bergsten and Marcus Noland, editors
May 1993   ISBN 0-88132-196-6
Economic Consequences of Soviet
Disintegration*   John Williamson, editor
May 1993   ISBN 0-88132-190-7
Reconcilable Differences? United States-Japan
Economic Conflict*
C. Fred Bergsten and Marcus Noland
June 1993   ISBN 0-88132-129-X
Does Foreign Exchange Intervention Work?
Kathryn M. Dominguez and Jeffrey A. Frankel
September 1993   ISBN 0-88132-104-4
Sizing Up U.S. Export Disincentives*
J. David Richardson
September 1993   ISBN 0-88132-107-9
NAFTA: An Assessment   Gary Clyde
Hufbauer and Jeffrey J. Schott/*rev. ed.*
October 1993   ISBN 0-88132-199-0
Adjusting to Volatile Energy Prices
Philip K. Verleger, Jr.
November 1993   ISBN 0-88132-069-2

The Political Economy of Policy Reform
John Williamson, editor
January 1994　　　　　ISBN 0-88132-195-8
**Measuring the Costs of Protection
in the United States**　　Gary Clyde Hufbauer
and Kimberly Ann Elliott
January 1994　　　　　ISBN 0-88132-108-7
**The Dynamics of Korean Economic
Development***　　　　　Cho Soon
March 1994　　　　　ISBN 0-88132-162-1
Reviving the European Union*
C. Randall Henning, Eduard Hochreiter, and
Gary Clyde Hufbauer, editors
April 1994　　　　　ISBN 0-88132-208-3
China in the World Economy
Nicholas R. Lardy
April 1994　　　　　ISBN 0-88132-200-8
**Greening the GATT: Trade, Environment,
and the Future**　　　　Daniel C. Esty
July 1994　　　　　ISBN 0-88132-205-9
Western Hemisphere Economic Integration*
Gary Clyde Hufbauer and Jeffrey J. Schott
July 1994　　　　　ISBN 0-88132-159-1
**Currencies and Politics in the United States,
Germany, and Japan**　　C. Randall Henning
September 1994　　　　ISBN 0-88132-127-3
Estimating Equilibrium Exchange Rates
John Williamson, editor
September 1994　　　　ISBN 0-88132-076-5
**Managing the World Economy: Fifty Years
after Bretton Woods**　　Peter B. Kenen, editor
September 1994　　　　ISBN 0-88132-212-1
**Reciprocity and Retaliation in U.S. Trade
Policy**　　　　　Thomas O. Bayard
and Kimberly Ann Elliott
September 1994　　　　ISBN 0-88132-084-6
The Uruguay Round: An Assessment*
Jeffrey J. Schott, assisted by Johanna Buurman
November 1994　　　　ISBN 0-88132-206-7
Measuring the Costs of Protection in Japan*
Yoko Sazanami, Shujiro Urata, and Hiroki Kawai
January 1995　　　　ISBN 0-88132-211-3
**Foreign Direct Investment in the
United States,** 3d ed.,　　Edward M. Graham
and Paul R. Krugman
January 1995　　　　ISBN 0-88132-204-0
**The Political Economy of Korea-United
States Cooperation***　　C. Fred Bergsten
and Il SaKong, editors
February 1995　　　　ISBN 0-88132-213-X
International Debt Reexamined*
William R. Cline
February 1995　　　　ISBN 0-88132-083-8
American Trade Politics, 3d ed. I. M. Destler
April 1995　　　　ISBN 0-88132-215-6
**Managing Official Export Credits: The Quest
for a Global Regime***　　John E. Ray
July 1995　　　　ISBN 0-88132-207-5
Asia Pacific Fusion: Japan's Role in APEC*
Yoichi Funabashi
October 1995　　　　ISBN 0-88132-224-5

**Korea-United States Cooperation in the New
World Order*** C. Fred Bergsten/Il SaKong, eds.
February 1996　　　　ISBN 0-88132-226-1
Why Exports Really Matter!* ISBN 0-88132-221-0
Why Exports Matter More!* ISBN 0-88132-229-6
J. David Richardson and Karin Rindal
July 1995; February 1996
**Global Corporations and National
Governments**　　　　Edward M. Graham
May 1996　　　　ISBN 0-88132-111-7
**Global Economic Leadership and the Group of
Seven**　　　　　C. Fred Bergsten
and C. Randall Henning
May 1996　　　　ISBN 0-88132-218-0
The Trading System after the Uruguay Round*
John Whalley and Colleen Hamilton
July 1996　　　　ISBN 0-88132-131-1
**Private Capital Flows to Emerging Markets
after the Mexican Crisis***　Guillermo A. Calvo,
Morris Goldstein, and Eduard Hochreiter
September 1996　　　　ISBN 0-88132-232-6
**The Crawling Band as an Exchange Rate
Regime: Lessons from Chile, Colombia,
and Israel**　　　　John Williamson
September 1996　　　　ISBN 0-88132-231-8
**Flying High: Liberalizing Civil Aviation
in the Asia Pacific***　　Gary Clyde Hufbauer
and Christopher Findlay
November 1996　　　　ISBN 0-88132-227-X
**Measuring the Costs of Visible Protection
in Korea***　　　　Namdoo Kim
November 1996　　　　ISBN 0-88132-236-9
The World Trading System: Challenges Ahead
Jeffrey J. Schott
December 1996　　　　ISBN 0-88132-235-0
Has Globalization Gone Too Far? Dani Rodrik
March 1997　　ISBN paper 0-88132-241-5
Korea-United States Economic Relationship*
C. Fred Bergsten and Il SaKong, editors
March 1997　　　　ISBN 0-88132-240-7
Summitry in the Americas: A Progress Report
Richard E. Feinberg
April 1997　　　　ISBN 0-88132-242-3
Corruption and the Global Economy
Kimberly Ann Elliott
June 1997　　　　ISBN 0-88132-233-4
**Regional Trading Blocs in the World
Economic System**　　Jeffrey A. Frankel
October 1997　　　　ISBN 0-88132-202-4
**Sustaining the Asia Pacific Miracle:
Environmental Protection and Economic
Integration**　　Andre Dua and Daniel C. Esty
October 1997　　　　ISBN 0-88132-250-4
Trade and Income Distribution
William R. Cline
November 1997　　　　ISBN 0-88132-216-4
Global Competition Policy
Edward M. Graham and J. David Richardson
December 1997　　　　ISBN 0-88132-166-4
**Unfinished Business: Telecommunications
after the Uruguay Round**
Gary Clyde Hufbauer and Erika Wada
December 1997　　　　ISBN 0-88132-257-1

Financial Services Liberalization in the WTO
Wendy Dobson and Pierre Jacquet
June 1998　　　　　ISBN 0-88132-254-7
Restoring Japan's Economic Growth
Adam S. Posen
September 1998　　　　ISBN 0-88132-262-8
Measuring the Costs of Protection in China
Zhang Shuguang, Zhang Yansheng,
and Wan Zhongxin
November 1998　　　　ISBN 0-88132-247-4
Foreign Direct Investment and Development:
The New Policy Agenda for Developing
Countries and Economies in Transition
Theodore H. Moran
December 1998　　　　ISBN 0-88132-258-X
Behind the Open Door: Foreign Enterprises
in the Chinese Marketplace　Daniel H. Rosen
January 1999　　　　ISBN 0-88132-263-6
Toward A New International Financial
Architecture: A Practical Post-Asia Agenda
Barry Eichengreen
February 1999　　　　ISBN 0-88132-270-9
Is the U.S. Trade Deficit Sustainable?
Catherine L. Mann
September 1999　　　　ISBN 0-88132-265-2
Safeguarding Prosperity in a Global Financial
System: The Future International Financial
Architecture, Independent Task Force Report
Sponsored by the Council on Foreign Relations
Morris Goldstein, Project Director
October 1999　　　　ISBN 0-88132-287-3
Avoiding the Apocalypse: The Future
of the Two Koreas　　　Marcus Noland
June 2000　　　　ISBN 0-88132-278-4
Assessing Financial Vulnerability:
An Early Warning System for Emerging
Markets　　　　　Morris Goldstein,
Graciela Kaminsky, and Carmen Reinhart
June 2000　　　　ISBN 0-88132-237-7
Global Electronic Commerce: A Policy Primer
Catherine L. Mann, Sue E. Eckert, and Sarah
Cleeland Knight
July 2000　　　　ISBN 0-88132-274-1
The WTO after Seattle　Jeffrey J. Schott, ed.
July 2000　　　　ISBN 0-88132-290-3
Intellectual Property Rights in the Global
Economy　　　　　Keith E. Maskus
August 2000　　　　ISBN 0-88132-282-2
The Political Economy of the Asian Financial
Crisis　　　　　Stephan Haggard
August 2000　　　　ISBN 0-88132-283-0
Transforming Foreign Aid: United States
Assistance in the 21st Century　Carol Lancaster
August 2000　　　　ISBN 0-88132-291-1
Fighting the Wrong Enemy: Antiglobal
Activists and Multinational Enterprises
Edward M. Graham
September 2000　　　　ISBN 0-88132-272-5
Globalization and the Perceptions of American
Workers　Kenneth Scheve/Matthew J. Slaughter
March 2001　　　　ISBN 0-88132-295-4

World Capital Markets: Challenge to the G-10
Wendy Dobson and Gary Clyde Hufbauer,
assisted by Hyun Koo Cho
May 2001　　　　ISBN 0-88132-301-2
Prospects for Free Trade in the Americas
Jeffrey J. Schott
August 2001　　　　ISBN 0-88132-275-X
Toward a North American Community:
Lessons from the Old World for the New
Robert A. Pastor
August 2001　　　　ISBN 0-88132-328-4
Measuring the Costs of Protection in Europe:
European Commercial Policy in the 2000s
Patrick A. Messerlin
September 2001　　　　ISBN 0-88132-273-3
Job Loss from Imports: Measuring the Costs
Lori G. Kletzer
September 2001　　　　ISBN 0-88132-296-2
No More Bashing: Building a New
Japan–United States Economic Relationship
C. Fred Bergsten, Takatoshi Ito, and
Marcus Noland
October 2001　　　　ISBN 0-88132-286-5
Why Global Commitment Really Matters!
Howard Lewis III and J. David Richardson
October 2001　　　　ISBN 0-88132-298-9
Leadership Selection in the Major
Multilaterals　　　　　Miles Kahler
November 2001　　　　ISBN 0-88132-335-7
The International Financial Architecture:
What's New? What's Missing?　　Peter Kenen
November 2001　　　　ISBN 0-88132-297-0
Delivering on Debt Relief: From IMF Gold
to a New Aid Architecture
John Williamson and Nancy Birdsall,
with Brian Deese
April 2002　　　　ISBN 0-88132-331-4
Imagine There's No Country: Poverty,
Inequality, and Growth in the Era
of Globalization　　　　Surjit S. Bhalla
September 2002　　　　ISBN 0-88132-348-9
Reforming Korea's Industrial Conglomerates
Edward M. Graham
January 2003　　　　ISBN 0-88132-337-3
Industrial Policy in an Era of Globalization:
Lessons from Asia　　　Marcus Noland
and Howard Pack
March 2003　　　　ISBN 0-88132-350-0
Reintegrating India with the World Economy
T. N. Srinivasan and Suresh D. Tendulkar
March 2003　　　　ISBN 0-88132-280-6
After the Washington Consensus:
Restarting Growth and Reform
in Latin America　　　Pedro-Pablo Kuczynski
and John Williamson, editors
March 2003　　　　ISBN 0-88132-347-0
The Decline of US Labor Unions and the Role
of Trade　　　　　Robert E. Baldwin
June 2003　　　ISBN 0-88132-341-1

Can Labor Standards Improve under
Globalization? Kimberly A. Elliott
and Richard B. Freeman
June 2003 ISBN 0-88132-332-2
Crimes and Punishments? Retaliation
under the WTO Robert Z. Lawrence
October 2003 ISBN 0-88132-359-4
Inflation Targeting in the World Economy
Edwin M. Truman
October 2003 ISBN 0-88132-345-4
Foreign Direct Investment and Tax
Competition John H. Mutti
November 2003 ISBN 0-88132-352-7
Has Globalization Gone Far Enough?
The Costs of Fragmented Markets
Scott Bradford and Robert Z. Lawrence
February 2004 ISBN 0-88132-349-7
Food Regulation and Trade:
Toward a Safe and Open Global System
Tim Josling, Donna Roberts, and David Orden
March 2004 ISBN 0-88132-346-2
Controlling Currency Mismatches
in Emerging Markets
Morris Goldstein and Philip Turner
April 2004 ISBN 0-88132-360-8
Free Trade Agreements: US Strategies
and Priorities Jeffrey J. Schott, editor
April 2004 ISBN 0-88132-361-6
Trade Policy and Global Poverty
William R. Cline
June 2004 ISBN 0-88132-365-9
Bailouts or Bail-ins? Responding to Financial
Crises in Emerging Economies
Nouriel Roubini and Brad Setser
August 2004 ISBN 0-88132-371-3
Transforming the European Economy
Martin Neil Baily and Jacob Kirkegaard
September 2004 ISBN 0-88132-343-8
Chasing Dirty Money: The Fight Against
Money Laundering
Peter Reuter and Edwin M. Truman
November 2004 ISBN 0-88132-370-5
The United States and the World Economy:
Foreign Economic Policy for the Next Decade
C. Fred Bergsten
January 2005 ISBN 0-88132-380-2
Does Foreign Direct Investment Promote
Development? Theodore Moran,
Edward M. Graham, and Magnus Blomström,
editors
April 2005 ISBN 0-88132-381-0
American Trade Politics, 4th ed. I. M. Destler
June 2005 ISBN 0-88132-382-9
Why Does Immigration Divide America?
Public Finance and Political Opposition
to Open Borders Gordon Hanson
August 2005 ISBN 0-88132-400-0
Reforming the US Corporate Tax
Gary Clyde Hufbauer and Paul L. E. Grieco
September 2005 ISBN 0-88132-384-5

The United States as a Debtor Nation
William R. Cline
September 2005 ISBN 0-88132-399-3
NAFTA Revisited: Achievements
and Challenges Gary Clyde Hufbauer
and Jeffrey J. Schott, assisted by Paul L. E. Grieco
and Yee Wong
October 2005 ISBN 0-88132-334-9
US National Security and Foreign Direct
Investment
Edward M. Graham and David M. Marchick
May 2006 ISBN 0-88132-391-8
ISBN 978-0-88132-391-7
Accelerating the Globalization of America:
The Role for Information Technology
Catherine L. Mann, assisted by Jacob Kirkegaard
June 2006 ISBN 0-88132-390-X
ISBN 978-0-88132-390-0
Delivering on Doha: Farm Trade and the Poor
Kimberly Ann Elliott
July 2006 ISBN 0-88132-392-6
ISBN 978-0-88132-392-4
Case Studies in US Trade Negotiation,
Vol. 1: Making the Rules Charan Devereaux,
Robert Z. Lawrence, and Michael Watkins
September 2006 ISBN 0-88132-362-4
ISBN 978-0-88132-362-7
Case Studies in US Trade Negotiation,
Vol. 2: Resolving Disputes Charan Devereaux,
Robert Z. Lawrence, and Michael Watkins
September 2006 ISBN 0-88132-363-4
ISBN 978-0-88132-363-2
C. Fred Bergsten and the World Economy
Michael Mussa, editor
December 2006 ISBN 0-88132-397-7
ISBN 978-0-88132-397-9
Working Papers, Volume I Peterson Institute
December 2006 ISBN 0-88132-388-8
ISBN 978-0-88132-388-7
The Arab Economies in a Changing World
Marcus Noland and Howard Pack
April 2007 ISBN 978-0-88132-393-1
Working Papers, Volume II Peterson Institute
April 2007 ISBN 978-0-88132-404-4
Global Warming and Agriculture:
Impact Estimates by Country William R. Cline
July 2007 ISBN 978-0-88132-403-7
US Taxation of Foreign Income
Gary Clyde Hufbauer and Ariel Assa
October 2007 ISBN 978-0-88132-405-1
Russia's Capitalist Revolution: Why Market
Reform Succeeded and Democracy Failed
Anders Åslund
October 2007 ISBN 978-0-88132-409-9
Economic Sanctions Reconsidered, 3d. ed.
Gary C. Hufbauer, Jeffrey J. Schott,
Kimberly Ann Elliott, and Barbara Oegg
November 2007
ISBN hardcover 978-0-88132-407-5
ISBN hardcover/CD-ROM 978-0-88132-408-2

Debating China's Exchange Rate Policy
Morris Goldstein and Nicholas R. Lardy, eds.
April 2008   ISBN 978-0-88132-415-0
Leveling the Carbon Playing Field:
International Competition and US
Climate Policy Design   Trevor Houser,
Rob Bradley, Britt Childs, Jacob Werksman, and
Robert Heilmayr
May 2008   ISBN 978-0-88132-420-4
Accountability and Oversight of US
Exchange Rate Policy   C. Randall Henning
June 2008   ISBN 978-0-88132-419-8
Challenges of Globalization: Imbalances and
Growth
Anders Åslund and Marek Dabrowski, eds.
July 2008   ISBN 978-0-88132-418-1
China's Rise: Challenges and Opportunities
C. Fred Bergsten, Charles Freeman, Nicholas
R. Lardy, and Derek J. Mitchell
September 2008   ISBN 978-0-88132-417-4
Banking on Basel: The Future of International
Financial Regulation
Daniel K. Tarullo
September 2008   ISBN 978-0-88132-423-5
US Pension Reform: Lessons from Other
Countries   Martin N. Baily/Jacob Kirkegaard
February 2009   ISBN 978-0-88132-425-9
How Ukraine Became a Market Economy and
Democracy   Anders Åslund
March 2009   ISBN 978-0-88132-427-3
Global Warming and the World Trading
System   Gary Clyde Hufbauer,
Steve Charnovitz, and Jisun Kim
March 2009   ISBN 978-0-88132-428-0
The Russia Balance Sheet
Anders Åslund and Andrew Kuchins
April 2009   ISBN 978-0-88132-424-2

SPECIAL REPORTS

1   Promoting World Recovery: A Statement
    on Global Economic Strategy*
    by 26 Economists from Fourteen Countries
    December 1982   ISBN 0-88132-013-7
2   Prospects for Adjustment in Argentina,
    Brazil, and Mexico: Responding
    to the Debt Crisis*   John Williamson, editor
    June 1983   ISBN 0-88132-016-1
3   Inflation and Indexation: Argentina,
    Brazil, and Israel*   John Williamson, editor
    March 1985   ISBN 0-88132-037-4
4   Global Economic Imbalances*
    C. Fred Bergsten, editor
    March 1986   ISBN 0-88132-042-0
5   African Debt and Financing*
    Carol Lancaster and John Williamson, eds.
    May 1986   ISBN 0-88132-044-7
6   Resolving the Global Economic Crisis:
    After Wall Street*   by Thirty-three
    Economists from Thirteen Countries
    December 1987   ISBN 0-88132-070-6

7   World Economic Problems*
    Kimberly Ann Elliott/John Williamson, eds.
    April 1988   ISBN 0-88132-055-2
    Reforming World Agricultural Trade*
    by Twenty-nine Professionals from
    Seventeen Countries
    1988   ISBN 0-88132-088-9
8   Economic Relations Between the United
    States and Korea: Conflict or Cooperation?*
    Thomas O. Bayard and Soogil Young, eds.
    January 1989   ISBN 0-88132-068-4
9   Whither APEC? The Progress to Date
    and Agenda for the Future*
    C. Fred Bergsten, editor
    October 1997   ISBN 0-88132-248-2
10 Economic Integration of the Korean
    Peninsula   Marcus Noland, editor
    January 1998   ISBN 0-88132-255-5
11 Restarting Fast Track*   Jeffrey J. Schott, ed.
    April 1998   ISBN 0-88132-259-8
12 Launching New Global Trade Talks:
    An Action Agenda   Jeffrey J. Schott, ed.
    September 1998   ISBN 0-88132-266-0
13 Japan's Financial Crisis and Its Parallels
    to US Experience
    Ryoichi Mikitani and Adam S. Posen, eds.
    September 2000   ISBN 0-88132-289-X
14 The Ex-Im Bank in the 21st Century:
    A New Approach   Gary Clyde Hufbauer
    and Rita M. Rodriguez, editors
    January 2001   ISBN 0-88132-300-4
15 The Korean Diaspora in the World
    Economy   C. Fred Bergsten and
    Inbom Choi, eds.
    January 2003   ISBN 0-88132-358-6
16 Dollar Overvaluation and the World
    Economy   C. Fred Bergsten
    and John Williamson, eds.
    February 2003   ISBN 0-88132-351-9
17 Dollar Adjustment: How Far?
    Against What?   C. Fred Bergsten
    and John Williamson, eds.
    November 2004   ISBN 0-88132-378-0
18 The Euro at Five: Ready for a Global
    Role?   Adam S. Posen, editor
    April 2005   ISBN 0-88132-380-2
19 Reforming the IMF for the 21st Century
    Edwin M. Truman, editor
    April 2006   ISBN 0-88132-387-X
                         ISBN 978-0-88132-387-0

WORKS IN PROGRESS

Reassessing US Trade Policy: Priorities and
Policy Recommendations for the Next Decade
Jeffrey J. Schott
China's Energy Evolution: The Consequences
of Powering Growth at Home and Abroad
Daniel H. Rosen and Trevor Houser
China's Exchange Rates: Options
and Prescriptions
Morris Goldstein and Nicholas R. Lardy

Global Identity Theft: Economic
and Policy Implications   Catherine L. Mann
Growth and Diversification of International
Reserves   Edwin M. Truman
Financial Regulation after the Subprime
and Credit Crisis   Morris Goldstein
Globalized Venture Capital: Implications
for US Entrepreneurship and Innovation
Catherine L. Mann
Forging a Grand Bargain: Expanding
Trade and Raising Worker Prosperity
Lori Kletzer, J. David Richardson, and Howard
Rosen
East Asian Regionalism and the World
Economy   C. Fred Bergsten
The Strategic Implications of China-Taiwan
Economic Relations   Nicholas R. Lardy
Reform in a Rich Country: Germany
Adam S. Posen
Second Among Equals: The Middle-Class
Kingdoms of India and China   Surjit Bhalla

Global Forces, American Faces:
US Economic Globalization at the Grass
Roots   J. David Richardson
Financial Crises and the Future of Emerging
Markets   William R. Cline
Global Services Outsourcing: The Impact on
American Firms and Workers
J. Bradford Jensen, Lori G. Kletzer, and
Catherine L. Mann
Policy Reform in Rich Countries
John Williamson, editor
The Impact of Financial Globalization
William R. Cline
Banking System Fragility in Emerging
Economies   Morris Goldstein
and Philip Turner
The Euro at Ten: The Next Global Currency?
Adam S. Posen and Jean Pisani-Ferry, eds.
Special Report 20 The Long-Term International
Economic Position of the Unitied States
C. Fred Bergsten, ed.

DISTRIBUTORS OUTSIDE THE UNITED STATES

**Australia, New Zealand,
and Papua New Guinea**
D. A. Information Services
648 Whitehorse Road
Mitcham, Victoria 3132, Australia
Tel: 61-3-9210-7777
Fax: 61-3-9210-7788
Email: service@dadirect.com.au
www.dadirect.com.au

India, Bangladesh, Nepal, and Sri Lanka
Viva Books Private Limited
Mr. Vinod Vasishtha
4737/23 Ansari Road
Daryaganj, New Delhi 110002
India
Tel: 91-11-4224-2200
Fax: 91-11-4224-2240
Email: viva@vivagroupindia.net
www.vivagroupindia.com

**Mexico, Central America, South America,
and Puerto Rico**
US PubRep, Inc.
311 Dean Drive
Rockville, MD 20851
Tel: 301-838-9276
Fax: 301-838-9278
Email: c.falk@ieee.org

Asia *(Brunei, Burma, Cambodia, China,
Hong Kong, Indonesia, Korea, Laos, Malaysia,
Philippines, Singapore, Taiwan, Thailand,
and Vietnam)*
East-West Export Books (EWEB)
University of Hawaii Press
2840 Kolowalu Street
Honolulu, Hawaii 96822-1888
Tel: 808-956-8830
Fax: 808-988-6052
Email: eweb@hawaii.edu

Canada
Renouf Bookstore
5369 Canotek Road, Unit 1
Ottawa, Ontario KlJ 9J3, Canada
Tel: 613-745-2665
Fax: 613-745-7660
www.renoufbooks.com

Japan
United Publishers Services Ltd.
1-32-5, Higashi-shinagawa
Shinagawa-ku, Tokyo 140-0002
Japan
Tel: 81-3-5479-7251
Fax: 81-3-5479-7307
Email: purchasing@ups.co.jp
*For trade accounts only. Individuals will find
Institute books in leading Tokyo bookstores.*

Middle East
MERIC
2 Bahgat Ali Street, El Masry Towers
Tower D, Apt. 24
Zamalek, Cairo
Egypt
Tel. 20-2-7633824
Fax: 20-2-7369355
Email: mahmoud_fouda@mericonline.com
www.mericonline.com

United Kingdom, Europe
(including Russia and Turkey), **Africa,
and Israel**
The Eurospan Group
c/o Turpin Distribution
Pegasus Drive
Stratton Business Park
Biggleswade, Bedfordshire
SG18 8TQ
United Kingdom
Tel: 44 (0) 1767-604972
Fax: 44 (0) 1767-601640
Email: eurospan@turpin-distribution.com
www.eurospangroup.com/bookstore

**Visit our website at:
www.petersoninstitute.org
E-mail orders to:
petersonmail@presswarehouse.com**